Jim,
Best Wished

Don Schynnyer

POWER ON EARTH

POWER
ON EARTH

Nick Tosches

ARBOR HOUSE
New York

Manufactured in the United States of America

10 9 8 7 6 5 4 3 2 1

Library of Congress Cataloging-in-Publication Data

Tosches, Nick.
  Power on earth.

  Includes index.
  1. Sindona, Michele. 2. Commercial criminals—Italy—
Biography. 3. Banks and banking—Corrupt practices.
4. International finance—Corrupt practices. I. Title.
HV6766.S56T67   1986   332.1′092′4 [B]   86-10778
ISBN 0-87795-796-7

J.L.W.

Table of Contents

Preface

WHEN I MET MICHELE SINDONA, his power and days in the sun were done. Were they not, his story most probably never would have been told.

The idea for this book, which I later realized had lain behind my eyes since I first learned of Sindona, seemed to pronounce itself in one sudden moment. I glimpsed his image —for the hundredth, the thousandth time—amid the dead pastel drone of the TV news one night. That's him, I thought, that's the one. I was told by many that he was unapproachable, by others that the governments of America and Italy were set on his silence. As usual, those who spoke were of more tongue than truth. In any case, fortune was with me. We met. Two years later, I am writing these words.

It has been my desire to prove neither the guilt nor the innocence of Michele Sindona. While some of those whom Sindona paints darkly—Enrico Cuccia and others—have chosen not to give me their sides of the story, I was able to speak to many people in many places: London bankers and Vatican cardinals, judges and crooks, New York lawyers and Hong Kong brokers, and unsmiling gents in the outlying boroughs. But I spoke most of all to Michele Sindona. This book, above all else, is his tale. It is his tale tempered by me. Let those with eyes to see, see.

The pages that follow tell all else there is to be said; but they do not thank those to whom thanks, and more, are due.

This book is based on two principal sources: my interviews

with Michele Sindona (in New York in March 1984, in Voghera in May, August and September 1985) and several hundred pages of typescript memoirs supplied by him. The latter were written in Italian—an Italian that proved to be, like Sindona himself, alternately reserved and fulminating, elegant and rough, straightforward and complex, and ever-florescent with surprises: snatches of dialect, Latin, and words such as *"per antonomasia"* (in English, "antonomastic"; one proceeds from there). I was fortunate to know, and more fortunate to count among my friends, Linda M. Eklund, a translator of consummate skills. Without her talent and work, I do not know how much would still stand between me and the end of the job.

There were others whose help was valuable, often essential, to the making of this book. Among them are: Antonella Antonelli, Count Pietro Antonelli, Stanley S. Arkin, Dario Cella, John Corsiglia, Mary Ellen Eckelberg, Aldo Fabozzi, Judge Marvin E. Frankel, Judge Thomas P. Griesa (whose words, though he asked me not to quote them and I have not, were much appreciated), Paul Goldberger, Sergio Cardinal Guerri, Jocelyn and Richard Hambro, Robert J. Hawley, Dennis Linder, Joseph Macaluso, Camillo Passerini, Paul Rao, Wayne Seifert, Giuseppe Severino, Jonathan Silverman, Marco Sindona, Murray Stein, and Barbara Walters. Two who especially helped were Robert Costello and my brother, Richard Tosches. And, of course, without Michele Sindona, there would be no book.

There are three I want to thank most of all: Eden Collinsworth, the president of Arbor House; Russ Galen of the Scott Meredith agency; and Judith Wilmot. They know why. They were with me in this.

POWER ON EARTH

I.
The Three Beasts

I HAD WANTED TO MEET THE DEVIL, and now here I was, toward dark, alone on a bench in a piny garden in a place called Voghera.

Where birds had swirled, lacing the dusk with song, there was now nothing; and there was no sound but that of the trees' sullen sway. The rosy flush and blue of the Lombardy sky were gone now, too. In the distance, the shadowy tide of nightfall rippled like a timeless haunting through the Oltrepo hills.

A lizard scudded up the statue of Garibaldi that stood nearby. It rested on the image's blackened shoulder, gazing upward, as if mesmerized by the waning moon. Little bats appeared, darting wildly amid the tall pines and round the statue; and the lizard vanished.

An old man approached. He sat on a bench across the path, and he began to pick solemnly through the lapful of dandelion greens he had gathered in his slow walk through this place. When his culling was done, he straightened his back and lifted his head, looking for a moment toward where the lizard had looked. Then he rose and was gone.

I was alone again. I let the night breeze take me. I watched the low-rolling clouds drift past the moon, veiling it; and I thought about what had brought me here.

Like most people outside Italy, I had first become aware of Michele Sindona more than a decade ago. He had taken over the Franklin National Bank in New York, and it fell. That was in the autumn of 1974. It was the largest bank failure in Ameri-

1

can history, and it was followed, days later across the sea, by the downfall of Sindona's Banca Privata Italiana. In the first week of the new year, his Geneva-based Banque de Financement was shut down. By then the Italian government had issued two warrants for his arrest on bank-fraud charges.

Only as Michele Sindona's empire crumbled was its vastness revealed. Through Fasco, A.G., his spectral Liechtenstein-based holding company, Sindona had controlled at least 5 banks and more than 125 corporations in 11 countries. His North American real-estate interests had included the Montreal Stock Exchange Building, Paramount Studios in Hollywood, and the symbol of the American public's loss of political innocence, the Watergate complex in Washington, D.C. His personal net worth was estimated to have exceeded $500 million.

The ruin of the man whom *Business Week* had called "Italy's most successful and feared financier," whom *Fortune* had exalted as "one of the world's most talented traders," stirred a storm that shook the ashlar of international finance. But that storm was only a prelude to the tempest that followed.

Sindona's clients and partners had been among the most important and respected institutions in the world: Continental Illinois, Gulf & Western, the Hambros Bank of London, the Banque de Paris et des Pays-Bas, Nestlé of Switzerland, and others. But it was his relationship with the least affluent of those clients and partners, the Istituto per le Opere di Religione—the so-called Vatican Bank—that proved to be the most sensational.

It was rumored that the Vatican, which had long done business with Sindona, had lost some $30 million when his empire fell. Roberto Calvi, a Milanese banker whom Sindona had taken under his wing, had been placed by his mentor to assume charge of the Vatican's finances. In 1977, Calvi's Banco Ambrosiano began to crumble, and the following year a massive investigation concluded that the Vatican had been involved with Sindona and Calvi in numerous questionable deals. Later, prison sentences would be given to two senior administrators of the Vatican Bank, and the Catholic Church would be immersed in a scandal from which neither penance nor lies could deliver it.

It was alleged also that the secrecy with which Sindona had always surrounded himself hid from sight his darkest partner of all: the Mafia. "Sindona rarely speaks for the public record," *Newsweek* had stated. "As a result, rumors abound. One moment he is allegedly the Pope's chief financial adviser; the next, he is supposedly the Mafia's No. 1 banker." By the end of 1978, he was presumed to be both those things. In the months and years to follow, the flames of his infamy—fed by the corpses of the victims of strange and violent deaths, by tales of conspiracies beyond the ken of paranoia—rose wildly higher toward heaven and burned more deeply toward hell.

In early 1979 the U.S. Justice Department indicted and charged Sindona with ninety-nine counts of fraud, perjury, and misappropriation of bank funds in the matter of the Franklin National Bank. Four months later, Giorgio Ambrosoli, the attorney appointed by the Italian government to handle the liquidation of Banca Privata and Sindona's other state-seized holdings, was murdered near his home in Milan by Mafia gunmen. Soon after that, in the heat of a New York August, Michele Sindona, whose trial was scheduled to begin in less than five weeks, vanished. He reappeared in Manhattan in October, with a bullet wound in his leg and a tale of being kidnapped. In March 1980, he was convicted of sixty-eight of the counts that he had been charged with. While awaiting sentencing at the Metropolitan Correctional Center (MCC) in New York, he took an overdose of drugs and slashed his wrist. But he survived, and a month later, a federal judge sentenced him to twenty-five years in prison.

In March 1981, after Sindona had begun to serve his time in America, a detachment of the Guardia di Finanza, investigating his case in Italy, raided the office of Licio Gelli, a known associate of Sindona's. A man of Neronic wealth and ways, Gelli was the grand master of a secret Masonic lodge known as

3

Propaganda Due, or P-2. The raid led to a safe and a leather case marked "Fragile" and, within, a list of 962 supposed P-2 members. The list seemed to be nothing less than that of an underground, parallel state. It included the names of two current cabinet ministers, many members of the Italian secret-service and military hierarchy, diplomats, industrialists, police officials, bankers, and journalists, among them, the editor of Italy's most respected newspaper, the *Corriere della Sera.* Gelli, who had recently been seen at President Reagan's inauguration (the Republican Party of America was also found to be represented in the P-2 list), went into hiding, as the Italian government fell in the wake of the P-2 scandal. Gelli was later arrested in Geneva, while making a $50 million withdrawal from one of his Swiss accounts. He escaped from prison there and fled to safety. He is believed by many to be in Uruguay.

Roberto Calvi, Sindona's disciple and a revealed member of P-2, was arrested that same spring. He, too, disappeared; and in June 1982, his body was found hanging beneath Blackfriars Bridge in London.

While imprisoned in America, Sindona was charged in Italy with ordering the murder of Giorgio Ambrosoli, the state-appointed liquidator of his Italian empire. He was also indicted in Sicily, where he was accused of complicity in a $600-million-a-year heroin trade between Italy and America. In February 1984, as the government of Italy sought to extradite Sindona to stand trial for fraud and murder, Ambrosoli's killer, William Arico, was himself killed in what seemed to be a bizarre attempt to escape from a New York prison.

Sindona was rendered more and more as a dark and dangerous figure whose power within the Vatican and the spheres of international finance was equaled only by his power within the Mafia. From the presses of the United States, Great Britain, and Italy came sensational books about the entwined serpentine mysteries of the Vatican, Licio Gelli's P-2 lodge, and the death of Roberto Calvi. At the heart of these lurid mysteries was always Michele Sindona, who was no longer "the immaculate Italian banker" and "financial legend," as *Forbes* had described him before the fall, but rather "the Sicilian swindler who nearly bankrupted the Church" and "a powerful and respected member of the High Mafia." One book about him, an awkward blend of fact and gross fiction whose author (unbeknownst to the book's publisher and readers) was a convicted perjurer, was accepted by many at face value. By the spring of 1984, in another, more popular book, Sindona was even accused of having killed Pope John Paul I.

He had become the Antichrist, the Devil in chains, to whom the world turned to slake the cravings of its credulous paranoia, as if turning to the tree of the knowledge of good and evil itself. But none entered into him.

The mysteries enthralled me, as they enthralled many. I watched as his image shifted from flesh to fantasy, from the realm of notoriety to the realm of mythology; and I wondered at how, all the while, his own voice was unheard. And so one winter day, when the view of the world from where I stood was wearisome, I decided that I should meet the Devil.

I wrote a letter to him, federal prisoner Number 00450-054, and I got a call from his American attorney, Robert Costello. He told me that Sindona had received my letter and was willing to see me, if I could arrange a meeting through Warden Dale Thomas of the MCC in downtown Manhattan, where Sindona was being held awaiting possible extradition (and where, only two weeks before, William Arico, Sindona's alleged confederate in murder, also facing extradition to Italy, had fallen from the prison roof to his death below). The warden acquiesced, and on a March morning, winter's last, MCC executive assistant Wayne Seifert led me to be frisked and to have my wrist stamped with the password of the day—the ink was invisible, but would glow beneath the black light of a farther checkpoint—then to the third floor, to the attorney conference room, a small and sunless chamber within a vaster plan of bleakness. There arrived at the door a tall, gaunt man in a prison-issue orange jumpsuit and sneakers. His gray hair was brushed straight back from his high forehead. His eyes, which were dark brown and lambent, seemed to hold what remained of his will; and what remained in those eyes was considerable. He extended his hand, then smiled.

"I am Sindona," he said.

During the hours of that first meeting, as wariness ebbed, he began to tell me the tale of his rise and fall. It was a tale that wound from small-town Sicily to the papal palace, from the gold-spun web of international banking to the Washington, D.C., corridors of power; a tale peopled by popes, presidents, prime ministers, shahs, and denizens of the political and financial night. As he spoke, his voice now and then rising, his hand now and then turning in emphatic *fioritura,* he rendered as children's romance all the speculation and calumny that had raged around him. It was, he said, innocence masquerading as worldliness, folly pretending to wisdom: the secondhand fantasies of those to whom neither he nor the others in his story were flesh and blood, but rather distant phantoms in a callow dream; those who, fancying themselves exposers of wickedness and crusaders for truth, wielded wooden swords against what were only reality's shadows; those who spoke of good and evil, but not of the dragons beyond those comfortable conceits. Their world was different from the world he knew. They understood little of the powers among which he had lived, and their tales of him were not his own.

To be sure, his was a darker and more terrifying tale. The Vatican scandal, the Mafia executions, the multimillion-dollar wheelings and dealings, the strange deaths and disappearances —these were only the whitecaps, the stormy surface of his tale. Revelations of greater evil lay beneath—revelations of international terrorism, political blackmail, money-laundering schemes beyond the grasp of any government agency, vendettas on the grandest, deadliest scale, and even secret nuclear-technology deals that have invested the most dangerous and unlikely hands with the power to destroy the world.

Of course, there was no way of knowing if his tale lay

closer to the truth than the speculation and the calumny of those who never knew him. One thing was certain: The source of this tale, Sindona, alone knew the truth. And he had nothing left to lose.

There was something else. I remarked to him that it must have been an awful blow to have lost it all, to have gone from having nothing to having hundreds of millions of dollars to having nothing once again. His lips turned downward and he shrugged nonchalantly.

"If I were free tomorrow, I just start again. I make it all over," he said.

"Wouldn't it require a great deal of capital to get started?"

"Nothing," he said, his lips now turning upward, his eyes glimmering. "A thousand dollars. I go buy a Telex, a telephone connection. After that, no problem."

The possibility of laying open the system by which one of the world's wealthiest men acquired his fortune was, needless to say, no less intriguing than the arras-web of conspiracies, scandals, and mysteries that enwrapped him.

I visited him again the next morning. Toward the end of that long meeting, I handed him my pen and a sheet of ruled yellow paper, and he agreed to cooperate with me on a book. I looked at the signature that would later grow familiar—the *M* surging forward, the rest of the letters rising vertically as if to obstruct that initial assertive lunge—and I folded the paper and slipped it into my breast pocket.

Walking down to daylight, Wayne Seifert, the soft-spoken executive assistant who was soon to be raised to the rank of assistant warden, asked me what I thought of the MCC's most notorious resident. Like many Americans, he pronounced Sindona's first name as if it were a woman's, rendering the hard Italian *ch* as a *sh* sound. I told him that I was not yet sure, and I shrugged. I asked him what he thought of Sindona. "After a while, you just don't know," he said. "You stop trying to figure it all out."

Sindona's impending extradition became entangled in

governmental procedures. Not long after I last saw him that spring at the MCC, he was transferred back to the federal penitentiary at Otisville, New York. We were in touch throughout the summer. Slowly, my desk began to fill with documents in two languages, and with the transcriptions of our talks. By summer's end, I had begun in earnest my search through the netherworld into which Sindona had invited me.

Suddenly, on September 24, a new extradition treaty between America and Italy became effective, and, on the following day, Sindona was flown without notice to Italy, where he was taken under heavy guard to Rebibbia prison, in Rome, and placed in the maximum-security cell that had been occupied by Mehmet Ali Agca, the mad Muslim who had shot Pope John Paul II in the spring of 1981. On the last day of September, a Sunday, two judicial instructors from Milan moved him north to the Casa Circondariale Femminile on the outskirts of Voghera, thirty-six miles south of Milan. There, the sole male inmate of a women's prison, he awaited his trial.

On the day on which he had arrived in Italy, I read in *The Wall Street Journal* of "the hope that Mr. Sindona might shed further light on some of the darker mysteries of Italian political and financial life in the past decade." But the bank-fraud trial, which finally began on December 3, brought forth little light indeed. He smiled at first through the iron bars of his courtroom cage. Then he ceased smiling, and eventually, as the trial progressed, he refused to appear in court at all. On the ides of March, 1985, he was sentenced to twelve years in prison. The prosecutor, Guido Viola, calling Sindona "one of the most dangerous criminals in judicial history," had asked for fifteen years.

All the while, I had been trying to get permission to meet with Sindona for more interviews. In his letters to me from the women's prison, Sindona told me that he was being denied all visitors and that only orders from the U.S. Department of Justice could sway the Italian authorities to grant an exception. Trudging through the tortuous bureaucracy of the Criminal

Division, I found no one who was quite sure of exactly just what Sindona's present status was under the new extradition treaty. One gentleman, a Mr. White, professed an eager desire to be of help, and he assured me that he would personally attend to the matter during an official visit to Italy the following week. I never heard from him again. At last, I reached Murray Stein, the head of the Criminal Division's Office of International Affairs, and one of the authors of the recent extradition treaty. He told me that as long as Sindona was in Italy he was under the jurisdiction of that country alone.

"Every day he's there, a day is ticked off his sentence here," Stein said. "That's all. While he's there, he's theirs."

Meanwhile, one of my earlier inquiries to the Department of Justice had elicited a belated response from Mark M. Richard, whose letterhead identified him as a deputy assistant attorney general of the Criminal Division. "I suggest the following scenario," he wrote. "First, please contact the U.S. Consulate in Milan, and give the consular officer the name of an Italian official who can confirm that the authorization of the United States is required. . . . If such authorization is required, the State Department will contact the Department of Justice for our response, which in turn can then be communicated through official channels to the Ministry of Grace and Justice in Rome." He, too, assured me that, after all was said and done, the matter rested "solely with Italian authorities."

On April 16, a month after his sentencing, Sindona wrote to tell me that his lawyer Giampiero Azzali had obtained authorization for me from the Ministry of Grace and Justice in Rome, from the Magistrate of Surveillance of the Tribunal of Pavia, and from the director of the prison. But the Court of Assize in Milan, the remaining body whose permission I needed, was willing to grant us only two meetings of one hour each. Sindona said that the U.S. Justice Department had lied, that the Italian authorities would have yielded readily to instructions from Washington. Unless the Court of Assize could be made to bend, there was little hope of further interviews.

9

And there was not much time: Sindona's next trial, for murder, was to begin in June. "They will keep me here, in isolation, for as long as they can," he told me.

A few weeks later, on a rainy day in early May, I called at the U.S. Consulate in Milan's Piazza della Repubblica. I explained my problem to one of the Italians who worked there. He regretted that it was not within his power to help me, and he brought me to the consular officer in charge, a Mrs. Patterson. I told her of my situation. "We," she said, "do not want to be involved." She said that Sindona—and there was aversion in her voice when she pronounced his name—did not happen to be an American citizen, and therefore was not a concern of the consulate. I reminded her that I was an American citizen. "Nevertheless," she said, her frigid manner waxing timorous round the edges, "we don't want to get involved." It was still raining when I left.

Above the entrance of the Palazzo di Giustizia (the Palace of Justice) in Milan, august words are set in stone:

IURIS PRAECEPTA SUNT HAEC: HONESTE VIVERE
ALTERUM NON LAEDERE SUUM CUIQUE TRIBUERE

"These," says the Latin in the rock, "are the precepts of law: to live honestly, to harm no one, and to give each his due." The author of those words was the third-century Roman jurist Ulpian. Their presence above the entrance to the Palace of Justice attests to the undying nobility of something—law as we know it—that was born in Italy long ago. But the fate of Ulpian, who gave those words to Rome and to the world, and who in time was slain in the imperial palace beneath the light of day, attests to other undying things, greater than justice and more deeply set in ancient rock than any words, which dwell in palaces such as this.

I walked up the steps, past the pillars beneath the Latin, and entered the vast babel that is the legacy of the oldest judiciary heritage in the world. The swarm of the wronged and the wrongdoing filled the halls and winding stairways, poured forth onto mezzanines, wandered apprehensively through mazy corridors, vanished into dim cul-de-sacs. The pandemonium of their confluent disorder was leavened by the grander swarm among them—the magistrates and lawyers, the clerks and sinecured myrmidons, the politicians and prosecutors who were the sacristans and thralls of the unseen, undying things, whose labyrinths these were. The entire phantasmagoria seemed to be presided over, orchestrated, by an uncanny sense of the inevitable. A man with the eyes of a corpse was led shackled through the halls by blue-suited ranks of carabinieri. The mingled swarms drew back, fixing their eyes on his; then chaos resumed.

I made my way eventually to the office of the Central Chancellery of the First Court of Assize, where I was told that I needed to submit, through that office, a formal petition to the president of the First Court of Assize. My petition—the chancellor suppressed a grin—would be processed, presented, considered, and answered in due course. Upon his desk were disorderly piles of what I presumed to be petitions in various states of due course. One of his assistants, who had been searching through a nearby file cabinet, turned just then and diffidently remarked that the president happened to be in his office this morning. Raising his eyebrows, the chancellor pushed forth his lower lip and nodded slowly to express the possibilities presented to me by this propitious happenstance.

The third-floor office of the president lay in the relative quietude beyond the swarming din of justice. The outer door was ajar, and I entered. The antechamber was empty; the secretary's desk was vacant. The door to the inner office was open. President Camillo Passerini, the man who would soon oversee the trial of Michele Sindona for murder, rose gracefully from his desk and looked at me inquiringly. He was a tall, silvering-haired man of natural, Augustan dignity, and his serene eyes were those of one who had looked long at, and beyond, the Latin in the rock. We sat, and he listened silently to the tale of my pursuit through the bureaucratic miasma of two republics. He steepled his fingers and looked away, toward the faint sound of the spring rain; then he looked to me. He nodded. The authorization I sought would be granted; the necessary papers would be ready in the morning.

And so, there I sat in the falling night in the little park in Voghera.

I was still uncertain. I knew by now that much of what the world believed about Sindona and the events surrounding him was not true, that it was the stuff of both fatuous misknowledge and of deliberate falsity; and, during the last fourteen months, I already had uncovered strong indications that past and ongoing governmental prosecutions of Sindona were often conducted more to suppress than to serve the truth. But I still had no way of knowing if Sindona's rendering of the truth was not just a different, more sophisticated, and more convincing lie. His tale, as he had so far shared it with me, was a powerful one, and the consistency and conviction with which he delivered its complexities were equally puissant. I recalled the words of one of his own favorite philosophers: "With all great deceivers there is a noteworthy occurrence to which they owe their power. In the actual act of deception," Nietzsche said, "they are overcome by belief in themselves."

The unknown truth lay between light and dark. In my solitary stay in little Voghera, I glimpsed something that brought me closer to it.

The founding stones of this place were cut from the rock —again, the ancient rock—and laid to rise in the names of saints upon a vanishing crossroads from the second century before Christ. Seeming neither to have thrived nor to have fallen since then, but only to have somberly replaced the stones as they crumbled with the passing of the ages, Voghera had retained something of a timeless cast.

History here was a dream, vague stains upon the stones. Spray-painted swastikas faded upon a bare and further-fading Communist Party bulletin board upon a decaying wall near the southern end of the main street, Via Emilia, which bore the name of a forgotten Roman consul, Marcus Aemilius Scaurus, of more than two thousand years ago. Nearby, in Viale Carlo Marx, a carousel stood motionless and deserted amid the gloom of trees. Posters announced the forthcoming thousandth anniversary of the death of a saint who died here on a May day in 986. More plentiful were the black-edged posters advertising funerals, bearing the names of the dead beneath images of the thorn-crowned Christ.

In the Piazza Duomo, the endless work of the stones was tended to. Tapping and chinking, two men in their sixties laid cobbles into the dirt where the stones of another day had been sundered free. They moved slowly, choosing each stone carefully from the heap behind them, wielding their mason's mallets with deliberation. Upon a scaffold set against the wall of the cathedral, another man daubed mortar between some stones that the centuries had unsettled.

Matrimonial banns were posted near the Duomo's entrance. They declared that the condition of each named husband-to-be was *"celibe,"* that the condition of his intended bride was *"nubile."* In the arcade across the piazza, there was a painted phallus, still clear beneath the evidence of much futile scrubbing.

An old movie poster flapped in the damp wind outside a tobacconist's door. Here and there, store windows were filled with the glimmering currency of the American moment—record albums, designer jeans, computer software. But these were fleeting things. It was the morbid effigy entombed behind a grille, the dead virgin beneath the altar of the Duomo chapel, that endured.

The knelling and the shadows in the streets were hers. And, on the May day I first encountered her, the sky, too, was hers: a looming, sunless, silent-raining thing of gray upon gray upon gray. The world is mine and I am hers, it whispered.

On another May day, the piazza was flooded with sunlight, and the key of the stone chinkings had passed from minor to major. There was a carnival of stalls, and all that the sea and the earth yielded seemed to have come somehow to this obscure place. There were golden quails and rubicund boars, bright-eyed swordfish and casks of salted cod, peppercorn-studded cheeses and the fruit of trees. The Duomo was filled with sprays of white flowers and cascading light through painted glass; the blue sky above, with gliding swallows and darting swifts. The world is ours and we are the breeze of day's, they sang.

But—dark, light—the world belonged to neither. Lady death and life's bright breeze cast their illusions over the surface of the earth; but it was the business of the stones that truly mattered, that remained constant. Empires rose and fell, and all the grand conceits of politics and philosophy with which men swathed their avarice and impotence were fading ciphers on a wall not built to last. Beneath that play of shadows were the forces that, like ancient stones, prevail.

My thoughts turned to one of my meetings with Sindona the year before. In the course of the hours, our talk had strayed somehow to Dante. *"Nel mezzo del cammin di nostra vita,"* Sindona began to recite from memory, *"mi ritrovai per una selva oscura, che la diritta via era smarrita."* It was the opening of the *Commedia,* which Sindona had never forgotten: "In the middle of the journey of our life, I came to myself in a dark wood where the straight way was lost." He waved his hand in a way that was both weary and angry. "This is the real Inferno," he said, and he seemed to mean not only the walls that surrounded him, but what lay beyond as well.

In that dark wood where he had wandered lost, Dante became aware of three terrifying beasts, which were the forces of the world's evil. Dante emerged from the dark wood, and at his journey's end saw the stars of paradise.

Michele Sindona, in his way, had come to a dark wood where three beasts—Church, State, and Mafia, the forces that prevail beneath the play of the shadows of the world—spilled the blood of their pitting. This was the heart of the tale.

In the morning, I would finally see him again, in the prison on the edge of town, and the tale of his strange journey would continue. But on this night, no stars of paradise, no stars of any kind, shone down.

As it happened, that morning, May 8, 1985, was Michele Sindona's sixty-fifth birthday. In younger years, he had foreseen many possible fates, but entering the autumn of his life as an inmate of a maximum-security women's prison was one he had overlooked.

Newspapers called this place a *"supercarcere,"* or "super-prison." Barely four years old, it was the first fully electronic penitentiary in all of Europe. Three television cameras in Sindona's cell oversaw his every move. A cadre of twelve guards, working in shifts of two, watched over him around the clock.

I was taken to the office of the director of the prison, Dr. Aldo Fabozzi; then to a grimmer, grayer place in the compound's far reaches. After passing through a Friskem metal detector, I was locked in a room that was divided by a screen from another, identical room. I sat at the narrow table on my side of the partition, and I waited until the door of the other room opened.

The orange jumpsuit, like the thousand-dollar tailored suits from Donini and Carraceni that had preceded it, was gone now. In his baggy brown corduroy pants, with the tail of his red sweater sticking out from under his brown sweater, with his worn leather eyeglass case protruding from his pocket, he might have been one of those old cavalieri who had not gone beyond the towns of their birth, whose wanderings from sun to shade, from shade to sun, were as familiar to those towns as the flight of birds above.

I saw immediately that he looked much better—healthier, calmer—than he had the last time I saw him. His brown eyes were bright, and though there had been reports in the Italian press that he was fasting from mortal fear, he had obviously gained some needed weight.

"The tortellini is good in this town," he said, patting his

15

gut and smiling. There was an opening in the partition that allowed us to shake hands.

My first business was to have him sign an agreement stating that he would have no control over the book I was writing. As the eyes of a guard peered curiously at us through a small plate-glass window in the wall, this was done. The eyes vanished then, in time, returned again.

I told Sindona of the grace with which President Passerini had obliged me at the Palace of Justice in Milan.

Sindona nodded abstractedly. "He is not my enemy," he said. "I have no bad feelings for him. I don't think he has any for me. He only does against me what he must. Soon he must take part in the travesty of a trial, the outcome of which is preordained. The American lawyers tell me that I will be absolved, but they reason only in terms of the law and the facts, and do not take into account the political pressures that in Italy are decisive. I know otherwise, and I think the president of the court also knows otherwise."

His eyes, which had narrowed as he spoke, relaxed again, and he glanced at the pages of handwritten notes before me, displaying his uncanny and often disconcerting ability to read upside down anything that lay within arm's reach. It was, he had explained, a skill that had been his since childhood.

I asked, he answered, and slowly we drew closer to the woods beyond the shadows. As the hours passed, his spirits and the energy of his words were unflagging. Condemned to twenty-five years in prison in America, to twelve in Italy, and facing, at the age of sixty-five, yet another dooming, he was unvanquished; and the tale of his rise and ruin was as much marked by his savoring of its dark ironies as by the lingerings of bitterness. Toward the close of that first meeting in Voghera, I asked him what errant ray of hope sustained him. He looked at me and laughed softly, as if in wonderment that I did not already know.

"To die," he said.

II.
A Dream of Death

HE WAS BORN ON A SATURDAY, the eighth day of May 1920, and he was given the names of his grandfathers, Michele Sindona and Eugenio Castelnuovo, and at the font in that part of the church of San Nicola where the cool shadows gathered toward noon, he was wetted in the name of the Father and of the Son and of the Holy Ghost.

His Aragonese ancestors had sailed from Spain to Sicily, drawn by the Mediterranean wind that had risen in the wake of the Sicilian Vespers. Though the spilled blood of the French had possessed a special beauty for Sicily, the Vespers and the House of Aragon's ascension to that island's throne were only another upheaval in the long course of violent shifts of power that was Sicily's history. Through the ages, the island had known little peace from the dogs of empire. The Angevins, whose flag had been torn down and stamped into the dust that Easter Monday of 1282, had been preceded in Sicily by the Hohenstaufens; the Hohenstaufens, by the Normans. Before that, the Saracens had ruled for two hundred years. The Vandals then the Ostrogoths had come before, during the Western fall of the Roman Empire, under the domination of which Sicily had lain since the third century B.C. Before the Romans there were the Phoenicians and the Greeks, who had overtaken the native, prehistoric Siculi by 700 B.C., in the days of Homer. And it is likely that the Siculi, to whom the island owes its name, had displaced an even older people, the Sicani. The endless waves of dominion had wrought a culture like no other. By the late twelfth century, the prevailing languages in Sicily were Greek, Arabic, and Italian, while the court spoke Norman-French. There were large colonies of Jews and Muslims, and an increasing number of Italians from the mainland. Decrees were issued in Latin, Greek, and Arabic. The Muslims had their own, Koranic courts of law; Byzantine law was kept for the Greeks. Amid the rising power of the Roman Church, there were mosques, synagogues, and temples of Greek Orthodoxy. The capital city of Palermo—which had been Panormus under the Romans, al-Madinah under the Arabs—had an English-born archbishop. Beneath this carnival of tongues, laws, and creeds was Sicily's true and soundless spirit, the ingrained fatal sense, wrought also by those waves, that bound her.

The House of Aragon did not rule long in Sicily. The waves of the centuries' empires continued to roll and to break. Eventually, amid Sicilian execrations, the kingdoms of Sicily and Naples were merged, and in 1816, Ferdinand I, a Bourbon, proclaimed himself the king of the Two Sicilies. In 1860, Giuseppe Garibaldi wrested the Two Sicilies from the Bourbons, and in 1861, Victor Emmanuel II of the House of Savoy, to whom Garibaldi had handed his conquests, became king of a united Italy. Thus Sicily, which had been loosed from Roman rule fourteen hundred years before, once again lay under it.

Michele and Nunziata Sindona lived in the small town of Patti, on the northeastern coast, in the valley east of where the Timeto runs beneath Mount Litto. Facing the Tyrrhenian gulf that bears its name, Patti lies some thirty-five miles west of Messina, by winding coastal road; some twenty-five miles north of Mount Etna, through the hills. It was, and is, a town of dry sea breezes through narrow, whispering streets and bleached, open spaces; was, and is, one of those places that have neither thrived nor fallen, but tended to the stones.

The Sindonas were one of the respected families of Patti. Michele was a merchant, and he had done well with his hardware and his other goods. With Nunziata, he entered this century with strength in his arms and gold in his purse. Together they lived through the great earthquake that devastated Sicily and southern Italy, taking some 150,000 lives, on the third day of Christmas 1908. Together they rebuilt what God had destroyed, and their fortune grew. On a summer day in 1914, on the eve of Italy's entry into the looming European war, Michele went down to the sea, and he returned to his wife, and he left the world.

Antonino Sindona, the heir of his father's wealth, was his mother's only child. In 1914, not long after his father's death, he went to war. He was nineteen then. He returned four years later to find that the family business had been all but destroyed by credulous trust. Relatives and strangers, with smiles and tears and God-witnessed promises, had stolen from Nunziata, in her innocence, all that her husband had left of gold and strength.

Antonino married a woman named Maria Castelnuovo. She was a bride of dark, striking beauty, but she was eight years older than Antonino, and her body was frail. After bearing the two sons, Michele Eugenio and Enio, through whom the Sindona name would live on, her health worsened, and the raising of those sons fell to the care of their grandmother, Nunziata.

Trust beckoned Antonino, too. There were so-called friends with decks of cards and sheaves of lire. What the laws of chance did not take from Antonino and give to them, their cheating did. He quit gambling forever in 1922, and he forbade his sons to play at cards even without stakes. In time, he became a florist of sorts, fashioning wreaths for funerals, bouquets for graves.

One of the little boys was to become a quiet man, a scholar of renown. The other, whose eyes were darker and who smiled at the sea, was to become Sicily's most notorious son.

"People"—he smiled, a lifetime later, those dark eyes shining—"said I was a financial genius. But I understood the balance sheets because of Latin. Numbers meant nothing.

19

They were just a way of seeing. Through them I interpreted the life of a company."

The man who led Sindona to Latin, and to much else, was Professor Sardo-Infirri, who taught in the secondary schools, the *ginnasio* and the *liceo*, of Patti. He was Sindona's first, perhaps his only, mentor. From him, at the *ginnasio*, Sindona learned the Italian of Dante, the Latin of Virgil and Cicero, and the history that encompassed them all. Later, at the *liceo*, where Sardo-Infirri was the head of the school of arts, he introduced Sindona to philosophy. Until then, young Sindona had read novels, Tolstoy and such, for his pleasure. Now he turned to the Greek philosophers; from them, to the Germans. He fell under the fascination of Hegel's "absolute world spirit," of that vast attempt to fathom the force beneath history. He moved through sunless Schopenhauer, then to fulminating Nietzsche. In time, he came to Pascal. This seventeenth-century Frenchman, who had invented a computer, pioneered the calculus of probability, and produced a treatise on conic sections before writing his *Pensées*, possessed a special appeal for Sindona, who would say always that the greatest philosophers were also the greatest mathematicians. Throughout his life, he would read and read again, through his rise and through his fall, in the gardens of fortune and in prisons, the philosophers to whom Professor Sardo-Infirri steered him; and he would say that it was that rare man of Patti who had opened his eyes to see.

From the age of fourteen, in addition to pursuing Latin, mathematics, and philosophy at the *liceo*, Michele worked as a typist and bookkeeping assistant at the office of his cousin Vittorio Cappadona, who had a small law practice in Patti. It was there, while still in his teens, that Michele gained a working knowledge of civil law; and it was there, studying the trade contracts that passed before him, that he came to see that there was more to business than selling flowers to those who tend the dead. The absolute world spirit was a series of deals, each deal a moment unto itself, its possibilities bound only by the limits of the minds of the men whose deal it was. At his cousin's little office, he saw where his future lay.

It was at Cappadona's office, too, that Michele lost his political innocence and discovered the mundane reality of Pascal's lofty dictum "We are equally incapable of truth and good." He saw that bureaucratic corruption was common. Several of his cousin's clients—"important men," Sindona explained, then laughed quietly, "by Patti standards"—routinely bribed local authorities to obtain construction permits, to avoid taxes. It was petty. But soon, when Sindona began to rise through the years, he saw that it was everywhere, that its breath and the breath of power were one.

At the age of fifteen, in addition to his classes and his work at Cappadona's law office, he began to tutor younger students in mathematics, Italian, and Latin. He was honored when Professor Sardo-Infirri sent his own children to him to learn algebra.

In 1938, his excellence at the *liceo* earned him a full scholarship to the University of Messina, the revered Sicilian institution that had been founded near the sea, beneath the rule of Spain, in 1549. He quit working for his cousin, and he took a job in Messina at the Ufficio delle Imposte, the local tax office. His starting salary, 330 lire a month, was barely enough to subsist on. After his first three months, it was doubled. He worked at the tax office for two years, while attending the university and tutoring—philosophy and physics now, as well —in the evenings. (For a while, in 1941, he took on additional, managerial work, at Bosurgi, Sicily's major citrus producer.) Though he was studying for a degree in tax law, the Ufficio delle Imposte offered insights into the recondite workings of the Italian tax system as no course could. As he foresaw, they were insights that would later prove invaluable.

He watched the light of the seasons wane toward winter, under the greater westerly darkness of another nearing war, and he wondered what would be left. He had written his dissertation on *The Prince* of Machiavelli, the sixteenth-cen-

21

tury philosopher whom all knew but few read, and whose wisdom, to Sindona, seemed to have grown brighter with the accruing westerly darknesses of every passing age. In the spring of 1942, a few weeks after his twenty-second birthday, Michele Sindona—Avvocato Sindona now—left the walls of the university.

Back in Patti, he found his first clients. They were two brothers named Caleca; one was a pasta-maker, the other a producer of stoneware. He was in business.

The sky over Sicily, and over Italy, was changing. In the year after the death of the grandfather Michele had never known, thirty-two-year-old Benito Mussolini—schoolteacher, journalist, civil servant—had organized his *fascio d'azione rivoluzionaria* (revolutionary action group), whose aim was the entry of Italy into World War I on the side of the Entente powers. After the war, the *fascio d'azione rivoluzionaria* had blossomed in the night, becoming first the *fasci di combattimento* (combat group), then finally, in 1921, the Partito Nazionale Fascista (National Fascist Party). A year later, following his March on Rome, Mussolini was granted unrestricted powers by Parliament, and in the elections of 1924, the Fascists took the majority of the votes. In 1926, Mussolini, hailed now as *Il Duce del Fascismo*, took his place beside the king. Elections were suspended; government by decree had begun.

Michele Sindona had grown up under that Fascist government. While attending university, he had refused to wear the military uniform that Mussolini had decreed upon male students. His perfect grade of 110, he later recalled, was lowered accordingly, to 105, in punishment.

Though he hated Fascism for what it was and, even as a boy, found Mussolini's Napoleonic delusions to be as ridiculous as they were dangerous, he knew that some good had come from it. He knew that Alfredo Rocco, the minister of justice under Mussolini from 1925 to 1932, had been a brilliant man. Indeed, *Il Codice Rocco*, his overhauling of the Italian penal code, enacted in 1931, would, with modifications, remain the basis of Italian criminal law. And he knew that Mussolini, in the vanity of his sovereignty, had subdued the black forces of the island of Sicily.

The Roman dominion of the island had transformed it into a territory of immense landed estates, called *latifundia,* which were worked for the profit of wealthy landlords who dwelled on the mainland. This system of landed estates survived through the Sicilian reigns of the Goths, the Byzantines, and the Arabs. Under the Normans, the island was divided into seigniories, after the French feudal system. Throughout the centuries, there were peasant uprisings, but, as *latifundia,* as seigniories, or as *feudi,* as the Italians came to call them, these landed estates of faraway lords remained the system of Sicily's economic hell through the time of Garibaldi's conquest; and it was not until April 1870 that the feudal system was abolished by Italian law. In the small private armies, the *compagnie d'armi,* which protected the *feudi* of the absentee barons and which were the arbiters of unseen might among the peasantry, the black forces had their origin.

In oriental Sicily, where, since Norman times, middle-class commerce rather than the feudal system had dominated the economy, those black forces held little power. As Luigi Barzini wrote of the Mafia in this century, "It rules over only one part of Sicily; its threats are terrifying in Palermo, Partinico or Agrigento, but are ignored in Messina, Catania and Syracuse." According to the testimony of Don Tommaso Buscetta, the most important Sicilian Mafioso to turn against his own kind (he was extradited to America under the same treaty that effected Sindona's return to Italy, in 1984), Messina and Syracuse are today the only two of Sicily's nine provinces that have remained free from the Mafia.

As a boy in Patti, Sindona had not known those dark forces that lay over the west, that had given Sicily its air of foreboding and doom, its air of endless slumbering beneath a dream of death. Even in the west, in the years of his boyhood, that darkness had been lifted. Mussolini, who could bear no forces that did not kneel before him, had the beast of the honored society driven down. Prefect Cesare Mori, the man ordained by Il Duce to destroy the beast, in 1924, had carried out his crusade with a passion. Fingernails were removed with pliers, genitals were crushed, and an electric-shocking device called the *cassetta* was used in the pursuit of information and confessions. In 1926, the first laws against the Mafia were decreed. In that same year, Don Vito Cascio Ferro of Palermo, who for a quarter of a century had been the unchallenged head of the Mafia, was arrested by Mori and committed to the Ucciardone prison, where he died. In 1929, conspiracy charges were brought against Don Calogero Vizzini, who had succeeded Don Vito to power. The regime was deemed invincible, and the beast lay still.

In June 1940, Italy under Mussolini had entered World War II, declaring war on England and France. Now, three years later, in July 1943, British and American troops landed on the southern coast of Sicily. By August, when Messina fell to the Allies, Mussolini had been removed from office, and a new government, without Fascist members, had been formed under the king. On September 3, the Allied troops moved on from their conquest of Sicily to the mainland, and five days later, Italy surrendered. It was a moment that Michele Sindona would never forget, a moment that illuminated the ages-old soul of Italy and the nature of Italian politics more perfectly than all the volumes of all her sage and learned men. He would grin sardonically whenever he remembered it: "Overnight, forty-nine million Fascists became members of the Resistance. They went to sleep singing 'L'Abissinia,' they woke up humming 'God Bless America.'"

The fall of Fascism was followed quickly by the resurgence of the honored society in western Sicily. It was, Sindona saw, a resurgence abetted by the Allies, who had enlisted the native aid of the Mafia in overtaking their common enemy. (Later, the purported role of Lucky Luciano in arranging this unholy alliance from his New York prison cell was offered as justification for his parole, in 1946, by Governor Thomas E. Dewey, the same man who, as a New York special prosecutor, had convicted Luciano a decade before. But it is likely that contributions to Dewey's presidential campaign of 1944 and his successful gubernatorial reelection campaign of 1946 had more to do with Luciano's release than either the patriotism or the Sicilian powers fancifully ascribed to him.)

British officers Sindona spoke with in Messina expressed their disapproval of the Americans' behavior. Sindona did not agree with them. He said that the end justified the means. But he was soon dumbfounded by the later actions of AMGOT, the Allied Military Government of Occupied Territories. Under such AMGOT officers as Colonel Charles Poletti, a former lieutenant governor of New York, the Mafiosi who had been driven down by Mussolini's reign were placed in positions of official power that they could only have dreamt of in the golden days before Fascism. In that hot summer of 1943, Don Calò Vizzini, whose indictment under Il Duce had signified the suppression of the honored society, received a contingent of Allied officers at his capital of Villalba. In a quiet ceremony, the American officer of civil affairs appointed Don Calò mayor of Villalba. Mayor Vizzini then presented AMGOT with a list of other respected victims of Fascism. They were all good men, and they deserved to be the mayors of their towns.

"To reward men like Don Calò for their help, that is one thing," Sindona recalled saying to an American soldier in Messina. "But to make them mayors, to give Sicily to them on a golden salver—that is awful. It is a great mistake." The soldier shrugged.

And so America had loosed the beast again. The United States, Sindona would say repeatedly, was a very young and naive nation. The beast was old and wise. It would never be driven down again, but would grow and roam wider and more ravenously. Sicily would remain its mother, but the world would be its whore.

As the sky changed in 1943, Michele leased one of the

25

army trucks that had fallen into civilian use. He began to journey every few weeks toward the center of the island, where grain and legumes were plentiful but citrus fruits were scarce. He would bring a truckful of lemons with him. He would sell the lemons at a good profit, then fill the truck with wheat, lentils, fava beans, carobs, chick-peas, and other foodstuffs that were scarce in the east; then he would return home and turn another profit.

But every time he bought goods to load his truck, he realized those goods were costing him more. He began to hedge by buying on margin against future inflation.

"How much wheat do you have?" he might ask.

"So many tons," he might be told.

"Costo?"

"Five hundred."

"I give you five percent now," he would tell the baffled farmer. "Hold onto it till I come back in a few weeks."

If inflation during those few weeks caused the price of grain to rise so much that Sindona made too striking a profit, he would allay the farmer with bolts of fancy fabrics for his wife. Like lemons, cloth came cheap in Messina.

Thus, Michele Sindona, under that changing sky, brought commodity futures speculation to rural Sicily. He continued hustling back and forth, from law in Patti to lentils in the high country, for close to a year. In 1944, he passed a special examination that enabled him to practice law anywhere in Italy. On September 4 of that year, he took a bride.

In Patti, where the furtive innuendo was both an industry and an art, Sindona had long been regarded as something of a womanizer, as a philanderer among the flashing skirts of Messina's cafés and scented parlors. But the woman, pretty Caterina Cilio, who walked with him that sultry day from the old church of the Madonna del Tindari in the hills above Patti, was one he had known since those childhood days of the tales.

He and Rina moved to an apartment in Messina, where his law practice grew. He wrote articles on the injustices of the fiscal system for *Il Bollettino Economico della Sicilia,* a publication of the chamber of commerce; and his practice grew greater still. Soon he knew and was known by all who did business in Messina or Catania.

On March 29, 1945, Rina gave birth to a baby girl. She was named Maria Elisa, for the mother whose illness and frailty had held her from her son.

A new Italy was born the following spring. King Victor Emmanuel III abdicated and left the country, leaving his son on the throne as Umberto II. A plebiscite abolished the monarchy, and Umberto followed his father into exile. On June 18, the Republic of Italy was proclaimed.

Two months after that, in August 1946, Michele Sindona kissed his wife and his blood good-bye. He crossed the Strait of Messina—the narrows, said the ancients, where Scylla and Charybdis lay—to the mainland; and he headed north, toward the world and all its might, toward where the dream of death and other dreams conspired.

III.
Fortuna

"LA FORTUNA É DONNA"—"Fortune is a woman"—Machiavelli said, "and it is necessary, if you wish to master her, to conquer her by force; and it can be seen that she lets herself be overcome by the bold rather than by those who proceed coldly."

So went young Michele Sindona, past Scylla and Charybdis, northward, past holy Rome, where the will of another world lay buried with its gods, northward, to Milan, where the fortunes of a new Italy stirred. It was languorous August, the *ferragosto.* Beneath the pealing of her campanile bells, in the shadow of the little madonna atop the towering Duomo of San Ambrogio, the city slept; and as she slept, he entered her.

The only person Michele Sindona knew in Milan when he arrived was Nino Cappadona, the brother of the cousin at whose law office he had worked in Patti. The elder Cappadona, a machine-tools dealer, opened his door to Michele and welcomed him to his table. But it was not long before Michele established himself in that city of fortunes.

He was befriended by Giuseppe Orlando, the young president of Milan's Mercantile Association. Back home, Michele had learned that declaiming the unfairness of the tax system in public print was a very effective way to lure new clients. In Milan, he began to publish articles in *Il Commercio Lombardo,* which had been founded by Orlando and others the previous year as the official organ of the Unione Commercianti of the province of Milan. (In Milan, the Unione Commercianti comprised sixty-four branches of business—steel, textile, chemical, and so on—each organized into its own association.) Sindona's first piece for *Il Commercio Lombardo*, a proposal for the restructuring of income-tax laws, was published on the front page of the issue of November 15, 1946. He would continue to write for *Il Commercio Lombardo* for the next two years, eventually becoming a legal consultant to the steel, chemical, paper, leather, and other associations of the Unione Commercianti.

His first client in Milan was Arturo Doria, an industrialist marquis whose companies were involved in chemicals, machinery, and rubber. Marchese Doria gave Sindona his first home in Milan, in the northern Affori area, accepting his legal services in lieu of rent.

Having in the breadth of six months laid his hand to that place where the hairs curled on fortune's neck, Michele summoned his family—his mother and grandmother and brother, as well as his wife and daughter—north to join him in February 1947. On March 5 of the following year, a first son was born to him and Rina, and he was named Nino, in honor of Michele's father.

The one whose name the child bore remained in Sicily, where he found a job with the Consorzio Agrario Provinciale, the local agricultural administration. But Michele had designs that would end that.

As Michele paid his rent with his wits, so he began to acquire stocks in the same manner, seeking as payment shares instead of cash from certain companies that retained him. This was a system he used with great discretion. Preferring cash payment in general, he sought shares only from ailing companies in which he perceived latent possibilities. The greater the spread between a company's potential and the devaluation of its stock, the more he pursued it. Studying the books and balance sheets of the companies that hired him, he searched for hidden veins of gold beneath the numbers; and when a glimmer caught his eye, he moved.

The first company he took over in this way was the pharmaceutical company Farmeuropa, in 1949. With the help of importers Sindona knew through the Unione Commercianti, Farmeuropa began bringing in marlin oil from Norway, and agar-agar, a seaweed-extract jelly valued as a solidifying agent in bacteriology, from Japan. But Sindona's primary purpose in taking over Farmeuropa was not to capture the agar-agar market in Italy, but rather to acquire a company—any company—of which he could appoint his father manager. So, in 1950, after acquiring 50 percent of the company from its original owner, a man named Monteverdi, Michele succeeded in removing his father north to Milan. "Don't give him too much work," said Sindona with a smile to his partner; and Monteverdi, grateful to the man who had given new life to his company, smiled in return.

And 1950 was the year Sindona bought Fasco, A.G. Though this small Liechtenstein stock company was then, as Sindona later described it, an "empty shell," it would become the holding company for all the vast and various wealth of his empire to come.

His enterprising ranged farther. Through the aunt of Marchese Doria, the actress Gina Faver, he became the chief executive officer of San Giorgio Film, S.p.A. When the production company went to Cortina d'Ampezzo, in the Carnic Alps, to make a movie called *24 Ore in Cortina,* Sindona went along because he liked the mountains and he liked pretty girls. Another of his clients, Piero Tramarollo, was married to the Florentine actress Germana Paolieri. One of the celebrated young stars of the past decade, her blond, slender image had begun to fade from the screen. Though she had turned with success to the theater, her desire, after years of childless marriage, was to return to the cinema. With her husband's help, and with Sindona as her chief executive officer, she started the Castello Brianteo production company. Once again, Sindona liked the view. But to him moving pictures were folly. During the making of one of them, he watched as a director urged an actress to further unbutton her blouse and hike her skirt. A few months later, upon the picture's release, Sindona was amused to find that critics wrote of it earnestly in terms of art and various other desiccated nouns. Truly, this was a world for the taking.

By the time he turned thirty, in the spring of 1950, Michele Sindona was a millionaire. That first fortune, the foundation of what followed, was largely made in real estate.

He had been introduced by an acquaintance to Raul Baisi, a big *commercialista*—a business consultant and accountant— who abhorred doing his clients' taxes. As taxes were Avvocato Sindona's specialty, Baisi gave all such work to him. The two became friends.

Between 1947 and 1950, Italy's postwar inflation had been reined to a halt by the government of Prime Minister Alcide De Gasperi, and the country was on the verge of a tremendous and long-lasting economic surge. Sindona was one of the men who caught the sea scent of that forthrushing epoch, and he moved, seizing land on which the tide of that surge would rise.

With Raul Baisi, he began buying land outside Milan and near the Adriatic shore east of Ferrara. The land outside Milan cost them 100 lire per square meter. They spent another 200 lire per meter for sewage and electrical installations. They resold the land for 3,000 lire a square meter. Much of the land near Ferrara was marsh. While waiting for the inevitable developers, Sindona and Baisi reaped a profit marketing the eels —an especially toothsome and sought-after variety of *anguille* —that slithered there in plenty.

Michele's fortune and power rose as the Italian economy billowed throughout the 1950s. He moved his family into the newly built luxury apartments at Via Visconti di Modrone 30, near the historic heart of the city, and acquired a country estate in Brianza, about twenty-five miles north of Milan. Rina gave birth to the last of their children, Marco, on April 8, 1952. Like his elder brother and sister, Marco would grow up speaking the pure, high Italian that Michele had mastered long ago, and would never know the impenetrable, consonantal language of Sicily.

Michele's younger brother, Enio, whose mind ran far from the business of the world, had begun to establish himself as an art historian of some repute in Milan. In 1952, Michele acquired a publishing company, Istituto Editoriale Italiano, and placed Enio as the director of its art-book series, Libri d'Arte, for which Enio himself eventually contributed volumes on Paolo Uccello, Pietro Cavallini, and Pisanello. Enio also became the editor of the venerable journal *L'Arte.*

The painters on whom Enio dwelled were products of those centuries—the *trecento,* the *quattrocento*—that also gave birth in Italy to capitalism as we know it, from the bills of exchange and the international-trade credit devices of the 1300s to the founding of the first modern bank, at Genoa, in 1407. It was this latter legacy of the Renaissance, the power that bought the blows that hewed the *Pietà,* that bought the strokes that colored Iscariot's brow on the cloister wall of Santa Maria delle Grazie, it was this, the business of the power beneath the glory, that claimed Michele and that drew Michele on.

The economic philosophy of Sindona, espoused by him at the March 1951 Study Conference on the Costs of Distribution and elsewhere, did not change with the years. It was one of absolute freedom of trade. With a grin, he called himself "a direct descendant of Adam Smith." Like that eighteenth-century Scotsman, who advocated in *The Wealth of Nations* a system of "perfect liberty," Sindona damned all interference by the state in private enterprise. He read widely in the works of modern economists, but found little of worth in them. In Milton Friedman, however, whose *Essays in Positive Economics* he read in 1953, Sindona encountered a voice he respected.

Though he would say always that he was *homo economicus,* not *homo politicus,* economics and politics were, the one from the other, inextricable. Italy's democratic constitution, after eighteen months of debate, had finally been approved in December 1947, and had gone into effect on the first day of 1948. Like most other democratic constitutions of this century, it placed true power in a council of ministers, the *consiglio dei ministri,* depending on the support of an elected chamber of deputies, the *camera dei deputati.* This chamber and the senate, the *senato,* comprised the legislature, the *Parlamento.* Elected by Parliament rather than by the vote of the people, the president of the republic would always be little more than a figurehead whose power it was to nominate the prime minister (the *presidente del consiglio*) and other council ministers. The real sovereignty lay in the hands of Parliament.

The first election under the constitution was held on April 18, 1948. Emerging as prime minister was the sixty-seven-year-old leader of the Christian Democrats, Alcide De Gasperi, who had acted in the interim government since the war. With the taciturn support of the first president of the republic, Luigi Einaudi, a professor of economics and finance at Turin, De Gasperi sought to bring Italy more closely together with the anticommunist nations of the West. This was a state of affairs strongly supported by Michele Sindona and his politically concerned business allies in Milan. But during that first year of democracy, the Partito Comunista Italiano (PCI), which had risen as a partisan group three years before, established itself as the second strongest party in Italy.

To Sindona, whose belief in the "perfect liberty" of capitalism was as vehement as Caesar's belief in *imperium,* communism was anathema. "We can (and must) begin to build up Socialism," Lenin had said, "with the material bequeathed us by Capitalism." It was that bequeathing that Sindona fought to prevent. In January 1933, the Fascist government of Mussolini had founded the Istituto Nazionale per la Ricostruzione Industriale (IRI), a state-controlled holding company designed to rescue Italy's failing banks and their industrial interests. IRI was conceived as a transitory institution. All its holdings were to be resold and returned to private hands. But, in 1937, IRI had assumed permanence, and in the years since then, it had grown monstrously. This vast machine of nationalization, in the grasp of a communist government, could become one of the great bequeathers of Lenin's dream. In February 1953, the month before the death of Josef Stalin, the self-exalting Russian leader whose relentless ideology had begun to enchant the communists of Italy, the Italian government gave birth to another vast state entity, the industrial-energy conglomerate Ente Nazionale Idrocarboni (ENI).

To Sindona, and to many others, the increasing, converging forces of nationalism and communism were a menace that threatened to undermine Italy's current capitalist renaissance. In Palmiro Togliatti, the austere little leader of the PCI, Sindona perceived the enemy, the embodiment of the tyranny of the weak. To him, Togliatti, who had taken part in the Moscow Comintern of the 1920s, was "the eyes and ears of Stalin in Italy." During De Gasperi's years as prime minister, Togliatti represented the greatest opposition. After De Gasperi stepped down in 1953, the year before his death, the Christian Democrats continued to govern, but with the frequent changes— eventually, the toll would reach forty-five governments in the span of years since World War II—that inevitably gave Italy her reputation of governmental instability. In those years following 1953, the *democristiani* grew weaker and more fragmented, while the electoral gains of the communists, like those of the neo-Fascist Movimmento Sociale Italiano (MSI) and socialist Partito Socialista Italiano (PSI), grew ever greater.

Sindona saw that the blindness of many of the big-business men around him would contribute to their own undoing. These were men who did not understand that no coin bore their image, that their fortunes were of this world and therefore susceptible to its winds. He spent as much time fighting with those he called "dumb capitalists" as with communists. "You," he exclaimed to Giorgio Valerio, the president of the giant Edison company, later to fall to government control, "You are the best possible advertisement for communism."

"Capitalism," he would tell those who listened, "is the breast of the fecund cow from which the milk for all flows. With nationalization, the breast of the cow is cut off, and there is no more milk."

IV.
Church and State

ON THE JUNE DAY IN 1907 when ten-year-old Giovanni Battista Montini had made his first Holy Communion, in the Lombardy village of Concesio, near Brescia, his father, Giorgio, had given him a Bible, and that Bible had become the dearest possession of that son. He carried it with him still, forty-seven years later, when he—Monsignor Montini now—was sent from the Vatican Curia to the see of Milan by Pope Pius XII.

Consecrated archbishop of Milan on December 12, 1954, Montini, in the course of his Christmastide steps among that city's society, encountered that most striking young man of affairs, Michele Sindona. In the first weeks of the New Year, the communist labor leader Pietro Secchia fought to stop Archbishop Montini from saying mass in factories around Milan. With the support of his allies in industry, Sindona came to the aid of the new archbishop. It was a conflict Michele relished.

He became more involved in political matters the following year. In the east, across the Alps, in November 1956, the people of Hungary rose against the Soviet-satellite government that had been imposed on them. After bloody skirmishing, the communist army retreated before the native troops led by Colonel Pal Maléter. But the Western support that Hungary hoped for never came, and new Russian tank units crushed the revolution. Some 200,000 people fled the country. A handful of them, about fifty refugees, found protection in Sindona, who transported them to the sanctuary of the Carla and Rina Farm, Ltd., vacation property owned by him and his

37

partner Raul Baisi (named for their wives) in Blind River, Ontario. With Sindona's help, they all eventually found work in the uranium mines of that Canadian region, while Michele himself found the enduring enmity—which, too, he relished—of Italy's burgeoning Stalinist left.

Those were busy times for Sindona. On March 25, 1957, the Treaty of Rome established the European Common Market of Italy, France, Belgium, Holland, Luxembourg, and West Germany. In the ensuing conferences on taxes, distribution costs, and the unifying of European business laws, various trade associations of the Unione Commercianti chose Sindona to represent them. Eventually, in 1960, he published a small book on the tax and distribution-cost aspects of the Common Market, *Oneri fiscali e costi della distribuzione nel Mercato Comune Europeo*, with a preface by Giuseppe Orlando, the Mercantile Association president who had befriended him in his early days in Milan.

Nineteen fifty-seven was also the year in which Sindona lost his father, who fell from a sudden stroke. In gratitude for the years Monteverdi, his partner at Farmeuropa, had kept his father as manager of that company, Sindona sold him his shares at par value.

Not long after he relinquished Farmeuropa, he made what was one of the most momentous deals of his early career. His client and friend Ernesto Moizzi owned, among his other interests, Acciaierie Vanzetti, S.p.A., a steel factory that had been suffering under inadequate management and the control of banks with no expertise in steel. Sindona perceived the possibilities of the Vanzetti steelworks not only in terms of potential profits, but also, because of its location in Milan, in terms of real-estate value. During one of Italy's recurrent steel crises, he bought it from Moizzi for the equivalent of $200,000.

In the months that followed, Sindona spent more time at Vanzetti than he had dedicated to any other of his acquisitions. As the legal representative of the Assofermet, the steel association of the Unione Commercianti, he used his influence and connections to see to it that there were buyers for the steel Vanzetti produced.

"If you're going to buy a hundred tons of steel, buy ten from me," he would say.

In less than two years' time, Vanzetti, under his control, went from considerable losses to consistent profits, and in 1959, he sold it to Crucible Steel of America, the sixty-year-old company that was then the world's most important producer of special steels.

In a letter to Sindona expressing his satisfaction with the deal, Joel Hunter, the president of Crucible, later confessed that the balance sheets submitted by Sindona had been found, by the New York auditing firm of Deloitte Plender Haskins & Sells, to reveal unaccounted reserves of about $75,000, and that this was the first time those famous auditors had ever encountered an understatement in the balance sheets of a European seller. In an avuncular manner, Hunter advised him that such benign probity in business was equal almost to stupidity.

But neither Hunter nor the big New York auditors knew about those pieces of cloth with which Sindona had long ago charmed the farmers of the Sicilian high country, distracting their eyes from the immensity of his profits. Neither Hunter nor the accountants knew what Sindona knew—that honesty, besides any merits it might possess as a virtue, was the best racket, that it was an instrument of great and ever-accruing bargaining might in the hands of the one who wielded it.

In that 1959 Crucible deal, Sindona realized a net profit of $2 million. In addition, he became vice-president of the new Acciaierie Crucible Vanzetti, S.p.A. Though the deal eventually turned bad for the American company—the original mill was deemed too small, and Crucible built another, which never worked properly—Crucible's relationship with Sindona, whose skills proved to be of great value to the company before and during its difficulties, was a remarkably good one.

Through the Crucible deal, Sindona became close friends

with Daniel A. Porco, the Crucible international vice-president who would later come to work for him. And through the Crucible deal, Sindona established his presence and his powers in the grander, international realm. From now on, more and more, he would cast his will across the sea toward that New World of arrogance and innocence, *l'America,* born of the greed of Europe and by Europe's God so blessed.

In that year of the Crucible deal, Sindona came once again to the aid of the archbishop, this time by assisting in the financing and construction of a home for the aged that Montini had long been yearning to build.

Sindona had come to know the archbishop well during the first five years of his see. The prelate's soul was not a simple one. Pope John XXIII, who had raised him to the rank of cardinal in 1958, referred smilingly to him as "our Hamlet cardinal." Though his devotion to the church was unquestioned, there was about him an air of enigmatic brooding and anguish that set him apart from his fellow churchmen in the ecclesiastical hierarchy. While the Bible given him that spring day more than half a century before was still the book dearest to him, he had grown into a man who read widely in several languages, and who, as a cardinal, would write the preface to the Italian edition of the French philosopher Jacques Maritain's *Humanisme intégral.* Among the people of Milan, and within the Roman Curia, his reputation as a man of social conscience was great. Yet it sometimes seemed that the good works—the serving of the laboring poor, the caring for the elderly—seen as the bounty of his concern for humanity were in fact penance for the estrangement from the masses that he really felt.

The two men, Sindona and Cardinal Montini, were so dissimilar and yet so kindred in many ways. The one born of the falling, the other of the rising, of the same Christian breath; the one as earnest in his worldliness as the other in his renunciation of it; the ladies' man and God's man—they were destined, each in his way, for glory's passing warmth amid the thrones and furies of this world.

It was said that the Duomo of Milan, the great, ornate cathedral raised in the late fourteenth century, stood on the site of the baptistry of Saint Ambrose, the Roman lawyer who became Milan's first archbishop, and who here baptized Saint Augustine on the Easter eve of the year 387. Close to the cathedral, southeast of it, in the Piazza Fontana, lay the Palazzo Arcivescovile, the palace of the archbishop. There, within the cloistered and tapestried quietude of the cardinal's quarters, the two men talked, coming to know each other in the shifting afternoon light of seasons' passing, but each to never cease wondering at the soul of the other.

Cardinal Montini's father was a lawyer who had been active in the Partito Popolare, the anti-Fascist group that had become the Christian Democrats; and his older brother, Lodovico, was a member of Parliament. He himself, however, as Sindona had discovered, knew little of politics and economics. Their common ground, other than their belief in the God of their ancestors, lay in the classics and in philosophy. The cardinal never failed to be provoked by Sindona's admiration for Nietzsche, the philosopher who had declaimed that "Christianity was the vampire of the *Imperium Romanum*," who had written "I *condemn* Christianity, I bring against the Christian Church the most terrible charge any prosecutor has ever uttered. To me it is the extremest thinkable form of corruption, it has had the will to the ultimate corruption conceivably possible."

The cardinal would shake his head disgustedly. "You like Nietzsche because you believe in his *Übermensch*, his superman," he would say.

"No," Sindona would say. "I like Nietzsche because he believed Socrates was greater than Napoleon."

And as the light shifted, as the seasons passed, neither man could know that the one would soon be pope, and that the other, soon to be among the earth's richest men, would raise

41

the gold-wrought sword of that church into which they both were born and in which they both would die.

"Money answereth all things," it was written in the Book of Ecclesiastes.

Through the Gate of Saint Anne into the Vatican City State, left to the little, high-walled Courtyard of the Triangle, to the fifteenth-century Tower of Saint Nicholas, there, atop that olden bulwark, was the IOR.

The Istituto per le Opere di Religione (Institute for Religious Works) was founded on June 27, 1942, by a special charter, a *chirografo*, of Pope Pius XII. As an institution thus founded and directed by the pope, the IOR was not the Vatican bank, as it wrongly came to be known, but rather the pope's bank.

Absorbing the older Administration of Religious Works that had been set up by Leo XIII in 1887, the purpose of the IOR was twofold: to guarantee the clergy secrecy in banking, and to manage fiduciary deposits in a manner that would yield profits that the pope could then use in his various works. Under the Lateran Treaty of 1929, in which Mussolini gave sovereign independence to the Vatican City State, such profits from investments by the IOR were exempt from taxation by the Italian government; and that treaty, alone of Mussolini's works, was later confirmed by the constitution of 1947.

It was decreed that the nominal president of the IOR must be a prelate. But the highest-ranking lay officer of the IOR, its *delegato*, was its true director. In the late 1950s, as Sindona and Cardinal Montini sat in the north disputing supermen and Virgil and the endless feud of blood between mankind and the snake, the *delegato* of the IOR in Rome was a man named Massimo Spada. A reserved and modest man by nature, his figure was a familiar and respected one in the social and financial spheres of the capital. His manner was of the old aristocracy, and so thoroughly Roman that it was fondly said of him that he did not speak *italiano*, but only *romanesco*. His knowledge of the economic history of Italy was renowned, and an invitation for coffee at the Spada home in Via degli Scialoia, where chapters of that history might be recounted in a style that was equally renowned, was coveted as an honor by many of those who knew or who hoped to know him.

Michele Sindona was one of those who hoped to know him, but he knew that the way to do this was not through the ethereal cardinal of Milan. As fortune had it, his cousin Anna Rosa—the daughter of his mother's brother—had married the younger brother of Monsignor Amleto Tondini, a respected *vaticano*. Born in Ravenna in 1899, Tondini was the author of several volumes in Latin. The first, *De ecclesia funerante ad norman c.j.c.*, published in 1927, four years after his ordination, was a treatise on church funerary rites; the most recent, issued at Rome in 1947, was a collection of ancient inscriptions. These, and his editorship of the publication *Latinitas,* had brought him acclaim as the Latinist of the Vatican. His standing in the Vatican would soon be further advanced by his appointment, under Pope John XXIII, to direct the office known as the Pontifical Secretariat for Letters to Princes, whose esoteric duties included the development of Latin terms for concepts that were unknown when Latin lived. Among the verbal inventions that would win Tondini the esteem of popes were *pyrobolus atomicus,* for the atom bomb, and *irritatio belli* ("stirring up of war"), to describe the escalation of fighting in Vietnam.

It was through this demure but formidable Latinist of the Vatican, whom the chain of the flesh had rendered kin, that Sindona in 1959 received his introduction to Massimo Spada.

Under Spada's guidance, the IOR had come to enjoy a prestige that surpassed by far its modest financial means. The fifty-four-year-old *dottore commercialista* had secured almost unlimited credit for the bank. This credit helped him to establish the Vatican as an important part of Italy's economic life, not so much as an entrepreneur, but as a guarantor and as an arbiter in delicate situations involving state and private companies. Spada's true desire, however, was to find a way to enhance both the Holy See's assets and its role in international finance. The solution, Spada felt, lay in developing the IOR as a financial intermediary, an empowered investor of the funds of others.

Ernesto Moizzi, the man who had sold Sindona the Vanzetti steelworks, was still a client and friend. The heart of Moizzi's fortune was Banca Privata Finanziaria, which he had founded in Milan after World War I. It was a small bank, but a special government authorization allowed it to operate as a financial intermediary throughout Italy. Thus the little bank in Via Giuseppe Verdi was a unique financial entity, with the characteristics of both an ordinary credit bank and a Geneva-style investment bank. Through the expertise of Moizzi and his partner, Mino Brughera, Banca Privata Finanziaria had attracted a small but select investment clientele, which included some of the most commanding names in Lombardy finance, from Pirelli to Marinotti, from Falk to Juker. Of all the banks in Italy, it was the first to take steps toward becoming a modern, British-type commercial bank, a true *banca di affari.*

Sindona had long been retained as the bank's tax lawyer, and as the personal financial manager of both Moizzi and Brughera. Indeed, Brughera, a man not greatly known for his trust in others, had, in 1952, invested Sindona with full powers of proxy in his affairs.

Now Mino Brughera was dead, and old Ernesto Moizzi lingered on alone. Neither Brughera's nor Moizzi's children showed any interest in the bank their fathers had built. In 1959, knowing of Sindona's acquaintance with Spada, Moizzi asked him to discreetly inquire as to whether the IOR might be interested in acquiring the bank's stock.

Spada required little persuading. He had already asked Sindona to study the possibilities of founding a financial institution that would give the IOR a base in Italy's economic capital and enable it to pursue work as a financial intermediary. Banca Privata Finanziaria was that envisioned institution.

To maintain Sindona's involvement, Spada wanted him to acquire 40 percent of the stock, with the IOR buying the other 60 percent. At the same time, he asked Sindona to offer some of his 40 percent to Franco Marinotti, a friend of Sindona's who was both the head of Italy's biggest textile firm, Snia Viscosa, and a director of the Confindustria, the powerful national federation of industries. Spada felt that, in both his capacities, Marinotti would be able and likely to steer important clients to the bank.

The IOR purchased the entire stock of Banca Privata through a fiduciary account at the Credito Lombardo, a bank with which the IOR had close relations. Then, while remaining the registered holder of 100 percent, it underwrote the resale of 20 percent each to Franco Marinotti and to Fasco Italiana, a limited partnership wholly owned by Michele Sindona.

At this point, Sindona was approached by Tito Carnelutti, a wealthy and ostentatious lawyer he had known since his early days in Milan. Carnelutti was himself in business with the IOR, with whom he and the Credito Lombardo shared a controlling interest in the Banque de Financement de Genève, commonly known as Finabank. He expressed to Sindona a desire to become a partner in Banca Privata, telling him that, since the IOR would be involved in both banks, he could work out an accord between the Italian bank and the Swiss bank whereby all would benefit. Sindona went to Spada, and Spada sighed. "In Rome," he told Sindona, "they say, if you want someone to know something, but you don't want to tell him yourself, tell it to Tito in strictest confidence, and your purpose will be served." As for Marinotti, he would have nothing to do with Carnelutti. Old rancor, which Sindona suspected to be more personal than professional, divided them. Even old Moizzi, who had been asked to stay on as the bank's president, declared that he did not want Carnelutti near him. He was not to be trusted, Moizzi said; he was a vain man with a womanly mouth, a *chiacchierone*.

Sindona thought in silence, and in silence he took Carnelutti's money and registered half of Fasco Italiana's Banca Privata stock in Carnelutti's name.

Meanwhile, in the Vatican, Monsignor Giuseppe De Luca, the classical scholar and theologian, had come to Spada for 100 million lire—the equivalent of about $63,000—which would allow him to buy books and to complete his vast history of piety, *Archivio per la storia della pietà*, three volumes of which had been published since 1951. Spada was fond of the eccentric old bibliophile; but Alberto Cardinal Di Jorio, the seventy-five-year-old president of the IOR, despised the monsignor and all his erudition. Over the years, Di Jorio had refused De Luca's requests. Spada had argued with him, saying that De Luca's work would bring honor to the Holy See and that his magnificent personal library would in time be donated to the Vatican Library; but Di Jorio had steadfastly waved his fellow Roman away. Spada had never liked Di Jorio, and had felt that the presidency of the financially inexpert prelate had been more of a hindrance than a help in his work for the IOR. In the months since Pope John XXIII had raised him to the cardinalate, in November 1958, Di Jorio had grown in his arrogance, and the rift between him and Spada had widened. So, upon Monsignor De Luca's renewed request, Spada spoke with Pope John. The pope suggested that Spada help De Luca through other means. Spada then went to the Credito Lombardo and convinced that bank to give De Luca the loan he sought.

Tito Carnelutti, in the course of his dealings with the Credito Lombardo, must have discovered the loan. News of it reached Rome and eventually the ears of Di Jorio. The old cardinal commanded Spada to return the Credito Lombardo's money. Furthermore, in the wrath of his indignation, he ordered him to resell the Banca Privata stock that had been assumed through the Credito Lombardo fiduciary account, as he, President Cardinal Di Jorio, did not approve of the acquisition. Spada threw up his arms and explained to the cardinal what the bank in Milan could mean to the IOR; but the cardinal waved his rubied hand, and turned his glance away. The matter was ended.

Sindona assailed Carnelutti and his washerwoman's mouth; and he wondered at the vipers' nest of envy and prideful folly that was the Vatican, in whose ever more venomous ways he was to become entangled in the years that neared.

On October 28, 1960, the controlling stock of Banca Privata Finanziaria was acquired by Fasco, A.G., the Liechtenstein holding company whose sole owner was Michele Sindona. Franco Marinotti remained as a partner, and Massimo Spada, who had encouraged Sindona to take over the bank in the hope that it might be brought back into the fold of the IOR, assumed a place on the bank's board of directors.

The little bank in Via Giuseppe Verdi prospered under Sindona's control. Franco Marinotti mentioned to him one day that John McCaffery, the representative in Italy of the Hambros Bank, Ltd., of London, had voiced a desire to meet Sindona, and to explore the eventual possibilities of a rapport between Banca Privata and Hambros.

Sindona's meeting with the elder Scotsman was a pleasant one. McCaffery, who had come to Italy as a student in 1924 and remained until the outbreak of war in 1939, had later been one of the chief British organizers of the European Resistance movements on the Continent and, after the war, had been honored as such in Italy by the highest decoration of the tottering House of Savoy. He had quit British government work— Sindona was intrigued to hear—after disagreements with Winston Churchill over Churchill's participation in the accords of Teheran and Yalta. Back in Italy, in 1945, the interim prime minister, Ferruccio Parri, offered McCaffery honorary citizenship of the Italian city of his choice. He chose Milan, where he founded a small insurance-brokerage firm, and eventually became the representative for Hambros.

The two men regaled each other with tales of anti-Stalinism, and recalled the story of how in 1859 Hambros had

47

financed the second war of Italian independence. McCaffery spoke of the letter of thanks from Conte Camilo Benso di Cavour that graced the office of the Hambros chairman in Bishopsgate, London.

A few months later, at McCaffery's urging, the venerable British merchant bank acquired 24.5 percent of the capital of Banca Privata. Sindona then talked to Dan Porco, the Pittsburgh steel executive he had come to know through the Crucible deal. He asked Porco to find an American bank of great prestige to join Hambros and Sindona in Banca Privata. Porco spoke with a friend of his who was the president of Continental International of New York, a wholly controlled branch of the Continental Illinois National Bank and Trust Company, one of the largest commercial banks in the United States. Porco's friend advised him to meet with the new chief executive officer of Continental Illinois in Chicago, a man named David Kennedy.

Aside from his years at Continental Illinois, David Matthew Kennedy's life had been spent in fealty to his God and his government. Born in Randolph, Utah, in 1905, he had been raised in the Church of Jesus Christ of Latter-day Saints, believing in the golden Book of Mormon that the angel named Moroni had revealed to Joseph Smith, alone of men, in the century past. He had served two years in England as a Mormon missionary, then joined the staff of the Board of Governors of the Federal Reserve System, in 1930. He had remained there, in Washington, D.C., for sixteen long years, a servant of the angel's golden light, and of that more palpable golden might. He had come then to Continental Illinois, and within five years had been raised to its vice-presidency. He had left two years after that, in 1953, to be special assistant to Secretary of the Treasury George M. Humphrey; then returned the next year. By 1957, the bank's centennial, Kennedy was its president; by 1959, the chairman of its board; and now, its chief executive officer.

After his meeting with Dan Porco, Kennedy sent examiners to Milan to look into Banca Privata. Not long after they returned to Chicago, Continental Illinois purchased, as Hambros had, 24.5 percent of the capital of Banca Privata. Franco Marinotti, like Sindona, made a stunning profit. But Sindona, by retaining 51 percent of the bank's stock, also retained its control, while acquiring, in Hambros and Continental Illinois, partners of the highest international order. Their power was now his, and his will was theirs.

As these things came to pass, Michele's grandmother, old Nunziata, lay drifting toward the shadows of those tales of her lulling long ago, of the sea swelling bright, and of the sun that was greater than the dream of death. He watched her enter into those shadows; and on the first morning of July 1961, he laid her into the dirt beneath a stone that bore her name.

Sindona's friendship with Cardinal Montini, though anchored fast by mutual respect, had begun to grow turbulent. The cause of this turbulence was the small, rat-faced priest Father Pasquale Macchi, who was the archbishop's secretary.

Macchi, a former seminary professor and prison chaplain from Varese, had been thirty years old when he came to the Segreteria dell'Arcivescovo in 1954. In the years since then, his growing closeness to Montini had given rise to rumors that the archbishop and his vassal were lovers. Sindona knew that there was in these rumors no truth. But he perceived in that growing closeness an increasing influence by Macchi on Montini's thinking that struck him as far more insidious than any fancied folly of the flesh.

In August 1959, during the controversy caused by a private visit to Moscow by the Christian Democrat leader Giorgio La Pira, Cardinal Montini had publicly denounced the sympathy of some Catholics for Marxism. Since then, however, the cardinal himself had seemed to turn sympathetic to that tyranny of the weak that Sindona so despised.

The year 1960, when Sindona took control of Banca Privata, had been an epochal moment in the shadow play of Italian politics. In February of that year, soon after Palmiro

Togliatti's confirmation as general secretary by the Communist Party Congress, President Giovanni Gronchi, a Christian Democrat, had gone officially to Moscow at the invitation of the Soviet premier, Nikita Khrushchev; while, at home, the government of Prime Minister Antonio Segni resigned and was replaced, in March, by a minority government under the lawyer Fernando Tambroni. Reveling in the need that Tambroni's new Christian Democrat rule had for the support of its deputies in the chamber, the neo-Fascist MSI grew more arrogant. The old Fascist salute reappeared in the breezy light of spring; and in July, when the Missini—as the MSI rank and file were called—converged at Genoa for their party's sixth national congress, rioting broke out in that city of strong liberal traditions. Communist-led riots erupted also in Turin, then in Rome, where the Soviet Trade Office and the PCI headquarters were bombed in retaliation by the Missini. In the assembly, the left-wing parties drew together in response to the threatening Fascist resurgence. Fearing the advent of a popular front, the Christian Democrats persuaded Tambroni to resign. At the end of July, Amintore Fanfani, a shrewd little man from Tuscany, became prime minister. It was he, a Christian Democrat, who introduced the coalition government that, in February 1962, resulted in an alliance of the Christian Democrats and the more moderate of the country's two socialist parties, the Partito Socialista Democratico Italiano (PSDI), led by Giuseppe Saragat. In the elections of April 28, 1963, Fanfani's Christian Democrats suffered setbacks, while the PCI won more than 25 percent of the votes, giving the *comunisti* twenty-five seats in the chamber. In May, Prime Minister Fanfani and his cabinet resigned. For months to come, the shadows tossed and were blurred in the winds.

Father Macchi, Sindona saw, was a great believer in the platitudes of socialism, and a defender of the *compromesso storico,* the historic compromise that opened the Italian government to the communists. In the political and social concerns of Macchi, wrapped always in the gift paper of Christian altruism, Montini, the Hamlet cardinal to whom the world and all its shadows were as sighs in a morning dream, found the balm that assuaged the guilt he felt for his estrangement. Sindona watched as Macchi's thinking slowly became Montini's own. At Macchi's urging, the cardinal visited Sesto San Giovanni, the little industrial town near Milan that was known as the *Stalingrado d'Italia* because of the consistent and overwhelming communist majority of its vote. There he echoed words that flowed from the pen of Macchi. Returning again and again to Sesto San Giovanni, the cardinal in time came to be laughingly referred to as the *Vescovo di Stalingrado,* the Bishop of Stalingrad.

"Macchi," Sindona would utter with vague loathing a quarter of a century later, sitting in his cage, "Macchi," he would say. "He was like the rest of them. He talked Mao Tsetung and lived Louis Quatorze." And then he would wryly grin, recalling the notorious collection of modern art that was Macchi's true delight.

The collection was cultivated as an oblation to Cardinal Montini, as an endless and ever growing offering from Macchi to the beloved master whom he governed. To obtain these great and costly—and often unsightly—paintings, Macchi turned to the men of wealth in the archdiocese. Copiously employing the name of the cardinal, he besought them to collaborate in this fine churchly honoring. Sindona was one of those whom Macchi approached. He declined Macchi's invitation, and did not hide the fact that he did not care to present a painting as an homage, especially as the real purpose of that homage was to gain further favor for Macchi in the eyes of Giovanni Battista Montini. It was a refusal that the priest would never forget.

As the seasons between the hot summer of 1960 and the changing winds of three years later passed, the meetings between Sindona and Cardinal Montini turned far from matters of philosophy and the classics, to more immediate and volatile matters of church and state. As if ever doubtful of the direction in which Macchi was guiding him, Montini called Sindona often for his thoughts on issues of politics and economics. Sindona told him of the breast of the cow, and of the blade of socialism; and he explained that the betterment of mankind's lot lay in enlightening capitalism, not in crippling it. Their talks erupted more and more into arguments. One day, in the Palazzo Arcivescovile, a silence passed between them.

"If you had chosen Palmiro Togliatti as your secretary, he would have done far less damage to the Church than Father Macchi is doing," Sindona said. The cardinal moved one slender hand through his dark and thinning hair, and his eyes beheld Sindona's own.

On the eve of the fateful April elections of 1963, Sindona was in America to negotiate a takeover of Libby, McNeill & Libby, the big packaged-foods firm centered in Chicago. As the shadows tossed in the winds of the coming weeks, the growing American concerns of his empire occupied him. Cardinal Montini's attention, too, was commanded from the events of those winds, for, on June 3, Whitmonday, Pope John XXIII passed from the world to faith's estate, and, on June 21, Cardinal Montini, to be known evermore as Paul VI, was elected to the papal throne. Nine days later, the burning flax was held before him, and the Latin was chanted. The tiara, a gift from the city of Milan, was placed upon his head; and he slowly raised his hand.

At the end of 1963, both of Italy's socialist parties, the PSDI and the PSI, were joined with the Christian Democrats, under Prime Minister Aldo Moro. This was the first of many left-leaning coalition governments, which in the years to come would tend ever leftward in a struggle to divert allegiance from the growing forces of the Communist Party. In 1964, Italy embraced a socialist president, the PSDI leader Giuseppe Saragat; and when old Togliatti, the Communist Party boss, died that year, it seemed that he closed his eyes to Italy more as a victor than as a loser.

Sindona foresaw that, as a consequence of the new, left-leaning government, the Italian economy would be irreparably harmed. He could feel the balance between the private and the public sectors shifting dangerously more toward the state, and he was convinced that state intervention, the killer of private initiative, would lead to economic collectivism, the bitter-breasted mother of communism. His hatred of communism grew more intense, as he heard the song of its pipers rise in the breeze at his empire's gate. From now on, a great part of his business would be devoted as much to fighting the stateward shift that threatened the foundation rock of his empire as to the enrichment of that empire.

And, by now, his empire was considerable. After acquiring Banca Privata Finanziaria in Milan, he had, in 1961, taken control of another, larger bank, with several branches throughout Italy: the Banca di Messina, which once had cast its shadow on a moneyless Sicilian childhood and on that child's fallen family name. With Hambros and Continental Illinois, his partners in Banca Privata, he acquired control of yet another bank, the Banque de Financement of Geneva, in which the IOR, one of the bank's preceding controllers, remained as a 30-percent partner. He chose his partners in banking—Hambros, Continental Illinois, the IOR—with great care, for he knew that prestige was as valuable and as negotiable a currency as cash. He cultivated partners in his other affairs with the same care.

Many years later, peering toward the morsels of Lombardy sunlight that drifted through the bars beyond his visitor's shoulder, his eyes narrowed and he smiled faintly, remembering those years before all that was his, even unto his name and his share of that sunlight, had been usurped; and he slowly nodded in abstracted assent. "I had the best partners in the world," he said—then the faint smile tightened for a moment in a breath that rose toward wrath, then suddenly burst into a grin—"for a criminal." He laughed.

The General Foods Corporation had become his 50-percent partner in Tindaris, the caramel company he owned in his native Patti (the sweet tooth of his childhood poverty having remained long after poverty's passing), and in Merx, his candy-distributing firm centered in Milan. The world's biggest bank, the Bank of America, was his 10-percent partner in Patti, S.p.A., a $3.5 million luggage manufacturer. His partners in the $7.2 million tender-offer takeover of Libby, McNeill & Libby were Nestlé of Switzerland and the Banque de Paris et des Pays-Bas (known as Paribas), whose executive director, Jean Reyre, had approached Sindona at the request of the new French prime minister, Georges Pompidou. The Banque Bruxelles Lambert, a part of the Rothschild banking group, was his 50-percent partner in a resort development along the Adriatic shore. (By this time, 1964, Sindona, through Fasco, A.G., controlled some $50 million in mortgage-free real estate.)

His numerous and ever increasing concerns ranged from petrochemical engineering (the Compagnia Tecnica Industrie Petroli, or CTIP) to textiles (Stabilimenti Tessili Italiani), from publishing (Istituto Editoriale Italiano) to biscuit making (Alsacienne Biscotti), from printing presses (Andreotti-Stabilimenti Rotostar) to magnets (SAMPAS-Magneti Permanenti), and from cellulose (the Società Industriale Agricola per la Produzione di Cellulosa, or SIACE) to microfusion (Microfusione Italiana). He was, all told, the president of seven companies, the vice-president of three, and a director of more than two dozen boards, including those of Snia Viscosa, Remington Rand Italia, Edizioni Condé Nast, and Chesebrough-Pond's Italia. He was also the *consigliere generale,* the director of the board, of the ASSONIME itself, the Associazione Nazionale delle Società per Azioni, the Italian association of corporations. He remained, too, the economic spokesman of the Unione Commercianti, and delivered the key address, on monetary stability, at its general assembly before the minister of industry and commerce on March 2, 1964.

Meanwhile, his tax-law practice had become the most respected in Milan. His mastery of the arcane and multifarious fiscal laws of his country had brought him great renown as *il mago dei modi legali di ridurre la contribuzione fiscale*—the mage of tax shelters. His office had more clients—about 300—than any other such firm in Italy; and not one of those clients ever left him for another firm.

The center of his operations was Studio Sindona, which occupied the third and fourth floors of Via Turati 29 (the Milan address also of Raul Baisi, *Fortune*, and Time-Life International), a modern building near the Piazza Cavour. It was to Studio Sindona that his black Mercedes would deliver him at eight on those weekday mornings when he was not abroad, and from where that black Mercedes would carry him to his luncheon meetings in the private room of Savini in the Galleria Vittorio Emanuele II, one of Milan's oldest and most elegant restaurants, or at Crispi, the other, less formal of his favorite restaurants, on the Corso Venezia.

His private office at Studio Sindona was not big. It seemed, really, more of an adytum, a sanctum, than an executive office. Its furnishings were princely, and evocative of an era of grander earthly winds. There were volumes of Latin, of philosophy and economics; two small paintings—a Saint Jerome and a crucifixion—by Giovanni Battista Piazzetta; a wooden statue attributed to Francesco Laurana, and a smaller wooden bust attributed to Antonio Pollaiuolo; a pair of eighteenth-century armchairs for guests; and a stately sixteenth-century *"fratino"* table that served as his desk. One window overlooked a slanted sprawl of red-tiled rooftops; the other, the centuries-old church of San Giuseppe. In this sanctum, as he entered his forty-fifth year, he thought for a moment that the fortunes he commanded and all that he had done were as nothing, that his true mistress yet beckoned.

Out in the breeze, there were shadows: that of a great and newfound enemy, come like himself from the southern isle, and that of an enemy not yet known, approaching now, in friendship's skin.

V.
Serpents and Friends

AGAIN MACHIAVELLI: "Men do you harm either because they fear you or because they hate you."

Like spring rain on hammered gold, the clear and simple, splendid truth of those words would reverberate in the thousand upon thousand nightfalls of Michele Sindona's imprisonment. The young man who had written his university dissertation on *The Prince* had himself become a prince of worldly powers; but that simple truth like rain on gold had been obscured by grander storms. He thought he had comprehended Machiavelli completely, and had grasped only too late what many never grasp at all, that arrogance is the magnifying glass through which men view whatever wisdom they possess. And on the sixty-fifth anniversary of his birth, he would listen to the more palpable rain that the breeze blew against the barred and wired panes in Voghera, and he would hear that other rain, that softer and more haunting rain; and he would think once more of Machiavelli, of that wisdom that had eluded him.

"This has been my mistake," he would say, as if he were indicating an accounting error in a ledger, as if the satisfaction of having at all discovered the error outweighed for a moment the disaster it had wrought. "I did not follow him. I trusted."

He smiled. Then the images of the two men whom he held to have been his undoing came to him, and he did not smile.

Enrico Cuccia was a *palermitano,* born in Palermo thirteen years before Sindona, in that occidental province that was, in those years, the demesne of Don Vito Cascio Ferro, and of the beast that had suckled Don Vito to power. He was, this Cuccia, a closemouthed and uncomely man whose snout and stealthy manner inspired some to liken him to a shrew mole. In his twenties, he had left Sicily for Rome, where he went to work for IRI, the state leviathan founded in 1933 under Mussolini, that subduer of Don Vito and of the beast.

Two of his co-workers at IRI, Tullio Torchiani and Loris Corbi, later told Sindona about those days in Fascist Rome. Every morning, the three of them—Cuccia, Torchiani, and Corbi—had coffee together at a small café near the IRI offices. One morning, Cuccia arrived at work and told his two companions that he had become engaged the previous night to the daughter of Alberto Beneduce, the president of IRI and a man of great influence. Torchiani and Corbi had occasionally marveled at the ugliness of Beneduce's daughter, a woman with the stultifying name of Idea Socialista; and they regarded Cuccia curiously as they congratulated him. When the time came for their coffee that morning, Torchiani and Corbi, as usual, summoned Cuccia. He declined, letting them know that, in light of his new stature as the fiancé of Signorina Beneduce, it was perhaps no longer proper for him to mix with them. The marriage took place soon after, and Enrico Cuccia's true rise began.

In April 1946, two years after his father-in-law's death, Cuccia became the *consigliere* of Mediobanca, the powerful state-controlled merchant bank founded that month in Milan by him and Raffaele Mattioli. In the years since then, as the imperious director of this bank, whose might traversed the machinations of the state and the private sectors, Cuccia had become the lord of Italian banking. His power and reputation —like Sindona's—were enhanced by the secrecy and mystery in which he cloaked himself. Ruling Mediobanca, and often the will of the financial establishment, he shied away from society and from all publicity. As Leopoldo Pirelli, the chairman of Pirelli, S.p.A., and the heir of his family's fortunes, was to say, "What Cuccia wants, God wants, too."

And, in 1960, what Cuccia wanted was to meet that much-bruited newcomer to banking, Michele Sindona. When he had taken over Banca Privata Finanziaria, Sindona was unaware of Enrico Cuccia's true importance, and he neglected to observe protocol by calling on him upon his entry into the banking fraternity. In time, through one of Banca Privata's senior officials, word came to Sindona that Cuccia would gladly deign to call on him. The senior official apprised Sindona of Cuccia's stature and advised him to respond. Sindona then did what seemed to be the most courteous thing: He called at Cuccia's office at Via Filodrammatici 10, the eighteenth-century building behind La Scala where Mediobanca's headquarters were. Cuccia rationalized his desire to meet Sindona by saying that the late Mino Brughera had spoken very highly of him.

Cuccia struck Sindona as a very introverted and reserved man, but a man whose libidinous urge to power was unrestrained. Sindona was surprised to hear him claim, in the course of expounding upon his own virtues, that he had been the true promulgator of the banking laws of 1936. And he was bemused by Cuccia's telling him, in a voice that wavered between confidentiality and detachment, that whenever someone gave him a present, he quickly sent an object of equal value, to have him know that he would rather avoid any such gift-giving.

After their meeting, Sindona spoke with Ernesto Moizzi, who had known Cuccia for many years. Old Moizzi, with a smile, said, "Remember, Sindona, what my father taught me: When someone tells you how honest he is twice in the course of a conversation, check before you leave to see if your wallet is still in your pocket."

Not long after this, Cuccia visited Sindona at his office in Via Turati. Cuccia complimented him on the décor of the place, then began to complain about the bad taste with which many of their mutual acquaintances had furnished their offices. He then began to criticize the table manners of many of those acquaintances. Sindona understood that this meeting was to ascertain whether or not Cuccia deemed him presentable. It was a game that Sindona found entertaining. Their third meeting took place at the Palace Hotel restaurant, where Cuccia was insistent on paying the check.

"To get what you want from people, to be able to dominate them," Sindona would explain many years later, "you must know their weaknesses, their Achilles' heels.

"After our third meeting, however, I had no doubt that Cuccia's weakness was his vanity. All you had to do was to imply that he was a man without equal in human affairs, or to offer him a glimpse of some new way to increase his power."

Remembering Cuccia's words about gift-giving, Sindona sent him a lavish art book published by the Istituto Editoriale Italiano, foreseeing that Cuccia would in turn send him an expensive volume—which, in fact, arrived promptly by return post. Sindona quickly informed him that the book he had sent Cuccia had cost him nothing, as he owned the company that published it. At the same time, he declared his admiration for Cuccia's code of behavior and assured him that he would never again compel him to squander any of his income on an exchange of gifts.

"Part of Cuccia's vanity, you see, lay in his feigning of poverty. Though he had his suits tailored by Donini and Carraceni, and sent his children abroad for breeding, he claimed to live on his salary alone. He was more snobbish in his pose of humility than any nobleman in his pretentions of grandeur."

Their meetings—Cuccia would later deny this—became more frequent, and the two men became involved together in several deals.

Cuccia, in 1959, had set up a holding company called Fidia, in which Mediobanca, Snia Viscosa, FIAT, Pirelli, the IOR, Assicurazioni Generali Venezia, Edison, and Montecatini were important partners. Fidia was, to Sindona's thinking, one of the few true Italian conglomerates to achieve success. Knowing that Mediobanca habitually financed all of Fidia's endeavors, Sindona happily accepted the company as an 80-percent partner in a resort-development project on the Adriatic coast.

Some time later, Cuccia told Sindona that Fidia was in serious trouble due to errors committed by Bruno Visentini, one of its fiscal advisers. Fidia, Sindona discovered, had profited considerably from an exchange of stock in the venerable chemical companies Vetrocoke and Montecatini, carried out in collusion with the Istituto Finanziario Industriale (IFI), the Agnelli-FIAT group, and executed through the good offices of the Vatican IOR. Unsympathetic parties, however, had brought to light the fact that several billion lire in taxes had been evaded. The Ufficio delle Imposte, the office of taxation, subsequently was about to levy an assessment on both Fidia and IFI, the immensity of which threatened the very survival of Cuccia's dearest creation. Cuccia decided to assign the matter to Sindona, and was advising Gaetano Furlotti of IFI to retain him immediately.

Sindona drew up lengthy legal briefs for the tax office in Milan and for the Direzione Generale delle Imposte Dirette in Rome, trying to persuade them, with complex technical arguments, that the deal was proper and should therefore be accorded some understanding. He also prepared a confidential memorandum for Fidia and IFI, telling them that their dishonesty had not been properly veiled and that the tax office's assessment was valid. One way or another, he said, they would have to render unto Caesar.

Sindona's technical arguments—which owed no less to his mastery of the convolutions of Latin syntax than to his mastery of the convolutions of Italian tax law—provided a rationale with which the regional inspector in Milan and the head tax office in Rome could justify their possible reappraisal of the matter. But before any understanding might be reached, a further rationale was needed. That rationale was supplied to the authorities by Bruno Visentini, the Fidia adviser whose carelessness had stirred the problem.

This added rationale, Sindona saw, consisted of approximately 2 billion lire in cash, furnished by IFI and Mediobanca.

An agreement of settlement was signed, enriching Fidia and IFI at the cost of government revenue.

Sindona recalled his days—a life ago, it seemed—at the local tax office in Sicily; and he smiled crookedly to see how his impressive legal briefs had become so much more impressive as wrapping paper for the bundles of cash delivered forth by Bruno Visentini. He would smile again, some years later, when Visentini became Italy's minister of finance; and again, after that, to find that his dossier on this affair had somehow disappeared, like so much else, from the files confiscated from Studio Sindona by the Guardia di Finanza—the armed troops of the Ministry of Finance.

Enrico Cuccia's minion Adolfo Tino, the president of Mediobanca, was also the president of the Snia Viscosa stock syndicate, of which Mediobanca was a part. When old Franco Marinotti, the president of the Snia Viscosa company, decided to name Sindona to his board of directors, he needed first to confer with Tino, who, as the syndicate president, readily assented. Before the appointment, Cuccia assured Sindona that he supported the nomination.

"That is good of you, Enrico," Sindona replied, "but President Tino has already expressed his approval."

"You should know," Cuccia barked, "that I am the only one who makes decisions at Mediobanca."

Later, Cuccia observed to Sindona that his entry into Snia Viscosa was perhaps his first step toward the presidency of that immense company. After all, Marinotti was now seventy-three years old. Sindona perceived in his elder's suggestion the implication that any further steps would involve bowing the knee of fealty to the will of Enrico Cuccia.

"I work for myself because I have never cared to be in the employ of others," Sindona remarked.

Cuccia drew back slightly but suddenly—more in embarrassment than in anger, Sindona thought; he was, after all, a glorified employee of the state—and his dark eyes widened.

"This," he said, "is a problem that we'll discuss some other time."

CTIP was a growing petrochemical-engineering company that Sindona had acquired in 1960. Through CTIP, which was based in Rome, Sindona helped Cuccia obtain rights to an American patent for one of Mediobanca's clients. Cuccia's interest in the company was kindled, and he repeatedly pressed Sindona for facts about CTIP's operations and ties with Esso (now Exxon) and other American companies. At the time, CTIP was on the verge of winning a contract from Egypt to build a $25 million refinery in Suez.

Cuccia was close, too, to Piero Giustiniani, the director of Montecatini, a major chemical company that had retained the services of CTIP for several of its installations. One day, in early 1962, Cuccia came to Sindona and told him that he might be able to convince Montecatini to buy CTIP.

"If Montecatini were to acquire CTIP," Sindona told him, "both companies would find themselves in a most delicate position. CTIP, you understand, has a great many substantial orders from firms that are in direct competition with Montecatini. If it were to become known that Montecatini was the new owner of CTIP, hell would break loose. The company would lose a large part of its clientele, and its value would plummet."

"There are ways," Cuccia said. "There are ways."

Sindona met then with Giustiniani and Cuccia. They asserted to him that the sale should be conducted in secrecy and that Sindona should remain on the board as the fiduciary stockholder and overseer of Montecatini's interests. At the same time, Montecatini would place two of its personnel at CTIP to watch over the technical business of Montecatini's installations.

A complicated and purposely obfuscating contract of sale was drawn up, and the deal was consummated. It was not long, however, before one or both of the men Montecatini had transferred to CTIP began to talk. Giustiniani felt the financial foundations of Montecatini start to quake, and Cuccia worried that his baptism of an arrangement plotted completely in secret, *in nero,* if laid before the public, might do great damage to his image as the protecting saint of Italian financiers. He turned to the man across the sea who was his mentor: André Meyer.

Meyer was sixty-four years old, and he had been with the French investment banking firm of Lazard Frères since 1927. In the spring of 1940, after the German invasion of France, he had fled from Paris to New York. In the years since then, as the head of the American branch of Lazard Frères, Meyer had come to be regarded with great ambivalence by the financial community in New York. He was perhaps the best known of that community's investment bankers, and, like Cuccia in Italy, he was respected for his power. But he was a despotic and imperious man who seemed to grow ever more unpleasant with age. His frequent shrill and choleric tirades had led him to be called—but never to his face—the Callas of Wall Street; and his irrational hatred of the British had inspired more than a few English bankers to compare him, unfavorably, to the Nazi dictator whose forces he had fled. Through Enrico Cuccia's influence, André Meyer had become central to the investment-banking affairs of many Italian companies that did business in the United States. To Cuccia, Sindona had noticed, Meyer, the European prince of Wall Street, was a figure of great reverence.

Meyer persuaded the Sociéte Financière de Transports et d'Enterprises Industrielles, the Belgian financial group commonly known as Sofina, to assume Montecatini's interest in CTIP. Cuccia reported to Sindona that Sofina was willing to buy 60 percent of CTIP, allowing 40 percent to return to Sindona's hands. He assured him that Sofina's capabilities would empower CTIP to realize projects on the grandest scale, which would lead to immense profits for Sindona. While Reconta, an accounting firm under the control of Mediobanca, studied the CTIP books, Sindona met Pol Boel, the young man who recently had been named the chief executive officer of Sofina. His credentials, Sindona later would say, consisted mainly in his being the son of a more able and respected Boel.

Though Sindona had doubts about Sofina's competence in the refinery-construction business, papers were drawn up and the deal was finalized, with Snia Viscosa assuming an eighth of Sindona's resumed interest in CTIP. Piero Giustiniani and Enrico Cuccia breathed easily again.

It developed, however, that Sofina's people did not get along with the Egyptian authorities, and CTIP's involvement in the Suez refinery, the company's most important standing project, was brought to an end. Boel, berated by his father, rushed to Cuccia, complaining that the projected billions from the Suez refinery had been a guaranteed part of the CTIP deal. Cuccia discounted his complaint as the folly of an innocent abroad, and he assured Sindona that he had set straight the young man.

But the elder Boel had meanwhile called André Meyer, accusing him of having advised his son to conclude an unsound deal. Sindona then heard from Cuccia again. His tone of voice had changed.

"We have to help the boy out," Cuccia said. "Any criticism of him could prove harmful to you, too."

Sindona responded by saying that any concessions to Boel could be construed as amends for an attempted swindle.

"Just give up another five percent of the stock without payment, and I'll render everyone thankful for your generosity."

Sindona grudgingly assented. By this time, he was involved in a series of American takeovers; the CTIP trouble was a distraction.

Cuccia had urged Sindona to call on André Meyer's services in the Libby, McNeill & Libby deal. But Sindona had already been introduced in New York to Bob Lehman, the head of the Lehman Brothers firm, whose expertise in the field of mergers and acquisitions was widely held to be greater than that of Lazard Frères. He got along well with Bob Lehman. They shared an interest in art as well as in the gold that bought it. (Lehman, in fact, possessed one of the most celebrated private collections in the world. Valued at over $100 million, it had been exhibited in the Louvre in 1959; and a few years hence, upon his death in 1969, it would be given to the Metropolitan Museum of Art.) It was Lehman whom Sindona chose to assess Libby for him.

There was bad blood between Lehman and Meyer. Bob Lehman considered Meyer an arriviste. He was a man without class, Lehman said; he was a man who would do anything to grab a commission.

Upon learning of Sindona's arrangement with Bob Lehman, Meyer asked Cuccia to set up a meeting between him and Sindona. The meeting took place, with Cuccia in attendance, at the Paris office of Lazard Frères. Meyer expressed his unhappiness at Sindona's having gone to Lehman instead of to him, and said that he would have appreciated the opportunity to have been a part of the Libby deal. When he said this, Cuccia paled, for he had arrogantly told Sindona that the proposed deal would be disapproved by Meyer and that Sindona should only offer it to Meyer for the sake of decorum. Sindona savored Cuccia's uneasiness, marveling at how timorous he suddenly was in Meyer's presence. When Sindona told Meyer that he would be pleased to consult him in the future, he saw Cuccia sigh with relief.

So, in the summer of 1964, when Sindona had set out to gain control of Brown, a New Hampshire–based paper company listed on the New York Stock Exchange, he called at Meyer's office at 44 Wall Street. Meyer told him that he should like to meet whomever it was who had led Sindona to believe that a tender-offer takeover of Brown was possible. Sindona arranged an appointment for him with David Bellows, the stockbroker who was assisting Sindona in his plan. Soon after that, Meyer invited Sindona to his office to tell him that Bellows was neither up to the task nor in control of all the stock he claimed to have at his disposal. Then, to the amused perplexity of Sindona, Meyer brought up the Libby business, telling him once again of his unhappiness. As his sentences rushed toward incoherence and his voice rose to shrillness—Sindona realized presently that he was experiencing one of the virtuoso arias of the Callas of Wall Street—Meyer yelped that it was a matter of principle, that he had two hundred goddamned million dollars and could live without any goddamned Libby commissions, but that such disrespect simply maddened him. Sindona silenced the fool with his eyes, then he rose and left.

Back in Milan, he told Cuccia of his esteemed friend's hysterical performance. "That simply isn't him," Cuccia responded. "A man such as André would never flaunt his net worth."

Sindona returned to America, where the takeover of Brown was successfully concluded, with the aid of David Bellows, on July 13, 1964. At a cost of $9.4 million, Sindona had acquired 23 percent of Brown's stock, enough to give him the controlling hand.

This was more than Meyer's twisted pride would bear. There were conversations between the Lazard Frères office in New York and the Sofina headquarters in Brussels; and a telephone rang in an eighteenth-century building in Milan. The vassal obeyed the lord, and the wills of André Meyer and Enrico Cuccia were one.

Cuccia told Sindona that the consolatory gift to Sofina of an additional 5 percent of CTIP, which he had recently cajoled Sindona into granting, simply would not do. The skin at Sindona's temples tightened, as Cuccia explained that Boel now suspected he had been presented with falsified books in the CTIP deal.

In cadences of restrained wrath, Sindona told him that he had never before been accused of falsification and that the books of his corporations, as in the Crucible deal, had yielded only pleasant surprises for buyers. Furthermore, in the case of

67

CTIP, the books had been examined by Reconta, a firm under the control of Mediobanca and therefore Cuccia himself.

Reconta examined the books again. After this new audit, it was concluded that Sindona owed Sofina 600 million lire (about $1 million). Sindona said that he was willing to pay that amount as a final adjustment, but that he was no longer willing to surrender the extra 5 percent of the stock.

Boel of Sofina, however, responded that the second audit was not satisfactory. He claimed that Sindona was indirectly liable for billions of lire in losses that had been incurred by CTIP since Sofina assumed management.

Cuccia, meanwhile, had heeded the decree of André Meyer: Sindona was a man whose breath would never mingle with their own.

Sindona stood fast against the triumvirate of Boel, Cuccia, and Meyer. The matter was consigned to formal arbitration before a committee in Geneva headed by the president of the Swiss Constitutional Court. While Cuccia busied himself slandering Sindona's name, whispering to Giovanni Agnelli, Leopoldo Pirelli, and other noblemen of Italian industry that Sindona was a falsifier of books and was not to be trusted, Sindona discovered that Sofina had registered strange items in the CTIP books for the purpose of diminishing its visible capital and thus considerably reducing Sindona's participation. The *collegio arbitrale* then invited Boel to reach a private agreement with Sindona in order to avoid a judgment that might make Sofina look bad. In a Geneva office adjoining the arbitration room, Sofina satisfied itself with a quittance of 500 million lire—100 million less than the 600 million Sindona had offered to pay but that had not been accepted by the triumvirate.

Though Sindona wondered, he was unable to find out if Meyer and Cuccia, the Octavian and Antony of the triumvirate, reimbursed the lost difference to Sofina out of their own pockets. One thing he did know was that Cuccia's slandering of him had, for the moment, rendered the saint a fool in the eyes of the financial nobility he had sought to sway.

In 1966, a few months after the settlement in Geneva, Sindona was further vindicated in his contention that CTIP was a sound company suffering only from the incompetence of its new owner. The Cleveland, Ohio, engineering firm of Arthur G. McKee & Co. bought control of CTIP from Sofina, and quickly won a much-coveted contract for a $12 million addition to the Empresa Colombiano de Petroleos refinery in Barrancabermeja, Colombia.

Thus began the *grande scontro,* the great clash, between Michele Sindona and Enrico Cuccia, the two Sicilian sons whose breaths were never meant to mix—the one born to illusions whose glories were set in stone, the other to that deathless court whose dogs those illusions truly were.

There was one more dooming encounter between them, when Cuccia, in seeming reconciliation, came to him with an idea for Sindona's Banca Privata Finanziaria. The elder Sicilian told Sindona that he could convince Giovanni Agnelli to buy a majority, 51-percent share in Banca Privata through IFI, the Agnelli family holding company. Cuccia could then see to it that some 27 billion lire of available Agnelli funds, which Cuccia managed on behalf of the Agnelli group, were deposited with the bank. He would further see to it, he assured Sindona, that Banca Privata came to be quoted on the Borsa. As Sindona knew, there was at this time only one bank quoted on the Milan stock exchange: Cuccia's Mediobanca.

Sindona said it was an attractive scheme, but he did not wish to relinquish control of his bank. Cuccia then proposed, as Sindona knew he would, that Mediobanca be given 2 percent of the bank's stock, thus enabling Cuccia to serve as an arbiter—with Sindona's interests in mind, of course—during any possible difficulties. As Cuccia spoke, he noticed the odd smile that crept across Sindona's lips. He had no way of knowing that Sindona by now had discovered some of the dark deals by which Cuccia and André Meyer were bound.

He had discovered that Cuccia had negotiated, in 1958, a secret pact between the IRI banking group (Banca Commerciale Italiana, Credito Italiano, and Banco di Roma), which owned 51 percent of Mediobanca, and Lazard Frères and its partners, which held less than 4 percent. Under the astounding terms of this pact, the voting power of the Lazard block was equal to that of the Italian consortium. Sindona had learned from Meyer himself, before their falling out, the explanation for this bizarre arrangement: his company had credited considerable sums of money abroad to Cuccia's accounts, *in nero*. With this *denaro nero*, this black money, and through fiduciary companies controlled by Meyer, Cuccia had been able to acquire, among other occult assets, a 4-percent interest in Assicurazioni Generali, Italy's largest insurance firm.

Sindona now knew these things and more, and he knew that Cuccia's proposal for Banca Privata was a last attempt to control him. So he listened, and he smiled; and he told the little man, politely, to spit blood.

All hope of controlling Sindona was forsaken by Cuccia. From that moment on, Sindona would later say, the dream of his destruction became the mistress of Cuccia's sainted will.

The second enemy, the one whose sword was trust, came to him in the autumn days of 1964. His name was Carlo Bordoni. He was two years older than Sindona, and fat, balding, and undone.

In September 1962, the First National City Bank of New York had resumed operations in Italy, which it had abandoned at the start of World War II. Its Milan office, in the Piazza della Repubblica, became the ninety-first of Citibank's overseas branches, part of its growing international division under the direction of forty-three-year-old Walter B. Wriston. The bank, which in 1963 became the first American bank to open a Swiss branch, was following the lead of the wiser and more sophisticated British banks, which dominated the seas of international finance.

The Eurodollar market was evolving wildly in those years following Regulation Q, by which the U. S. Federal Reserve

Board had limited interest rates on deposits at home; and competition was increasing to service the ever more complicated, and ever more lucrative, needs of the world's growing multinational corporations. The seas the British ruled waxed fiercer and more turbulent. Here and there amid the waves and the winds were the flimsy and devious-cruising vessels of those seeking a short route to the Indies, sudden riches in a new, uncharted world of brokerage and speculation.

One of these devious-cruising seekers was Carlo Bordoni. The Milan branch of Citibank had hired him as a foreign-exchange broker in 1962, and had fired him in 1964 for engaging in unauthorized currency speculation.

He was a desperate man when he came to Sindona. Since being fired by Citibank, he had not been able to find employment elsewhere. He showed Sindona a proposal for an international money-brokerage company, and he explained its possibilities. Sindona was intrigued by the proposal, but he had doubts about Bordoni. He had been told that Bordoni was a clever man but a rash man, that, while he had never been known to steal, his speculative gambling had been a curse to his career.

"In all the world," Sindona told him, "not one man ever became wealthy by gambling." Bordoni squirmed a bit, and Sindona continued, "I would rather bankroll an alchemist than a gambler. Their visions and their chances of success are the same; but alchemy is a far less costly delusion, and the alchemist might at least fall upon some learning along his way."

Bordoni swore that his gambling was done, that he had learned his lesson, and would hence play only the percentages. Sindona perceived something of truth in the fat man's words.

Neither Continental Illinois in Chicago nor Hambros in London, Sindona's partners in Banca Privata, wished to involve the Milan bank in Bordoni's designs. Sindona relayed their objections to Bordoni, who swore once again that his gambling days were finished. He gave his word of honor that if Sindona helped him to create his proposed company, he

71

would never operate in a way that might endanger him or his banks.

In the cold, sleety days before Christmas 1964, Euromarket Money Brokers, also known as Moneyrex, S.p.A., was founded in Milan. Under their arrangement, Sindona gave Bordoni an annual salary of 7.2 million lire (about $12,000) and a 2-percent interest in the company. Later, through an option, that 2 percent became 10, and eventually it rose to 20.

Moneyrex—and how Sindona savored the imperial, Latin flavor of that name—dealt in debt brokerage and in the buying and selling of spot and future currencies for its clients on a commission basis.

"We had ten Telex machines, twenty telephones," Sindona later recalled, moving his outstretched hand before him in a slow arc, compassing cell walls bare of any electrical outlet. "Say Barclays Bank of California needed $100 million. We go to the Telex, the telephone. We call Banca Nazionale del Lavoro, Bank of Tokyo, Chase Manhattan. We quote a rate of interest that Barclays is willing to pay, say eleven and a quarter percent. They say OK, and they transfer $100 million automatically. To our account then is automatically credited one-eighth of one percent of $100 million, or maybe one-sixteenth, one thirty-second of one percent, depending on the fickleness of the market. We never took risks, there was no speculation with Moneyrex—just commissions, brokerage fees."

In its first two years of business, Moneyrex operated at a slight loss, as Sindona encountered more reluctance than he had foreseen in convincing the financial community to work anew with Bordoni. But the proven skills of the two men turned the tide of that reluctance. Eventually, more than 1,000 of the world's banks, among them the central banks of several governments, sought the services of Moneyrex. Its business grew until it handled more than $40 billion in transactions in a single year—more than the Bank of America, the biggest bank in the world.

Moneyrex served as Sindona's window. Through it, he

could see, as no one else quite could, the movement of the world's wealth, the meshings and clashings of the immense and recondite machinery of earthly power in flux. In a sense, Moneyrex was the world's shylock, letting neither its right nor its left hand know what the other was doing, profiting equally from the greed of the one as from the need of the other. It connected him with the great banks of the world, and gave him an edge of rare knowledge with which to conduct the other business of his empire. In time, through Moneyrex, Sindona spied conspiracies beyond the realm of greed and gold, saw the secret plottings, nation against nation, of destruction.

Carlo Bordoni was being true to his word. There was no gambling in foreign exchange. There was only the steady, calculated harvesting of profits. Bordoni, who had come begging as a desperate man, became a man of wealth and standing, who in time would be appointed to the boards of several of Sindona's banks.

"You saved my life," he would tell Sindona more than once, holding out his arms and turning his wrists to the sun. "I would cut off both my hands for you."

Sindona looked neither hard nor long enough at those hands.

Though continuing to veil his business dealings with great discretion, Sindona by now was becoming a figure of fame, in America as well as in his native land. In late September 1964, *Time* published a profile of him. There was a photograph of him, smiling coolly as the fourteenth-century wooden nobleman of Francesco Laurana gazed over his shoulder with the dead eyes of the ages; and there were words of his "spectacular success." Two weeks later, *Business Week* published a long article on him, calling him a "whirlwind operator in business circles and a banker regarded by many as Italy's outstanding postwar financier." In 1965, he made his debut in *The International Who's Who,* the red-bound British registry of the world's aristocracy.

His dealings in America flourished. In April 1965, he

bought 150,000 unissued shares, at slightly more than $3 each, in the Oxford Electric Corporation, taking effective control of that Chicago maker of paints and automobile parts. By the close of 1968, Oxford Electric would be quoted at $14 a share on the American Stock Exchange, bringing a value of over $2 million to Sindona's original investment of less than $500,000.

In 1965 he also acted as the middleman in the $31 million sale to the Celanese Corporation of SIACE, the Sicilian eucalyptus plantation and cellulose producer that Snia Viscosa had commissioned him to organize in 1950, and of which he was the president, having stayed in charge of the company after Snia Viscosa's sale of its controlling interest to a French-Canadian group operating through a Liberian holding company in 1962 (which sale had also been engineered by Sindona). The Celanese Corporation, which bought SIACE with an eye on the European cardboard-box market, ended up writing off the company as a $40 million loss three years later, after the Sicilian eucalyptus pulp proved unsuitable for its purposes. The mistake, which might have been prevented by a few thousand dollars' worth of research, had nothing to do with Sindona, and Celanese laid no blame at his door.

That same year, 1965, he acquired from his old friend Arturo Doria the Angelini-Universal rubber-goods company. He reorganized it, then sold it to Reeves Brothers, Inc., of New York. In addition to his quickly realized net profit of about $1 million, Sindona was retained as a director of Reeves, S.p.A.

In January 1966, through the Brown paper company, controlled by him for the past eighteen months, Sindona acquired K.V.P. Sutherland, another paper company, twice the size of Brown, listed on the New York Stock Exchange. He merged the two firms into a new and grander Brown Co.

Libby, McNeill & Libby had fared well since his takeover of it in concert with Paribas and Nestlé. In May 1967, he and Paribas, which by now was the largest investment bank in Europe, sold their shares at a 5-percent net profit to Nestlé, the century-old Swiss company that was intent on acquiring all of

Libby—an endeavor that would take Nestlé ten long years.

"Millions, millions, millions," he would say. "For many years, millions." Such was the Sindona system: buy, reorganize, merge, sell. A million here, a few million there, it all added up; for many years, millions.

"Wealth," the Bible said, "maketh many friends." As Sindona's business in America increased, so did the number of those who called him friend.

Through Francesco Chiarini, the Snia Viscosa public-relations director who had introduced him to Bob Lehman, Sindona had come to know Judge S. Samuel Di Falco.

Born in Italy in 1906 and raised on New York's Lower East Side, Judge Sam Di Falco was a short, fast-witted man who shared Sindona's fondness for finely tailored suits and beautiful-ankled women. A familiar figure in the Democratic circles of Tammany Hall under Carmine De Sapio, he had been elected to the New York Supreme Court in 1948, following seven years as a city councilman. In 1956, a year or so after Sindona first met him, Di Falco had run successfully for surrogate judge, a position that gave him jurisdiction over the estates of Manhattan residents, and a position he would hold until he reached the mandatory retirement age, twenty years later.

It was a well-kept secret that Judge Di Falco was a favored protégé of the New York Mafioso Frank Costello, who was known to refer affectionately to the judge as "one of my boys." Costello's own mandatory retirement from power had occurred on a May evening in 1957, when his skull was grazed by an admonitory bullet as he entered the foyer of his home on Central Park West.

Though Di Falco remained close to Costello until Costello's death from a heart attack in 1973 (four years to the month after the fatal heart attack of his younger nemesis, Vito Genovese), Sindona never met Di Falco's *compare,* and Di Falco did not speak much of him to Sindona.

"Di Falco was a crook," Sindona would later say with a laugh, "but he was a good man, an honorable man. He enjoyed the respectability he had achieved in society, and he was careful to maintain it. At that time, my own reputation was immaculate. I think perhaps that Di Falco, though he loved Mr. Costello, would have been embarrassed to introduce him to me. Also, most of my dealings with Di Falco were social, and Frank Costello by then was an old man who did not much run around."

Together, Sindona and Judge Di Falco would make the rounds of the uptown nightclubs. To Sindona's surprise, he discovered that the older man seemed to sleep even less than he himself did. Sindona, who did not smoke (he did, however, practice the Japanese paper-folding art, origami, with a smoker's compulsiveness), was not much of a drinker either. A shot or two of single-malt Scotch, or a Chivas Regal on the rocks, usually would be the sum of his drinking at any one sitting. Often, he drank just tomato juice, telling whoever asked that it was a Bloody Mary. (His liking for tomato juice had been one of the reasons he had bought Libby.) But there was that shared enthusiasm for those ankles of women, girls whose lips were painted the color of blood, and for the nights filled with laughter not meant to last.

Judge Di Falco turned sometimes to Sindona for counsel. When he needed a place to stash the money his left hand had raked into his robe through the years, Sindona led him to Switzerland, to a numbered account.

And Judge Di Falco had a son, a boy named Anthony, who followed in his Democratic footsteps beneath the shadow of blind justice that lay downtown. He was little more than a child, a uniformed student of St. Francis Xavier High School, when Sindona first met him. Sindona saw the paternal pride in the judge's eyes as Anthony began his law practice in 1963, joining Di Falco, Field, Florea & O'Rourke, the firm the judge had founded; and he saw that pride grow greater still five years later, in 1968, as Anthony, barely thirty years old, was elected assemblyman of the sixty-first district of New York. The following year, he became a member of the Assembly's Minority Committee on Crime and Safety in the Streets.

Sindona shared the judge's happiness for the young man's fortune, and he helped the boy as he had helped the father. But in ten years' time, he would curse the seed that had brought Anthony G. Di Falco into this life, and he would damn his soul to the Iscariot ice of hell's ninth circle.

Daniel A. Porco, the steel executive who befriended Sindona during the Crucible deal and later brought him together with David Kennedy of Continental Illinois, had been treated well. As Sindona's American representative, he had been made a director of Libby, McNeill & Libby, and had been appointed the interim president of the Brown Co. after its takeover by Sindona.

The man chosen to run Brown on a permanent basis was Frank T. Peterson, a descendant of several generations of Swedish papermakers and the former president of the Black Clawson Co. He took over from Porco at the Brown headquarters in Berlin, New Hampshire, in April 1965.

Peterson introduced Sindona to a friend of his, an oilman who was in grave financial trouble due to a few crooked dealings that had backfired. As a favor to Peterson, Sindona agreed to meet with and advise the oilman's lawyer.

The lawyer turned out to be Richard M. Nixon, the fifty-three-year-old Quaker who had served eight years as vice-president of the United States under Dwight D. Eisenhower. After losing the 1960 presidential race to John F. Kennedy, the Quaker had returned to his native California, where, in 1962, he had run unsuccessfully for the governorship of that state. Crestfallen in his political ambitions, he had then moved to New York City, where, in December 1963, after fulfilling the New York State Bar Association's six-month residence requirement, he had resumed the law practice he had begun in the late thirties. Mudge, Rose, Guthrie & Alexander, the firm he had joined as a senior partner, promptly changed its name to Nixon, Mudge, Rose, Guthrie & Alexander. Though Sindona had never met Nixon, he was aware of him, as he had called on the services of Mudge, Rose, Guthrie & Alexander in the course of his American dealings, and had come to be friends with the firm's senior partner Randolph Guthrie.

Sindona and Nixon met at the Quaker's office in downtown Manhattan. Sindona listened patiently as Nixon proposed that Sindona support his oilman client in a joint venture that could rescue the oilman and also prove profitable to all. Sindona, regarding the nervous, heavy-jowled man through narrowed eyes, said that he would think about it.

Sindona quietly approached Randolph Guthrie and asked him about this strange Quaker, this new senior partner emerged from the slag of history's footnotes. Guthrie hesitated a moment in silence, then he looked at his friend.

"Don't tell our esteemed partner this"—Guthrie smiled—"but all his clients are"—he searched for a word, a phrase—"second-class characters. Don't become involved."

Sindona followed Guthrie's advice. Nixon, however, pursued him, and the two men lunched together several times in the months that followed. During the course of those lunches, Sindona perceived in Nixon, beneath the abundance of faults that seemed to define rather than to flaw his character, an understanding of international politics that, to Sindona's thinking, was rare in an American.

"Nixon told me he knew and loved Italy," Sindona later recounted. "He told me that during his visits to Venice, he'd had a chance to meet politicians and businessmen who had analyzed Italy's situation, and who had told him of the need for the United States to help prevent the Mediterranean region from falling into enemy hands. Nixon said he agreed with this view of Italy's strategic nature and with the desirability of supporting the democratic parties, the friends of the United States, in Italy."

It struck Sindona that Nixon was more a politician than he

was a lawyer. It did not surprise him, after the lunches had ended, to hear that Nixon was once again casting his eye to the presidency of America. He won the Republican nomination in the hot days of 1968, and a few months later, narrowly defeating Hubert Humphrey, he won the election.

Sindona watched as the strange Quaker with the second-class clients was sworn in as the president of the most powerful nation on earth, and he recalled their luncheon conversations, and he grinned. But he did not yet truly know how strange this Quaker was.

Of all the men he came to do business with in American, Sindona admired none more than he did Charles Bludhorn, the founder, chairman, and chief executive officer of Gulf & Western Industries.

Like Sindona, he had risen from nothing, armed only with will and wits. Born in Vienna, Austria, in 1926, he had emigrated in 1942 to America, where, after serving in the Army Air Force and studying at Columbia University, he began working, for $15 a week, at a cotton-brokerage house in Manhattan. In 1949, he had started an import-export business, which he ran until 1956, the year he acquired the small auto-parts company in Grand Rapids, Michigan, that was to become Gulf & Western Industries two years later. Under Bludhorn, Gulf & Western had grown rapidly. Taking over the New Jersey Zinc Company in 1966, Paramount Pictures in 1967, and Simon & Schuster in 1968, Gulf & Western, the company that Charlie built, had joined the front rank of American corporations.

In the spring of 1967, a federal court barred Sindona from buying stock in the Riegel Paper Corporation, charging that his move to force a merger with his Brown Co. constituted a violation of antitrust laws. Some months later, in January 1968, Sindona was in Milan when he got a call from Charlie Bludhorn in New York. Bludhorn asked Sindona to meet him the next morning at the Grand Hotel in Rome, saying that he had an interesting deal to propose.

The meeting took place at eleven o'clock, and it was over by noon.

Though the deal was a complicated one, and it would take the appointed lawyers several days and nights to transform the handshake between Bludhorn and Sindona into a legally precise contract, Sindona in that hour had sold the Brown Co. to Bludhorn for $15.5 million in cash, common and preferred stock, and warrants. On February 20, 1968, Brown officially passed from Fasco to Gulf & Western. It was a deal that pleased both men, and for Charlie Bludhorn it was the first step toward a place he had never thought he would see: the Vatican.

VI.
The Systems of Evil

THERE HAD BEEN only two days of sunshine. The rain would not end. The front pages of the Milan newspapers carried photographs of flooded streets and spoke of the *"maledetta primavera"* ("the cursed spring").

On pages farther back, there were reports of a ceremony, on May 9, 1985, to dedicate the law library at the Palace of Justice in memory of Giorgio Ambrosoli, the state-ordained liquidator of Michele Sindona's Italian banks, gunned down on a summer night six years past. The reports closed with reminders that the trial of Sindona for Ambrosoli's murder would open in less than a month.

From the light-falling drizzle of a Saturday morning, I entered the high-vaulted place of darkness and radiance and big-pillared stone, the Duomo at Milan's heart, and I walked down the left aisle and sat near where the votive candlelight played. An old woman approached, stopping before the heavy bronze gate that separated a reliquary apse from the rest of the cathedral. She raised her hand to the sacred symbol on the gate, and held it there as her lips moved silently. Then she moved her hand from the holy place and pressed it to her right leg, her forehead, rubbing slowly, her lips still silently moving. She repeated the process several times, replacing her hand to the holy place every few moments, as if she was sure of precisely when the magical property left her hand and needed to be renewed. After a while, she moved on to another holy place along the wall of the cult of the dead, and she raised her hand anew.

I thought then of Sindona's wife, Caterina, whom I had recently seen for the first time, in Voghera. We had been talking, Sindona and I, nearing the woods of his downfall's tale, the deadly copse beyond the deals and trust's last light, when a guard had rapped upon the door of Michele's cage.

"La moglie fedele"—"The faithful wife"—the guard had heralded, as if announcing the entrance of a leading character in a tragic opera known by heart. Sindona had looked to me then with an expression that framed resignation to the inevitable in tacit apology. "I could have her wait," he said with a sigh, "or, if it is not too much trouble for you, we could continue tomorrow."

I had seen her then on my way out: a small, slender woman, on in years. She wore a simple, elegant blue dress, and she held her head high, keeping something of dignity and of pride as the guards led her through the metal detector. She nodded to me politely, smiling faintly, as we passed each other, escorted by our respective sentries on our respective ways.

"Did your wife ever know what you were doing?" I had asked Sindona the next morning, the delicate, silent image of her lingering behind my eyes.

"No," he said without hesitation, shaking his head. "She was a good mother," he said. Then he smiled, remembering. "Once in a while, she would say, 'Michele, why do you never sleep?' She worried, but she did not know." He fell silent, then suddenly he spoke. "That woman," he said, with something like admiration in his voice, "always believed that vanity was the worst thing in the world." Then, just as suddenly, he was quiet again, and he inhaled deeply, as if in acquiescence to some unsaid, unsayable thing.

And on this drizzly Saturday in the cathedral where the skeleton of Saint Ambrose lay, I remembered the small glass case that stood not far from there, in Room V of the Biblioteca Ambrosiana. Easily undescried among the treasures of the Ambrosiana—the *Codice Atlantico* of Leonardo Da Vinci, Raphael's *Sposalizio*, Petrarch's copy of Virgil—this dusty display, assembled by some forgotten curator at some forgotten time, seemed to contain shards washed forth by the tide of that unsaid, unsayable thing, that truth or that lie, which I had more than once discerned in Michele Sindona's deep-drawn breaths: that truth or that lie which is the vanity of history beneath the black heaven of mortality.

There were three objects in that case. There was a waxen triptych, some three hundred years old, that bore the words *"Anima Beata-Purgante-Dannata"* and showed those states of blessedness, purgatorial biding, and damnation with the face of a woman that was, in turn, serenely beautiful, disquieted, and gruesomely contorted. Beneath the triptych was a tawnied ringlet, identified in Latin as a lock of Lucrezia Borgia's hair, snipped at the hour of her death in 1518. To the left of it, simply labeled *"Guanti Portati da Napoleone a Waterloo 18.-6.1815,"* was the pair of chamois gloves worn by Napoleon on the day the wind changed for him.

A few strands of brittle hair, a pair of gloves lingering long after the hands that filled them have turned to dust—power's miserable remains, beneath the portrait of that self-blest, self-damned thing, the shade of every vain upward grasping for eternity. It was all there, in that case.

I rose from the pew where I sat. I put some coins into a slot, and I lighted a candle. Soon it would be time to return to Voghera.

I brought up the name of Rosario Spatola, a man Sindona came to know in the years between his downfall and his imprisonment, and a man whom the Italian press portrayed as one of the most dangerous Mafiosi in Sicily. Sindona corrected my pronunciation of Spatola's name—the accent is on the first syllable, he said—and then he laughed.

"I will tell you about Spatola later," he said. "I will tell you this now: The Rosario Spatola I knew and the Rosario Spatola in the newspapers are different. In the newspapers, he is a big, scary tough guy. To me, he was always . . ." And Sindona, laughing again, brought his fingertips together before him like a schoolgirl in prayer, and in a farcical feminine voice mocked, "Oh, please, Mr. Sindona, please." And then he lowered his hands, laughing again.

I watched him, and I smiled; and a thought occurred to me. "Did you ever meet anyone who scared you?" I asked.

The grin rushed from his face and he seemed for a second to turn to stone. Once before, I had—or so it had struck me—inadvertently insulted him, by asking him where he had bought his suits. "I never *'bought'* suits," he had said, sounding indignant, then, calming, turning his hand, added, "I had suits made"—then, smiling—"always in the classic style." Now it seemed I had done it again. His back straightened, and a new, stranger grin emerged as the stoniness ebbed.

"No one ever scared me," he said, stressing the final word ever so slightly more than the rest. And as I looked at him, expressing nothing myself, he began once again to laugh. "No," he said, "that is not true. There was one time, long ago, in the days of the lemons and the grain." For a moment, he receded into the memory of those days, then, with happiness in his voice, he talked.

"I was busy with legal work in Catania, and I sent a friend in my place to pick up a load of carobs in the town of Prizzi, in the west. When he returned, I saw that the entire truckload of carobs was completely *guasto,* completely spoiled. I became crazy. 'Come with me in the truck. We're going back to Prizzi,' I told him. 'But, these people there,' he said. 'I don't care,' I said, 'we go.'

"And we went. And when we got to Prizzi, I found the men and I said, 'You must change these.' 'But it is the will of others,' one of them said. 'I don't care,' I said. My friend was trembling. 'I go now,' I said. 'I will return tomorrow, and I want to find fresh carobs here.' The man stared at me. 'You will find something else,' he said.

"The next day, I returned alone—my friend was too faint. The fresh carobs were there. I continued to buy from those men, and they never cheated me again." Smiling, he shook his head. "I was crazy. No wife yet, no children." He tapped his temple with his forefinger. *"Pazzo."*

"The people who brought you down," I said, "have accused you of working for the Mafia."

"Yes." He nodded. "They have accused me of that. They have accused me of everything except nailing Christ to the cross." He laughed. Then he cleared his throat, and he drew a deep breath. "If I was going to be in that thing, I wouldn't be a damned soldier. I wouldn't be here.

"You see, I never needed them, and they never needed me. You must remember that my banks in Italy were first-class institutions with first-class partners. Banca Privata was a bank of the aristocracy. The Mafia always used second-class institutions and professionals." His eyes narrowed sagaciously. "Those men are not so stupid, I think. They are much smarter than the government people who think they understand them."

"Which banks does the Mafia use?" I asked him.

He hesitated for a moment. "That is a dangerous question," he reflected. I shrugged, he smiled. With no further thought, he said, "In Sicily, sometimes Banco di Sicilia. In Milan, the little Banca Rasini in Piazza Mercanti."

He sat quietly then, listening to the sound of the falling rain.

"No matter what they claim, governments will never understand the Mafia," he said slowly. "With their silly charts and their lying, know-nothing informants, they try to reinvent the Mafia in their own image, the only image they can comprehend: that of an ordered, homogeneous organization. Their delusion of 'organized crime' is one of an imagined ideal bureaucracy, and it exists nowhere but in the lacking minds of little men with big titles.

"Governments have unknowingly done a great deal to

abet the massing of criminal fortunes, through laws ostensibly enacted to protect their economies or their citizens' welfare. Trade and customs restrictions gave life to smuggling and trafficking in contraband. The prohibition of alcohol in America served to found that country's greatest centers of illicit wealth. Most of the respected families of the world—the Rothschilds and the Warburgs, the Agnellis and the Pirellis, the Kennedys and the Rockefellers—can trace the origins of their fortunes to various illegal profits, and to the avoidance of taxes on those profits. Over the years, their money became clean, and they became the world's establishment.

"The antidrug laws of today have allowed vast amounts of dirty money to accumulate in the hands of a few men—men who are often served and protected by the very governments that swear their every effort to kill drug crops and to fight with all their might against the producers and sellers of narcotics.

"The drug trade is the means by which so-called organized crime finances itself on every continent. If drug laws were liberalized, that means would no longer exist. But governments do not seem willing to strike at the heart." He shrugged, then grinned. "You see, these governments are not as good at finding dirty money as they are at helping to create it.

"Government agencies in America and Europe often capture intermediaries in the drug traffic. They see these people as crime lords, as the heads of criminal organizations. But, in reality, they are only entities of, at most, second-class importance, pawns who do not themselves understand the complex economy of which they are a part.

"James Harmon, the director of the President's Commission on Organized Crime, and Giovanni Falcone, the biggest of the anti-Mafia magistrates in Italy, both admitted to me that neither they nor their assistants knew anything about options on currencies or commodities, or about futures or forward contracts." His voice rose suddenly. "They told me that they had no idea how the international monetary system works!"

His eyes widened and he grinned sardonically. "It is ridiculous!" he howled. "They are babes in the woods! The Mafia could never have hoped for more."

He was silent then. He closed his eyes and he rubbed his forehead, then he rubbed his hand, staring at it. "Rheumatism," he mumbled.

"Take anything for it?"

"Ah." He grimaced lackadaisically. "Aspirin." He separated his hands.

"You see," he said, "this is why the so-called war on crime can never be won. They cannot find the front." He raised his eyebrows. "Never, in any book, any government report, any newspaper, any magazine, has there been published an accurate explanation of money laundering." He slammed his hand down. "Never."

"So," I said, "tell me about money laundering."

He inhaled deeply and exhaled slowly. He nodded abstractedly. He looked at me and he smiled.

"First," he began to explain, moving forward in his chair, "one must distinguish between black money and dirty money. Black money is simply money held or exchanged in secrecy— under-the-table money—usually for the purpose of avoiding taxes. The money placed in anonymous Swiss accounts is often black. Generally, it belongs to respectable people, who can freely use it because it is rarely noticed in the flow of their greater, legitimately accounted wealth.

"Dirty money is money made through crime—drug money. It is illegal gain. It can be hidden, but it cannot be used in the light of day unless its owner can make it appear to be legitimate, tax-paid income. Many people hide dirty money, but few know how to turn it into clean money. Most people confuse hiding and laundering.

"There are many near-perfect ways to hide dirty money. The most obvious is to deposit it in a country with strict banksecrecy laws. Switzerland was once popular with the Mafia. These days, Switzerland gets money that was made by evading taxes and currency laws. The Mafia has turned to countries where bank secrecy is more impenetrable. Austria, Holland, Ireland, Hong Kong, the Isle of Man, the Dutch Antilles, Luxembourg, Singapore, Malaysia, Thailand, Costa Rica, Paraguay, Uruguay, Lebanon—all these places, and others, offer more anonymity than Switzerland. Cooperative agreements exist with only a few of them, and where they do exist, they have no value at all, because they've been drawn up by people who are incompetent in international banking and monetary matters.

"Numbered accounts are not truly anonymous. The identities of their owners are hidden only from the eyes of bank employees, not from top management—two persons, at least, at every bank know the names behind the numbers. This is why smart depositors devise further screens. They operate through bearer-share companies, set up for them by lawyers or accountants who have—yet another screen—received their instructions from phantom fiduciary companies, which are protected by secrecy laws more rigorous than those that apply to banks. Sometimes the fiduciary companies assign terms to the governments of the countries they operate in, to ensure the efficacy of those countries' secrecy laws.

"The hiding of very large sums of money is done principally in two places: the Far East and Latin America. There are banks in Hong Kong, Singapore, and Kuala Lumpur that for years have catered to dirty money. Recently, they've been joined by the Bank of China. In Costa Rica, Paraguay, and Uruguay, banks are so eager to cope with their liquidity needs that they'd gladly accept money even if it was drenched in blood. Cash is taken into those countries as normal luggage by certain operators who have arrangements with customs officials. But in Latin America, things are not as sophisticated as in the Far East. Governments in Central America are prone to blackmail.

"These are some of the ways little criminals hide their money. Whenever one of them is caught scurrying around with a million or two, he is made out to be bigger than he is. This is not difficult, since he himself usually thinks he is bigger than he is.

"Laundering money is more difficult, but when it is properly done, it allows criminals to use their dirty money in the open, and allows the law absolutely no means of interfering. The real evil of laundered money is not that it deprives the government of revenue. Because when money is effectively laundered, taxes must be paid on it. The tax money used to fund the President's Commission on Organized Crime, for this reason, may be part of the dirty money that the commission is trying to trace." He smiled a smile that was slow to fade. "No," he said. "The real evil of money laundering is its power to allow dirty money—the instrument of crime—to enter the mainstream of economies undisturbed, to consume important sectors of those economies and transform them into *feudi* of an international criminal oligarchy beyond the reach of the law—an oligarchy that is to be brought down by men who do not understand money."

He leaned back in his chair.

"To launder relatively small amounts of dirty money—up to $150 million a year, say—all you have to do is set up a bearer-bond company in a tax-haven country. You deposit your dirty money in the account of the company. The company is protected by secrecy laws, so nobody knows that the company is you. Then you draw up a consultancy agreement or an employment contract between you and the company, providing the terms of payment for some imaginary services. You have those payments made to you accordingly, and that's that: Hidden money becomes laundered money.

"This system has already been discovered by some federal prosecutors and financial journalists. But it's still virtually impossible for lawmen to demonstrate that such an arrangement is false, especially if the papers have been drawn up properly and a file of work reports has been maintained.

"Then there's the 'double-pricing' system. Very popular.

What you do is buy some real-estate property officially worth, say, $3 million. You make a recorded payment of $1 million, and you pay $2 million in black money under the table. After the purchase, you lay out some money for development— $300,000, say. In a few months or a year, you sell the property at its actual value, $3.3 million. If you're an American citizen and you do this in America, you must pay about 25 percent in taxes on your $2 million 'profit.' At the same time, you render clean and untouchable $1.5-million in dirty money.

"People who operate legal importing businesses in addition to their illegal activities sometimes use the 'double-invoicing' system. Through his bearer-share company, the importer anonymously buys goods from a legitimate foreign seller at, say, $2 a pound. He then buys those same goods from himself —that is, from the bearer-share company—for, say, $1.80 a pound. The 20-cents-per-pound difference becomes a legal profit for the importer, while dirty money he owns in the name of the bearer-share company is cleaned by passing to the loss side of its profit-and-loss account.

"This was basically the system by which the Italian Communist Party financed itself in the years after World War II. Selected Italian commercial houses—I found out about them because some of them were clients of mine—were, with a nod from the party, granted the right to sell certain Russian products by that country. The Russian government factories invoiced as in transit, and therefore beyond customs controls, to Liechtenstein companies belonging to Italians, goods at, say, $2 a kilogram, when the market price was really $3 a kilogram. The intermediary company then invoiced the goods to the appointed Italian company at $2.80 a kilogram, and gave the 80-cent profit to a shell company owned by the PCI. For its services, the Italian company enjoyed a greater than usual profit of 20 cents per kilogram. The fiscal authorities in Italy were aware of what was going on, but they turned a blind eye to it; and the communists there are still using the same system today, though to a lesser extent, I think.

"Mutatis mutandis." He grinned in a less than pleasant way. "That which is dirty is rendered clean."

He leaned forward again. The dim, rainy light at the barred window was dwindling. Shadows in the chamber lengthened.

"There is another, more sophisticated method. It is a method used for two reasons: One is tax evasion; the other is the exploitation of special laws pertaining to financial easements and incentives.

"To use the method, you must own a construction company or some kind of industrial business; and you need the help of an engineering firm—one of the several in Europe and America that specialize in such assistance.

"If your purpose is tax evasion, you have the engineering firm invoice your company for industrial projects that you have already carried out—projects whose costs have already been borne by your company's account. Often, the engineering firm supplies a blank letterhead or forms, on which you can draw up your own projects and reports—based, of course, on projects your company has already completed and paid for. The letterhead is then privately returned to the engineering firm, which officially mails it back to you along with an invoice. Your company then honors that trumped-up invoice, paying for services it never received from that firm. In effect, your company has paid twice for the same installation, doubling its cost. The engineering firm, of course, returns some of the money to you under the table—money that has now become black.

"This 'double-cost' system either reduces in whole or in part the profit of the project against which it is debited, or it falsely increases the value of your company's installation, allowing a higher amortization that reduces taxable income for years to come. Besides offsetting taxes, the system permits you to create a reserve of black money, which can then be laundered by any of the methods I've explained.

"If your purpose is to exploit special financial laws, the procedure is not much different.

"In many underdeveloped regions of Italy—as in many American cities—industrial firms enjoy financial benefits and tax exemptions. The benefits consist of long-term financing at low interest rates—often as low as 3 percent in Italy—and subsidy grants to encourage companies to develop the most depressed areas. Normally, in Italy, special financial firms controlled by the state grant loans of up to 80 percent of the value of the developing company's installations, factory buildings, and warehoused materials. In addition, they give grants of about 20 percent of the value of the installations and factory buildings.

"Let's say that your installations and factory buildings cost $1 million. A foreign engineering firm—your accomplice—contract in hand, invoices you for $1.6 million. Your company obtains a financial easement from the state of $1.28 million and a grant of $320,000. This creates a black-money fund of $600,000.

"That black money is then laundered by means of the 'double-invoicing' system. That is, your company buys raw materials below cost from a foreign bearer-share company, anonymously owned by you, or from your Anstalt, your appointed Liechtenstein fiduciary. This below-cost purchasing is continued until the $600,000 in black money is cleansed through the false profit-and-loss process.

"You thus make an extra profit of $600,000—the laundered black money—on which you pay no income tax, as the laws pertaining to development in the depressed areas provide your company with a tax abatement that is effective for ten years following the inauguration of your project—a project that, to begin with, has been invoiced at an unreal and inflated price.

"I learned of these ways twenty-five years ago, when I bought CTIP," he said. "It had been one of the engineering firms that had pioneered such schemes for selected clients around the world. When I took it over, management asked me if we couldn't continue these deals for at least a chosen few of the big Italian industrialists. Among that chosen few were companies under state control. *Tutte le strade conducono a Roma.*" He smiled. "All roads lead to Rome." The smile became a weary laugh, then the look of weariness itself.

"I refused to continue these deals," he continued, "because through these ways, companies involved in legal activities but owned by the Mafia could increase the value of their projects while laundering the profits of crime. Look to America, to where the big derricks are."

He stretched his arms and breathed the chamber's chill air. It seemed as if his talking, for now, was done. But then, in his stillness, he drew his eyetooth slowly across his bottom lip, and his eyes narrowed, as if in forethought, or hesitation. And then those dark eyes glimmered.

"There is one more system," he said. "It is the most sophisticated and the most dangerous system of all." He was not smiling.

"To use this method, you must have knowledge of the international banking system and of the laws and regulations that govern the commodities and currency exchanges in various countries throughout the world. It is an extremely dangerous system—not for him who uses it, but for the economies of the world—because it allows the laundering of immense, almost limitless sums of dirty money.

"It is a system that has been used until now by only one or two small groups that operate in the Far East with the protection of several governments. You can forget about all this 'Pizza Connection' nonsense, all this 'Godfather' shit. It is these few men without names in the Far East who are the real *pontefici della mala.*

"In this system, you deposit your dirty money, in the name of your bearer-share company, at the Hong Kong & Shanghai Bank, at the Chartered Bank, or at one of the other banks in Hong Kong or Singapore.

"Now," he continued, "you know that the Philadelphia Stock Exchange trades currency futures options on British pounds, Canadian dollars, German marks, Japanese yen, Swiss francs, and U.S. dollars, and the Chicago Mercantile Exchange trades options on British pounds, German marks, and Swiss francs.

"Only about 5 percent of all the options traded are executed on behalf of corporations wishing to hedge the currency risks of their international trade. The vast majority of the trading is purely speculative in nature, carried out by banks on behalf of their clients or themselves.

"In the international currency flow of some $60 trillion a year, it is extremely hard to distinguish those transactions carried out simply to realize legal profits from those carried out to launder dirty money.

"So," he went on, "your dirty money has been deposited in Hong Kong or Singapore in the name of your ghost company. Now you buy, say, a yen option at 240 yen per dollar. This option gives you the right, but it does not obligate you, to buy 24 billion yen for $100 million six months from now. The premium for the option is $1 million.

"If, during those six months, the yen falls to, say, 260 per dollar, you can buy the 24 billion yen in the spot market for $92 million, or you can sell the option contract. In either case, you make a profit of $7 million. That is, $8 million less the $1 million premium.

"Your counterpart in the deal is officially the bank in Hong Kong or Singapore. But, in reality, that bank is acting only on behalf of the ghost company that deposited the dirty money with them. Your real counterpart is yourself. Therefore, the $7 million profit you earn is not recorded as the bank's loss, but as the loss of your anonymous bearer-share company.

"The deal has turned $7 million in hidden dirty money into a clean profit. You haven't even really lost the $1 million option premium, because it has been paid to the ghost company that was your counterpart in the deal—that is, to yourself. Your final profit from the transaction is reduced only by the commission you must pay the bank for the fiduciary transaction—here, about $20,000—and by the income tax you must pay to the American government.

"In practice, a man who is expert at this system might buy and sell the same option many times during the six-month period, according to the fluctuations of the market. In this way, he could launder hundreds of millions of dollars in a relatively brief time.

"All right," he then said. "But what if, during those six months, the yen rises? What if it goes up to 220 per dollar?

"In this case, you allow the option to expire unexercised, and you lose only the cost of the premium, $1 million, and the $20,000 commission to the bank. But, again, that $1 million loss is not actually a loss. It is offset by the $1 million in black profits earned by your ghost company as a premium for the option you have granted it. And, as you can deduct the $1 million 'loss' from your income, not only do you suffer no real losses, but you also, through this deduction, lower the tax you must pay on the laundered profits from other deals.

"In these days of floating exchange rates, there are often rapid fluctuations within a span of hours. Working prudently, a man who knows what he's doing can realize enormous profits without risk—profits that are not really profits, but dirty money made clean.

"The same system can be used with commodities. You buy a futures contract valued at $100 million. Once again, the counterpart of the American bank or broker you use will be, upon your request, the bank in Hong Kong or Singapore where your dirty money has been deposited in the name of your bearer-share company. The Far East bank will receive a notice that the contract proposed by the American bank or broker is to be stipulated for the ghost company. The Far East bank takes no risk, and asks only a very slight margin as a formality—perhaps $1 million.

"If the price of the commodity rises 10 percent, you make

$10 million in profit. The counterpart company registers a loss in the same amount. Thus you have turned dirty money to clean.

"If the price of the commodity falls ten percent, you officially lose $10 million. But since you are also secretly the counterpart company that profits by $10 million, your commission to the bank, $20,000, is your only real loss—and you can now deduct $10 million against your other taxable profits.

"Whether currency or commodities options are used, the system is invincible. It is"—he looked away, feeling for a phrase—"it is the system at the end of the world." He smiled wickedly then. "Your government, perhaps, should speak of this to Mr. Colby, the former CIA director, who is now privately employed by the Singapore government."

He fingered the corner of the manila folder, stuffed with papers, that lay before him; the manila folder on which he had written my surname in bold capitals, and which he brought daily from his cell to our meetings in this chamber.

"Several months ago, when I was still in America," he said, in a voice not much louder than the breath that carried it, "they secretly brought me to Washington, to explain these things to Mr. Harmon of the President's Commission on Organized Crime. He had me know that, in turn, he would provide me with an affidavit stating that I had worked with the government toward solving the very serious problem of money laundering, blah, blah, blah. Later, I was able to see a copy of the commission's subsequent *Interim Report to the President.* Harmon had completely misunderstood what I had told him. His big report was a bunch of gibberish, not worth the paper it was printed on. I wrote to him, and I told him as much.

"Then here, in Voghera, Magistrate Falcone came from Palermo to interrogate me. I tried to tell him that it was not the guns but the money. I told him that he and the Commissione Parlamentare Antimafia and their American counterparts—no matter how admirable their intent and dedication might be—had not yet even slightly grazed, nor would they ever graze, the actual centers of power created by the drug traffic. These financial centers, I told him, are the real engines, the real furnaces, of something that is hardly touched by the captures and confessions of the world's Buscettas and Badalamentis, or by the breaking of its so-called Pizza Connections and Sicilian Connections.

"You see," he continued, "the Harmons and the Falcones and all the tax-squandering self-important agencies and commissions in America and Italy, they can never, they will never, succeed. The only hope"—he slammed his hand down, then lowered his voice just as suddenly—"and it is perhaps not a pretty thing to say"—he smiled—"is to change the drug laws, to legalize heroin, to destroy the source of the wealth that fuels the furnaces, before it is too late.

"But no, they continue with their meaningless, sensational arrests, far from the furnaces' heat. And all the young prosecutors are celebrated by the press, and in that way they build their careers. And the dirty billions stay in the hands of those untouchable men who use them to buy death and stoke the furnaces of their power."

He tossed his hand dispiritedly. "And I never got that damned affidavit either."

The moments of daylight were dwindling. The face of a guard appeared at the small pane in the chamber's wall, then, turning, vanished.

"How did you learn of these systems?" I asked.

"Like everything else I know"—he tapped his index finger to his silvered temple, winking—"it began with those Latin lessons. *Homo sum: humani nihil a me alienum puto,* no?" He was smiling, but his voice was grave. "I bought and sold my share of this world." His eyes passed over the scar that crossed the veins of his left wrist. "I have been around a long time," he said. "Perhaps too long."

I asked him then if he had ever used the systems of which he spoke.

"Yes," he said. "I used them to transmute the taxable

profits of some of my clients. It was not for nothing"—he grinned—"that I had the most successful tax-law firm in Italy.

"You see, until 1972, tax evasion in Italy was punishable only under the civil code. The penalties one risked were generally only fines. But in 1972 tax evasion became subject to the penal code, the *codice penale*. And so, in 1972, I closed my practice.

"Never," he said, "did I launder dirty money. Never," he said, "did I lie down with the Mafia. Not until after my career was destroyed did I ever even meet any of those men. And never, despite their greatest efforts, blackmails, and dreams, have the prosecutors here or in America been able to produce one Mafioso to say otherwise. In all their wiretaps, not once have they ever heard the name of Michele Sindona mentioned." His voice had risen excitedly. Now it lightened. "Their truth and justice"—he smiled—"are not too unlike the Mafia's honor."

"How was it, then, that you and the Mafia came to be wedded in the public mind?"

"Cuccia," he said. "Dear, saintly Cuccia."

While Sindona's activities in America flourished, his ventures in Italy met with greater and greater trouble. His difficulties began with Enrico Cuccia and extended to the highest seats of power in Rome.

Throughout the sixties, the Italian labor unions, controlled in many areas by the PCI, grew enormously in strength. New labor laws prevented companies from firing workers. Consequently, many businesses that had increased their work forces during periods of expansion were now incapable of decreasing them during recessions. As a result, those businesses were driven to the verge of bankruptcy. Under the pretext of saving the livelihoods of workers, the state intervened to nationalize the endangered businesses. Eventually, the state conglomerates—IRI, EFIM, ENI, GEPI—came to control many of the industrial, commercial, and banking assets of Italy. Through the banks it came to control, the government stealthily seized other businesses—the industries that were indebted to those banks. These industries were enslaved to the will of their creditor banks, and therefore to the politicians who controlled those banks. Nearly every construction permit, nearly every permit to import or to export restricted goods, came to depend on under-the-table "contributions" to parties and politicians, to high-ranking government bureaucrats and the officers of state-run conglomerates.

At a time when companies abroad were beginning, as *The Economist* expressed it in 1964, "to think 'multinationally,' " to diversify and to expand, corporations in Italy were rotting, sinking into the ashes of that centuries-old patronage system, *il patronato italiano,* which was the true phoenix—Guelph and Ghibelline, democrat and communist—of Italy's endless history.

"It became virtually impossible to draw foreign investors to Italy," Sindona recalled. "They were now aware that almost all companies in Italy maintained at least five sets of balance books: one for the taxmen, one for the banks, one for the minority shareholders, one for the board of directors, and one that contained the truth. A foreign investor had no way of knowing which of these books he might be shown.

"This is why I had always had my companies audited by independent firms of international stature, such as Peat, Marwick. It was the only way to gain the confidence of foreign businessmen who had become leery of Italy.

"In the early sixties, I drew up legal proposals for the institution of obligatory audits by independent auditors of all companies listed on the Milan stock exchange. I thought that this might help to bring Italian industry into the international mainstream. While the central bank, Banca d'Italia, officially but timidly supported my proposals, the opposition of many politicians was overwhelming. I discovered that the black-money funds, the *fondi neri*, maintained by so many companies to finance and purchase favors from politicians, were much more than I had thought."

Sindona also discovered something known as the Trinacria Accord. He had never come across this strange word, "Trinacria," in his reading. It was, in fact, the Latin appropriation of an ancient Greek name for Sicily. Deriving from *thrinax*, Greek for "trident," it had alluded to that island's triangular shape. Here, as Sindona found out, it alluded to the three-pointed payment system, stipulated by a secret government pact, by which black money was disbursed to Italian political parties.

The Trinacria Accord placed a premium on all public-works contracts. Under its terms, the company awarded the contract was obliged to kick back a certain sum in black money —customarily 3 percent of the contract's worth—to the politician, or politicians, who had supported the company's efforts to procure that contract. This 3 percent black-money premium would, in turn, be divided into thirds and distributed thus: a third to the Christian Democrats; a third to the socialists, with a small redistribution to the less moderate Democratic Socialists; a third to be shared by the Liberals and the Republicans, with another small redistribution to the Democratic Socialists. The various parties would usually toss some crumbs to the neo-Fascist Missini. Only the communist and the radical parties, which did not yet have members in Parliament, were excluded from sharing in the black-money bounties of the Trinacria Accord.

"Of course," Sindona reflected, "when such large sums of money are hidden and expended without any sort of documentation or receipt from the recipient, it is impossible to know how much of that money goes to the political parties and how much of it sticks to the hands of the politicians, who, armed with the means of blackmail, feel themselves immune to indictment.

"Look at a man such as Ugo La Malfa, a member of every Parliament since 1946. For twenty years, I had heard about his austerity and humble manner of living. He was the Sicilian Abraham Lincoln, loved by all Italy for his frayed cuffs. He himself told me that he had been able to care for his failing eyesight only because his fellow *palermitano* Enrico Cuccia had generously given him the money to do so. He encouraged the populace to ride bicycles, to live more modestly." At this point in his remembrance, Sindona began to laugh. "Later, after I took over the CIGA hotel chain, I discovered that La Malfa had for a long time maintained a residence—and not for himself alone—at one of the most luxurious and most costly resorts in all of Italy, the CIGA Hôtel des Îles Borromées on Lake Maggiore, in Stresa.

"And La Malfa was not the only one. Parliament was full of politicians who secretly spent in a month more than they declared to be their income for a year."

In the mid-sixties, after Sindona had come to know of the Trinacria Accord, the Christian Democrats offered to set him up as a sure-to-win candidate for either the chamber of deputies or the senate.

"I think of that sometimes," he mused, shifting slightly in the cheap plastic chair the state provided him. "In Italy a senator cannot be sent to prison."

His knowledge of the Trinacria Accord convinced him, he explained, that the principles of democracy and capitalism had been distilled, Italian-style, into a system of corruption that was as maleficent as the suffocating communism that opposed those principles.

"I should have left Italy then," he said.

Instead he lingered, and he saw fortune's parted lips close into a bitter grin.

Emilio Colombo was forty-three years old when in 1963 he became the minister of the treasury under Aldo Moro. Like the doomed Moro, Colombo was a *democristiano;* and there were many in Italy who foresaw—as it later came to pass—that the dark-haired, bespectacled Colombo would himself someday be raised to the prime ministry of the nation.

It was widely known that Emilio Colombo had long been active in the leadership of Catholic youth groups and young men's organizations. Other things were not so widely known.

Count Stefano Rivetti—his family's ennoblement had come late, toward the end of the Savoy era—was a handsome man who owned several big textile mills.

"The count had a wife, beautiful daughters," Sindona said. "But"—Sindona grinned—"he was like Janus. He had two faces."

When Rivetti inaugurated a new mill, Lanificio Maratea, near the coast south of Naples, Colombo was supportive in every way. Enormous lines of credit were obtained from the Banca Nazionale del Lavoro, the Banco di Napoli, and the Banca Commerciale Italiana; and the maximum financing allowed by law was assigned to Count Rivetti at favorable rates through the state-operated Istituto Mobiliare Italiano (IMI).

In spite of all this, Lanificio Maratea failed to realize its plans. There were huge losses, and its prospects were bleak. IMI appointed its own man to the board of the mill to protect its interests as creditor. He was Luciano Francolini, a Genovese businessman who was also an executive of Sindona's Pierbusseti tourism agency in Milan.

Francolini discovered serious irregularities in the company's accounts. Minister Colombo, interceding for Rivetti, asked Francolini not to reveal these irregularities to IMI. Colombo then called Sindona to Rome.

"The Rivetti company must be saved at any cost," Colombo told him. He assigned Gaetano Stammati, his director-general of the treasury, to assist Sindona.

Sindona met repeatedly with the officers of the Banca Nazionale del Lavoro (which also represented the Banco di Napoli) and the Banca Commerciale Italiana. Eventually, he was able to convince the Banca Nazionale del Lavoro to consider a debt-restructuring agreement. But the Banca Commerciale Italiana would hear nothing of the sort. Carlo Bombieri, its new Czechoslovakian-born chief executive officer, was adamant: "Tell your friend Rivetti and Minister Colombo that we'll never give in."

Hours after Sindona conveyed Bombieri's message to Colombo, Bombieri heard from Guido Carli, the governor of Italy's central bank, the Banca d'Italia. The next day, when he spoke to Sindona, Bombieri's voice was different: "Tell your friend Rivetti that we're prepared to give in."

The agreements drawn up by Sindona were signed by the three banks. Together, the banks forgave some 5 billion lire in debts. Meanwhile, Colombo, with the help of Francolini, had obtained the continued support of IMI.

As the ink dried on the papers, as smiling faces beheld those that were not, Sindona was struck by the gross absurdity of what had transpired. The banking system and the treasury of Italy had been loaded with losses by the very men whose entrusted duty it was to prevent such losses. And for what?

There were other hidden dealings. When the Banca d'Italia needed, urgently and secretly, to salvage the Credito Commerciale e Industriale bank of Rome, Guido Carli hurried to Milan to meet with Sindona. He asked Sindona to have his Banca Privata Finanziaria take over the management, and cover the deposits, of the Credito Commerciale e Industriale. In return, Carli promised, the Banca d'Italia would authorize Sindona's Banca Privata to open a branch in Rome, at the exclusive Via Veneto location that had until now belonged to the Credito Commerciale. In addition, the Banca d'Italia would rediscount, on easy terms and for a twelve-year period, various bills of credit issued by inactive companies Sindona owned through Fasco. The unwritten proviso Carli imposed on Sindona, however, was that Luciano Francolini should be appointed vice-president of Banca Privata Finanziara.

"You travel so much, Michele, and are out of the country so often," Carli explained. "And Luciano, you know, is a man Minister Colombo truly trusts."

Under the administration of Francolini, whom Sindona eventually fired, Banca Privata suffered the first substantial credit losses in its history—losses due in part to the suspension of bank funds used by Francolini to finance companies in which he held an interest.

He had been drawn, Sindona, into the shadow play at the highest level of financial power, to find there only *fantoccini*, puppets on strings. Soon he raised his eyes, and he saw Enrico Cuccia's hands.

In 1968, thinking that he had earned the goodwill, such as it was, of Minister Colombo and Governor Carli, Sindona laid plans to found an Italian investment bank that would be able to rival the great British banks in the field of international commerce.

Paribas, the Hambros Bank of London, and the Lehman Brothers of New York agreed to join Banca Privata Finanziaria in promoting and underwriting an initial capital pool of 50 billion lire (the equivalent, at the time, of about $80 million). This initial pool would represent the largest inflow of capital for the founding of any such institution in Italy's history. Furthermore, David Kennedy—soon to be appointed secretary of the treasury under Richard Nixon—agreed to have the Continental Illinois National Bank and Trust Company take part in a planned capital increase.

Sindona was to be the chief executive officer of the bank. Jean Reyre, head of Paribas, was the chief representative of the foreign investing group.

Guido Carli told Sindona and Reyre that he thought their venture would be a blessing to the Italian economy, and he assured them of the coming approval of Minister Colombo. A meeting was scheduled at the Banca d'Italia offices in Rome, at which the formal authorization for the institution would be discussed.

At that meeting, however, Governor Carli, his eyes averted in embarrassment, told Sindona and Reyre that Treasury Minister Colombo had discouraged the authorization. Carli promptly excused himself, leaving Sindona and Reyre more nonplussed than angered. It was a long time before Sindona discovered what had gone wrong.

"Carli, realizing that our proposed investment bank might have harmed the power of Mediobanca, had gone to Mediobanca's director, Enrico Cuccia. What seemed to truly vex Cuccia was the size of our initial capital. For twenty years he had prided himself on the fact that Mediobanca had been founded with the highest capital pool—10 billion lire—in the financial history of Italy. Our investment bank would have deprived him of that cherished distinction.

"There were no legal, technical, or even logical arguments Cuccia could use to defeat our plans. He went straight to Rome, to IRI and to his friend Ugo La Malfa; and, armed then with political support, he arranged for Colombo to block the authorization that we needed."

In the months that followed, Sindona attempted twice more to found an Italian financial institution of international dimensions. He turned his eyes to the Italcementi company, the biggest cement manufacturer in Europe. Its financial-group subsidiary, Italmobiliare, governed three ordinary-credit banks and the equity holdings of the Riunione Adriatica di Sicurtà (RAS), the second largest Italian insurance company. The control of Italcementi would include the control of Italmobiliare; and in Italmobiliare Sindona saw the makings of the institution he envisioned.

After obtaining an assurance of support from the Union de Banques Suisses in Zürich, which held a large block of Italcementi shares for its clients—and which had little faith in the company's present director, Carlo Pesenti—Sindona, in concert with the Hambros Bank of London, began buying up Italcementi shares on the open market. Once their stake in the company, together with that of the Swiss bank, outweighed

Carlo Pesenti's shares, Pesenti agreed to sign a contract of collaboration.

It was then that Sindona received a call from Guido Carli, who strongly advised him and Hambros to back off. Governor Carli told Sindona to explain to his British friends that if Italcementi were placed in foreign hands, the Italian government —meaning Colombo and Cuccia's friends in Rome—would be forced to nationalize all cement manufacturers and insurance companies. Surely, the governor concluded, this was not a prospect that Michele Sindona, the great adversary of nationalization, should welcome.

Sindona and Hambros had little choice but to sell their Italcementi shares to Carlo Pesenti. Sindona knew that Pesenti at the time was in over his head in Lancia, the automaker. Yet Pesenti somehow came up with 60 billion lire to pay Sindona and the Hambros Bank for their stock. The source of that money was a mystery—a mystery whose answer Sindona thought he discerned in Enrico Cuccia's vague and pallid grin.

In the Società Nazionale per lo Sviluppo delle Imprese Industriali, the financial organization commonly known as Sviluppo, Sindona once again perceived the cornerstone of his elusive investment institution. The management of Sviluppo had long been delegated by the Gaggia family to Vittorio Cini, a man whom Sindona felt to be one of the very few world-class financiers active in Italy, despite his advanced years. Cini confided to Sindona that he wanted to retire, and he revealed to him how Sviluppo could be acquired from the hands that then held it.

Sindona entered into an agreement of proposed partnership with Paribas and the Banca Commerciale Italiana. Then he set about gathering Sviluppo stock, starting with the 12-percent block owned by the Compagnia di Assicurazione di Milano, a major insurance firm. Paribas and Banca Commerciale Italiana arranged to purchase Vittorio Cini's shares.

Enrico Cuccia had reason, beyond those of bad blood, to be apprehensive of Sindona's takeover. For, as Sindona knew,

Sviluppo held an important place in the stock syndicate of Montecatini Edison, the unwell colossus that had been formed by the 1966 merger of the Montecatini chemical and Edison electric companies. And, as Sindona also knew, the state agencies, IRI and ENI, that held the controlling interest in Montecatini Edison had placed it under the complete tutelage of Enrico Cuccia.

There was little Cuccia could do this time. His frustration, however, was short-lived. In its attempt to take over Credit Commercial de France, Paribas was strongly criticized at home for expanding beyond its capital means, especially in its ventures abroad. The president of France, Charles de Gaulle, privately told Jean Reyre that Paribas should withdraw from some of its foreign investments if it desired to maintain its position of power in France.

The departure of Paribas from Sviluppo led to Sindona's relinquishing his own shares—at a profit of 7 percent—to a new controlling syndicate, whose plans were different from his.

During the Sviluppo affair, a new element of intrigue had been employed by Enrico Cuccia. Sindona, with his customary secrecy, had declined to discuss his intentions or his partnerships with the European press. But that didn't stop the press from writing about them. Sindona believed that Cuccia, through his minions, propagated an answer to the great curiosity he had aroused—an answer that was piningly embraced: Michele Sindona was operating on behalf and with the support of the Mafia.

In January 1969, an Italian journalist writing in *Le Figaro* of Paris alluded to Sindona's "more or less occult protectors," and claimed that through him the Bank of America had come to serve "Frank Sinatra and the powerful financial interests of certain *Siciliens d'Amérique* who seemed to gather around the singer." A day later, in Milan, the *Corriere della Sera* echoed this concern for "the Sindona mystery."

"And this," Sindona said with a smile, "is how I became the big Mafioso that I am today."

VII.
A Christian
Darkness

CHURCH AND STATE, the beasts that crouched on opposite banks of the Tiber, renewed their ancient battle. In 1968, following a vote by Parliament, Italy swore to renew the taxing of dividends on Vatican-owned stocks.

The Vatican's investments were diverse, plentiful, and often imprudent. They included interests in Beretta, the handgun company, and in the Istituto Farmacologico Serono, which produced oral contraceptives called Luteolas. The Amministrazione del Patrimonio della Sede Apostolica (APSA), the agency that presided over the Vatican's holdings, had been created in 1967 by Pope Paul VI, through the merger of two other agencies, the Amministrazione Speciale della Santa Sede and the older Amministrazione Speciale dei Beni della Santa Sede, which had been the recipient of Mussolini's endowment of 80 million gold lire, as set forth by the Lateran Treaty of February 1929.

Contrary to what had been popularly believed, the Vatican's money had been managed in a manner that was far from brilliant. Smaller, profitable investments had been countervailed by large or controlling shares in cumbrous industrial giants that the Vatican had proved itself to be incapable of properly managing. Monsignor Bernardino Nogara, who ran the Amministrazione Speciale from 1929 until his retirement in 1954 (he was then eighty-four years old), had spent a good part of Mussolini's endowment on two such giants: the Società Italiana per le Condotte d'Acqua, a heavy-construction firm, and the Società Generale Immobiliare (SGI). The latter, the largest real-estate conglomerate in Europe, had been involved in many grand development projects—the Fiumicino airport, the 1960 Olympic village, and the Monte Mario Hilton among them. In 1968, at the time of the Vatican's looming tax troubles, SGI was involved in the development of the $78 million Watergate complex on the Potomac River in Washington, D.C. The financial soundness of SGI, however, was far less grand than its undertakings. The company's capital-renewal needs, like those of Condotte d'Acqua, were an increasing burden. In the face of the considerable tax outlays it soon would have to make, the Vatican decided that its controlling interests in SGI and Condotte d'Acqua must be relinquished.

The president of APSA at that time was Sergio Guerri, a stocky, good-natured, white-haired man, born on Christmas day, 1905, in the ancient Etruscan port of Tarquinia. At the end of March 1969, just a few months after Guerri had been appointed to APSA, Pope Paul VI raised him from the rank of monsignor to the cardinalate.

Massimo Spada had left the service of the IOR in 1964, to be replaced as the lay *delegato* of that bank by his colleague Luigi Mennini. Since then, Spada had served on the boards of Sindona's Italian banks, to which Sindona also would later welcome Mennini. Though he no longer represented the Vatican in an official capacity, Massimo Spada's ties to that walled state were still strong. When, in early 1969, Pope Paul advised Cardinal Guerri to seek the help of his old friend from Milan, it was Spada's intercession that brought Sindona to Rome.

Sindona met Cardinal Guerri at the Spada home, at Via degli Scialoia 28. After the customary serving of coffee by Spada's wife, the cardinal explained the Vatican's problem and proposed that Sindona take over SGI and Condotte d'Acqua. He stressed that it was a matter which the Holy Father wished to see dispatched with the utmost care and secrecy.

"Bring me the balance sheets," Sindona told the cardinal. "Then we will talk."

After inspecting the documents Guerri brought him, Sindona said that he could handle the job only if APSA agreed to contribute one final capital renewal of at least 100 billion lire and to guarantee bank loans for another 100 billion.

Cardinal Guerri frankly responded that he had no such funds at his disposition. Sindona was shocked. Mussolini's patrimony, had it been managed according to the most conservative, low-yielding methods, would by now easily have grown to at least a billion dollars. Instead, it had been squandered by incompetents—the senile Nogaras and theologians-turned-entrepreneurs to whom it had been entrusted.

"I looked at Guerri," Sindona remembered, "and Guerri looked at me."

With his friends Spada and John McCaffery, the representative in Italy of the Hambros Bank, Sindona flew to London and met with Jocelyn O. Hambro, the director and chairman of that bank. He explained the cardinal's proposal, and he underscored what Massimo Spada told him: that by helping the Vatican in a sensitive moment such as this, the Hambros Bank, like Sindona himself, could count on substantial support from the Vatican in the future.

In early May, Sindona and the Hambros Bank acquired the Vatican's holdings in Condotte d'Acqua and all but 5 percent of its controlling interest in SGI. The deal was executed through Distributor Holding, S.A., a Luxembourg joint-stock company owned in equal parts by the Hambros Bank and Sindona's Fasco, A.G. The final cost was about $50 million.

One of the few people who knew the identities behind Distributor Holding was Enrico Cuccia. He took it upon himself to speak with his crony Eugenio Cefis, the forty-six-year-old president of ENI, the state-run oil and gas conglomerate. Cefis, he knew, was a friend of Archbishop Giovanni Benelli, the Vatican's secretary of state.

Archbishop Benelli reproached Cardinal Guerri for his undue trust in dealing with Sindona, a man he barely knew.

111

"He will never pay," he said. Guerri was offended. He reminded the archbishop that the deal had been sanctioned by the Holy Father, that the contract had been negotiated with the assistance of Raffaele Politi, the adviser to the papal Prefettura Economica, and that the contract had been approved and initialed by Benelli himself.

Cardinal Guerri was transferred to the Governatorato della Città del Vaticano. He was replaced at APSA by Giuseppe Caprio, a balding dark-haired prelate who had spent the last decade as the apostolic pro-nuncio to China and then India.

Sindona, meanwhile, upon a closer examination of the records of SGI and Condotte d'Acqua, had found that the companies he and Hambros had taken over were in far worse shape than he had been led to believe. Furthermore, Condotte d'Acqua had long operated under the Trinacria Accord, expending enormous sums in *bustarelle,* black-money bribes.

The balance sheets and documents shown him by the Vatican had been audaciously falsified. After all these years, and with all that he knew, he had taken a shot in the shorts—from the church.

He talked to Cardinal Guerri, who was deeply embarrassed but obviously innocent and unaware of any wrongdoing. He then talked to Caprio, who lapsed into a flutter. "I defend your indignation, Avvocato Sindona," he bleated, "but if you don't pay, they'll send me back to India."

Caprio was not shipped back to India. Sindona, contrary to Archbishop Benelli's calumnies, had never thought of reneging. The Vatican was paid in full for its shares, and before the appointed deadline. It was a calmer Caprio who, with the basilica of St. Peter looming behind him, grinned to Sindona and said, "Look at it like this. You've been sent by God to help your church."

Later, the pope called his old friend to him in the papal palace. "They tell me, Avvocato Sindona," he said with a smile, "that you have been sent to us by God." Then his smile widened. "They say, Avvocato Sindona, that you are God's man."

Thus began the strangest, and the final, lustrum of Michele Sindona's career of earthly power.

Sindona transformed SGI into one of the world's most prosperous and important real-estate corporations.

In the early months of 1970, his friend Charlie Bludhorn, the chairman of Gulf & Western, traveled frequently to Rome, where Paramount was involved in film production. During one of his visits, he confessed to Sindona that Gulf & Western was passing through hard times, and he proposed to him a wedding of collaboration between SGI and the wholly-owned Canadian real-estate subsidiary of Gulf & Western. Sindona agreed to finance Bludhorn's acquisition of a 5-percent share of SGI through Distributor Holding, to which Bludhorn would give $5 million in promissory notes and a package of debentures in the stock of a company Gulf & Western controlled. (This company's primary asset was a 50-percent share in the future profits, if any, of a forthcoming Paramount picture called *Darling Lili,* produced and directed by Blake Edwards, and starring Julie Andrews and Rock Hudson. Though *Variety* found *Darling Lili* to be "smacking of b.o. promise," the movie ended up losing money.) Sindona also agreed to grant places on the SGI board to Bludhorn and Gulf & Western's thirty-six-year-old vice-president, Don Gaston.

Bludhorn, a Jew, was apprehensive of being received coldly by the Holy See representatives who still served on the company's board. To banish his friend's doubts, Sindona brought him to the Vatican and arranged a private meeting between him and Caprio. The deal was concluded; Bludhorn and Gaston joined the board of SGI.

Later, when Gulf & Western's liquidity problems worsened, Sindona bought back its SGI shares, then used Bludhorn's old promissory notes toward buying out the Hambros Bank's share of Distributor Holding, and thus its share of SGI.

In May 1973, Sviluppo, the firm whose takeover by Sindona had been thwarted a few years before, was merged with

Edilcentro. With an after-merger capital of 61 billion lire and fixed assets and stockholdings worth more than 70 billion lire, Edilcentro-Sviluppo emerged as the fourth largest nonstate holding company in Italy—and the object of Michele Sindona's sudden desire.

Enrico Cuccia rose against Sindona as he had in the past. This time, however, Sindona had the support of a powerful new friend, Giulio Andreotti, who had become prime minister the summer past. Barely a week after Edilcentro-Sviluppo had been formed, Sindona, at a cost of $140 million, acquired the 44-percent, controlling interest he sought, and in July 1973, with a subsequent recapitalization, Edilcentro-Sviluppo was incorporated into SGI.

SGI was then the world's most geographically diverse corporation of its kind. Through its control of Edilcentro-Sviluppo, it also controlled the Compagnia Italiana dei Grandi Alberghi (CIGA), the most important group of luxury hotels in Italy. In Paris, the holdings of SGI included the Grand Hôtel, the Meurice, and the Prince de Galles, and all the real estate opposite the Place de l'Opéra. In Montreal, it held the Stock Exchange building and the Port Royal Tower. Among its American holdings were Paramount Studios in Hollywood, the Watergate complex in Washington, D.C., and several hundred residential acres in Oyster Bay, Long Island.

Sindona inaugurated a financial division of SGI, concentrating on limited-risk copper and silver ventures in partnership with other Italian and American companies. In itself, this one division of SGI produced a first-quarter net profit of some $10 million.

When the SGI board of directors met in early 1974 to approve the first postmerger budget Sindona had drawn up, he told them that he held in his hands the most sound, and perhaps the best, budget any Italian company would present to its stockholders that year. True or not, his days were numbered.

* * *

Condotte d'Acqua was a different matter. Wanting not to be burdened by the Trinacria Accord, Sindona planned to fatten the company's portfolio and then sell it off.

A contract was signed between Condotte d'Acqua and the Pahlavi government of Iran. The project was a prodigious one: the $2 billion construction of the great port of Bandar Abbas on the Strait of Hormuz.

Iran at the time was seen as a secure anchorage for the will of the West. While E. F. Hutton opened a branch in Teheran, the American government happily negotiated a $2 billion arms-sale agreement with the shah. Great Britain joined in with another billion dollars' worth of weapons. The reports of the CIA, like those of the usually more astute international insurance agencies, declared that Iran would continue to be the steeled arm of United States policy in the Persian Gulf, and that the chances there of political upheaval were negligible.

While overseeing Condotte d'Acqua's construction in Iran, Sindona came to know well Shah Mohammad Reza Pahlavi and his prime minister, Amir Abbas Hoveida. He also came to know that the reality of Iran's political stability was very different from the pictures painted by Western intelligence agents and diplomats. Shah Pahlavi privately told Sindona what had once been told to him by his father, Reza Khan, abolisher of the veil and restorer of Persia to her olden name. The Iranian people, Reza Khan had said, are born to live beneath the shadow of dictatorship; but there is nothing they so love as the endless changing of that shadow's name.

Sindona saw that the day would likely come, as the shah and Hoveida secretly feared it might, when those Western guns would be turned against the West. Until within months of that day, in February 1979, the CIA and other observers would maintain a rosy view of Iran. But long before that day, Sindona would prepare for the shah a detailed plan to help him hold his ground. The plan explained how social upheaval could be avoided through the creation of medium-term liquidities that would permit the distribution of housing and small-business loans, how the Iranian currency should be made convertible to increase its international liquidity, and how Iran could reduce the risk of its strategic commodities being cornered by unfriendly countries.

Sindona's legal problems and Amir Hoveida's resignation stood in the way of that plan's success. Later, a revised version of Sindona's plan would come to the attention of the Saudi royal family. In time, it would find its way into the hands of the Libyan dictator Muammar Mohammed al-Qaddafi; and Sindona, a fugitive vanished from the grasp of the world, would then discover that Sicily was still a land of many gods, and that Islam's deadly dream, the power of terrorism, was traded daily on the stock exchanges of the West.

Once the construction of the great port in Iran was contracted, Sindona asked Jocelyn Hambro to find a foreign buyer for Condotte d'Acqua, a buyer who would be free from the surreptitious obligations of the Trinacria Accord. Hambro reported that the British construction firm of Taylor Woodrow was interested.

Sindona had previously given his word to Loris Corbi, the chief executive officer of Condotte d'Acqua, that, before any sale occurred, Corbi would be offered a chance to buy the company at the bid price. Carlo Bombieri, the CEO of the Banca Commerciale Italiana, was prepared to aid Corbi in his plans.

A few days after Sindona received word of Taylor Woodrow's interest, Bombieri told Sindona that a group organized by him would like to come in, fifty-fifty, in the British firm's takeover plans. The offer was relayed to Taylor Woodrow by Jocelyn Hambro, and Woodrow backed off. At that point, Sindona was approached by Raffaele Mattioli, the seventy-five-year-old state banker.

Sindona respected Mattioli more than he did any of the other bankers who served the state. The head of the Banca Commerciale Italiana from 1936, Mattioli had also been a life-long reader of philosophy and the classics. He owned the distinguished publishing house of Casa Riccardo Ricciardi, and was known for his own translations into Italian of Shakespeare and Coleridge. It was Mattioli who had overseen the founding of Mediobanca. And it was he who, in a private moment, had confessed, "You see, my dear Sindona, I created Mediobanca for Cuccia thinking I had adopted a son. I didn't see my mistake until it was too late." But the Mattioli who now approached him seemed to be a different man, a man who in his final years had made his final deal. He stood there, in his familiar wide-brimmed hat and his baggy countryman's suit, and he suggested that Sindona relinquish his Condotte d'Acqua shares at a *complessivo-di-lire* price that was a billion lire less than what Taylor Woodrow had offered. Sindona looked inquiringly at the old man and said that he did not understand.

"I asked him why I would want to do such a thing. He explained to me that IRI banks held some of Condotte d'Acqua's debt, and that those banks would call it in if I did not comply.

"I knew Mattioli was a gentleman. He never would have undertaken an extortionary swindle like this on his own. Rome, I surmised, was making him act as he was.

"Hambros and I had little choice then. In the end, I was told by the Banca Commerciale Italiana, 'Don't worry. You'll see. We'll find some way to recoup your loss for you.'

"I'm still waiting to recoup."

By this time, Sindona had become involved with two of the most curious characters in his tale, both of whom he had come to know in early 1969, the year he became God's man. One of them was a vain and prideful American bishop whose love for his church was equaled only by his love for himself. The other was a small and introverted man who sought to read in the scroll with seven seals, therein only to find, written large, his own and violent death.

Michele's mother had died in 1966. His daughter, Maria

Elisa, was married the following April to a young lawyer named Piersandro Magnoni. A year later, Sindona brought his son-in-law into his organization. In November 1968, Sindona acquired his fourth bank, Banca Unione at Via Santa Maria Segreta 5, in Milan, previously owned by the publisher Giangiacomo Feltrinelli and the IOR (which retained a 20-percent interest). Later, Carlo Bordoni stepped aside at Moneyrex, and Piersandro was allotted an interest in that flourishing company.

In the first days of 1969, Piersandro's father, Giuliano Magnoni, told Sindona that Roberto Calvi, an assistant manager of Banco Ambrosiano, wanted very much to meet him. Sindona had never before heard of the man, but he consented to have Magnoni introduce him.

Roberto Calvi was born in Milan, on April 13, 1920—three weeks before Sindona's own birth in Patti. Banco Ambrosiano, the bank at which Calvi had worked since 1946, had its headquarters in a quiet, shadowy piazza set off from the side entrance of La Scala. It was a bank quite like no other. Named for the patron saint of Milan and inaugurated in 1896 on the feast day of another Milanese saint, Carlo Borromeo, Banco Ambrosiano had been proposed by its founder, Giuseppe Tovini, as an institution of *"corpi morali,"* devoted to *"principi cristiani."* When Calvi joined the staid but wealthy little bank, it was still often referred to as *"la banca dei preti,"* or "the priests' bank." At the close of every fiscal year, a prayerful call was made that *la provvidenza,* divine providence, would care for the bank's finances. Calvi, a balding little man with a dark moustache and brooding eyes, decided to supplicate Sindona instead.

During their first meeting, at Studio Sindona, Calvi spoke at bewildering length of his family and of his farm-villa in Comasco, near the Swiss border, stressing the importance in his life of that place where he went every weekend to renew his energies. As if to substantiate his georgic rhapsody, he proudly showed Sindona his hand that lacked a finger—the result of a poorly aimed swing of the wood ax.

"He was a budding Cincinnatus," Sindona said with a laugh, recalling that first meeting. "Later he gave my little granddaughters a goat." He shook his head fondly. "We named it Federico."

Finally, Calvi broached business. He explained that the directors of Banco Ambrosiano were provincials in banking and that he desired to establish a working association between Banco Ambrosiano and Banca Privata Finanziaria in the international market.

After their meeting, Sindona spoke with Carlo Canesi, the president of the Ambrosiano, with whom he had long had excellent relations. Canesi talked of Calvi in a detached manner, implying that he was not a central figure at the bank.

"I myself," Canesi said, "appointed Roberto to handle our international division. There was only one problem: He was afraid to fly. I held his hand on his first air trip. Since then, he's been flying here and there, fancying himself a great cosmopolitan prince of affairs."

Sindona was amused by Canesi's words, but he sensed in them a certain jealousy toward the young man who was venturing into areas beyond old Canesi's expertise. A few days later, Sindona received Calvi again.

This time, there was no talk of the bucolic life. Calvi straightforwardly told Sindona that he had at his disposal, through the Ambrosiano, considerable medium-term funds abroad—funds that he wished to employ in joint ventures with Sindona. He confessed, however, that his lack of authority at the bank made it difficult for him to operate without the supervision of the board of directors. He asked Sindona to devise a way in which significant medium- to long-term deals could be undertaken without his superiors' knowledge.

"I saw then," Sindona said, "that, beneath the skin of a lowly functionary, there lurked in Calvi a man clearly set on winning wealth and power—not for the Ambrosiano, but for himself. In effect, he, the employee of a credit institution, was asking me to find him a way to achieve a position like mine, to become his own boss. So I laid it out for him. I explained how a series of financial institutions could be created—in Luxembourg, the Bahamas, Costa Rica, Vaduz—that would retain the aegis of the Ambrosiano while enjoying the lawful luxury of secrecy offered by those countries. It was, I explained, a luxury whose value had already been proven by the world's most important banks."

Calvi then surprised Sindona by telling him that he was afraid to proceed without first obtaining formal authorization from the Ambrosiano.

"Avvocato, you must help me," he said. "Introduce me to Massimo Spada and ask him to speak on my behalf to the board and the general manager of the Ambrosiano."

Sindona did indeed speak to Spada, suggesting to him the advantages of their gaining a friend—a hungry and submissive friend—who sat in power at the prestigious Ambrosiano. Spada agreed to intercede, and in the autumn of 1970, Calvi was appointed the *direttore centrale* of Banco Ambrosiano. Several weeks later, in November, Calvi had the Ambrosiano acquire from Sindona a Luxembourg holding company called Compendium, which was rechristened Banco Ambrosiano Holding. Later, with Sindona's permission, Calvi approached the board of the Ambrosiano with a polite ultimatum: "Either make me *direttore generale* with absolute powers to work abroad, or I will accept an offer to assume the management of Signor Sindona's banking network." He became general manager of the Ambrosiano in February 1971. In March, with the help of Sindona, he established the Cisalpine Overseas Bank in Nassau, the Bahamas. Controlled by Banco Ambrosiano Holding of Luxembourg, Cisalpine was partially owned by Sindona's Finabank and the IOR, each of which had underwritten 2.5 percent of Cisalpine's capital.

Calvi and Sindona easily and quickly attracted a wealth of long-term depositors to Cisalpine. Their success was due in great part to the lofty presence on Cisalpine's board of a figure beyond reproach, one who brought with him the sovereign and hallowed aura of the church itself. He was Bishop Paul Marcinkus, the new president of the pope's bank.

Paul Casimir Marcinkus, the son of a window washer from Lithuania, was born in Cicero, Illinois, on January 15, 1922. Ordained in 1947, he left America three years later to study canon law at the Gregorian University in Rome. In 1952, he joined the staff of the Secretariat of State of the Vatican. In time, he rose to serve as a Vatican diplomat in Bolivia and Canada. Owing to his size—Marcinkus stood close to six feet three and was heavyset—he was appointed the personal bodyguard and traveling aide of Pope Paul VI in 1964, and acted the following year as the interpreter at the pope's meeting with President Lyndon B. Johnson in New York.

"Chi sta vicino al sole si scalda," Sindona said, smiling. "He who stands near the sun grows warm. It is an old Italian saying—one, I think, that translates easily into many languages."

Pope Paul VI had seen to it that his secretary, Father Macchi, had been raised to the rank of monsignor. Since his master's ascension to the papacy, the little man's influence on him had increased rather than ebbed. The modern-art collection cultivated by Macchi in Milan had been brought to Rome, where eventually its growing unsightliness would arrogate several rooms of the Vatican museums. The pontifical suites and the pope's private quarters on the third floor of the Apostolic Palace had been modishly redecorated in cool grays and pale blues. A roof terrace had been built at great expense above the papal apartments. It was there that the Hamlet pope spent much of his time, descending only rarely to the gardens below. The devoted keeper of that distance between the Holy Father and the earth beneath him was Monsignor Macchi.

The reign of Paul VI had brought controversy and change to the Catholic Church. In September 1963, barely three months after his inauguration, he had reconvened the Second Vatican Council, begun by John XXIII. Within a month, the council had approved twelve amendments to the first chapter of the schema on liturgy. Vernacular masses were introduced in August of the following year. In January 1967—the year in which it was announced that the Latin mass would soon be fully abolished—President Nikolai Podgorny of the Soviet Union became the first communist head of state to be welcomed to the Vatican. The encyclical *Populorum Progressio,* Pope Paul's appeal for social and economic justice, was delivered in March 1967. It was an appeal that was taken up again by the thirty-ninth Eucharistic World Congress, held in August 1968.

Sindona was convinced that all this was Macchi's doing. "The Second Vatican Council, the Novus Ordus of the mass, the advocacy of socialism in the guise of piety, the embracing of communist rulers to whom God was anathema—this was Macchi's work. The pope's voice and the pope's power were the instruments of Monsignor Macchi's will. The church did not see until it was too late that to destroy the Latin mass was to destroy the ritual power of the sacred mysteries. The vernacular mass, instead of bringing people to the church, drove them from it. Through Paul VI, Macchi was destroying the church he had vowed to serve. Later, in the last years of his life, Paul VI finally understood all this. He saw what had been done, and it anguished him."

Marcinkus realized that the way to gain the favor of Paul VI was to ingratiate himself with Macchi. So, in Macchi's presence, the priest from Cicero became a wellspring of egalitarian truisms and socialist sympathies.

When Francis Cardinal Spellman, the archbishop of New York, died in December 1967, Marcinkus sensed his opportunity to seize the moment. Spellman had been for years the Catholic Church's great American moneymaker. Presiding over America's most affluent archdiocese—the real-estate holdings alone of the see of New York were valued at more than $500 million—Cardinal Spellman had channeled considerable sums to the Vatican, and had procured much financial assistance for endeavors of the Holy See. The sums and the financial assistance began to dwindle after his death, causing a great deal of concern in Rome. Lying profusely, Marcinkus told Macchi that he had many powerful acquaintances in the financial communities of Chicago and New York and that his own knowledge of the financial world—which, of course, he disliked for its lack of social conscience—was considerable.

At the end of 1967, Marcinkus was appointed to the secretariat of the IOR. A year later, he was named to the Cardinals' Commission of Vigilance for the IOR. In January 1969, he was consecrated bishop, and in 1971, several months after Sindona introduced him to Roberto Calvi, Bishop Marcinkus became the president of the IOR.

By that time, Sindona knew Marcinkus quite well. The two men had been introduced, at the request of the bishop, through a mutual acquaintance, Mark Antinucci, an American businessman living in Rome. Marcinkus had been aware of Sindona's relations with Massimo Spada, Luigi Mennini, and Pellegrino De Strobel, the *ispettore* (chief accountant) of the IOR and an executive committee member of Sindona's Finabank, in which the Vatican was a partner. At their first meeting, Bishop Marcinkus asked Sindona what he honestly thought of these men. Before Sindona could answer him, Marcinkus interrupted to say that his own opinion of Spada, Mennini, and De Strobel was low and that if he, Marcinkus, were the president of the IOR, he should quickly get rid of Mennini.

Sindona laughed, and he told the bishop that Luigi Mennini—who had been with the IOR since its founding, who had delivered two of his fourteen children, a priest and a nun, to the service of the church—was the only capable manager the IOR then had and that he was a man whose seriousness was widely respected.

There were other meetings, and in the course of them, Sindona became convinced that Bishop Marcinkus was absolutely incompetent in economic and financial matters and that he was, in mind and soul, a pompous fool. While playing the part of the pious proletarian priest for Macchi and the pontiff,

Marcinkus was, in reality, a vain *scalatore*, a social climber of the most graceless order.

"Marcinkus was very upset by the Vatican's sale to me of SGI. This was because SGI controlled the Olgiata Romana, the golf course it had constructed on the northern outskirts of Rome. As long as the Vatican had owned SGI, Marcinkus had been treated as a sort of *padrone* at the Olgiata. When the Vatican sold SGI, his princely status at the Olgiata was diminished.

"At Rome's other exclusive golf club, L'Acqua Santa, Marcinkus was treated as a nouveau riche by the Roman aristocracy that frequented the place. Only at the Olgiata had he been able to maintain his pose as *dominus maximus* of the club, too blind to see that the *antichi romani* of high society, beneath their smiles, regarded him as a cowboy who would be emperor.

"He asked me repeatedly to fire Aldo Samaritani, the SGI general manager who was the executive head of the Olgiata Romana. Samaritani was known, somewhat drolly and somewhat seriously, as the *Re di Roma*, the King of Rome. Since the Vatican had ceased to control SGI, his kingly shadow at the Olgiata, and elsewhere, had overtaken the bishop's own. This maddened the great egalitarian's soul to no end."

Sindona laughed and waved his hand. "Forget about theology. To understand the church of Rome, one first must understand the golf courses of Rome."

In 1971, immediately after being named president of the IOR, Marcinkus invited Sindona to visit him in his elegant new office. A beautiful secretary escorted him across the bishop's threshold. She was one of the many striking women with whom Marcinkus increasingly surrounded himself. These ladies—they were little more than girls, actually, and every bit as playful—delighted in behaving in public as if they were the bishop's secret mistresses; and the bishop loved it.

Marcinkus radiated self-importance as he greeted Sindona. "I asked for full powers as the condition *sine qua non* for my accepting the presidency, and the Holy Father granted them to me," he proclaimed. Sindona knew that the bishop was lying—and lying toward no end, at that—but he said nothing.

As the president of the IOR, Bishop Marcinkus entrusted some of the bank's money to a California exchange agent who ended up involving the IOR in several violations of the Securities and Exchange Commission regulations. As the powerful American acquaintances about whom Marcinkus had told Macchi and the pope were for the most part imaginary, he turned to Sindona for help. Sindona introduced him to his friends and partners at Continental Illinois, in the bishop's native state, and he asked them to help the new IOR president find his way. In time, Marcinkus came to see that men such as Mennini and De Strobel, whom he had boasted that he would fire, were invaluable to the IOR.

Sindona was amused to learn that Marcinkus knew little of the institution's less savory traditions. Though he had heard some talk of an unorthodox service offered by the IOR to its selected clients, the bishop confessed that he was unaware of precisely what that service was.

"Later," Sindona recalled, "that fool Harmon of the Commission on Organized Crime asked me to give him the names of Italian banks that engaged in the illicit export of cash.

"I had to laugh. I told him that there was not a single Italian bank that did not engage in the *in nero* transferal of money. 'It's incredible how naïve you Americans are,' I told him.

"'If you wish,' I said, 'you can go right now to Milan or to Rome with $1 million, $10 million in cash, with me or some other Italian who knows his way around. In a matter of minutes, we would find any number of persons or organizations offering us their services to transfer the money abroad, *in nero*, without risk. Ten minutes later, you would have confirmation that your money has been credited to you, in the currency of your choice, in Switzerland, Austria, or the Bahamas, minus a service fee.' Harmon was amazed.

"The pope's bank, the IOR, had been involved in such services since its founding. In general, the IOR catered to other banks, whose more privileged clients sought the added security and secrecy offered by Vatican channels.

"The IOR would open a running account with the Italian credit bank that wanted to export lire *in nero*. The client of the Italian bank would deposit the lire in cash in that account, and the IOR would then credit it to him abroad, in the currency and in the bank of his choice. In the process, the IOR would deduct a commission that was slightly higher than the going rate.

"The Banca d'Italia and the other authorities never interfered, as they were convinced that the Holy See, if pressed, would respond that, being a sovereign foreign government, it was not under obligation to furnish any information to Italy.

"I know these things very well," Sindona continued, "because the IOR acted in this capacity for clients of my Banca Privata and Banca Unione.

"Bishop Marcinkus, once he came to understand it, believed that the system used by the IOR to export funds was the 'perfect crime.' Later, the legislature of Italy made the unauthorized export of capital a penal, rather than a civil, crime. From New York, I advised Marcinkus to immediately suspend the Vatican's illegal currency transferals. I told him that if representatives of the Vatican were ever dragged into the courts as accomplices in black-money crimes—something that the Italian government would dearly love—the prestige of the IOR, and of the papacy itself, would never recover. But Marcinkus believed himself to be beyond the reach of the law. He continued to pursue the profits that he flaunted to the pope as proof of his competence and worth and that he hoped would bring him the scarlet *berretta*."

Whatever the case, the IOR eventually lost the respect that men such as Spada had won for it; and Marcinkus never became a cardinal.

In the early summer of 1971, a few months after Sindona, Calvi, and Marcinkus conspired to form the Cisalpine Overseas Bank in Nassau, Sindona heard that La Centrale Finanziaria, an important financial holding company, was in trouble due to disagreements among its stockholders. Two of La Centrale's board members, Ettore Lolli and Antonio Tonello, told Sindona that he might be able to convince La Centrale's owners to sell. Sindona and the Hambros bank undertook the takeover in concert. Calvi implored Sindona to allow the Ambrosiano to join them in the venture. He explained to Sindona that he yearned to gain the friendship of Jocelyn Hambro, as he wanted to send his eighteen-year-old son, Carlo, to learn banking in London. Sindona pointed out to Calvi that, under Italian law, Banco Ambrosiano was forbidden to involve itself in acquisitions of this particular sort. In the end, it was secretly agreed that Calvi's bank, like Sindona's Fasco, would be represented in a fiduciary manner by Hambros. The takeover was concluded in July, and on August 5, with Sindona's help, a beaming Calvi joined Jocelyn Hambro, Evelyn de Rothschild, and others on the board of La Centrale.

It was Sindona's desire to bring about a merger of La Centrale's construction subsidiary, Cogefar, with the Agnelli group's IMPRESIT. He met privately with Giovanni Agnelli at the Agnelli-FIAT headquarters in Turin.

"Look," Sindona recalled Agnelli telling him, "your ideas and proposals are wonderful, Michele. I would be happy to help marry the two companies if I could. But you have far too many enemies, and my own position right now has become far too vulnerable."

Sindona well understood Agnelli's position of vulnerability. FIAT, as the largest company in Italy, was under increasing attack by trade-union militants. Recurring strikes and the government's prohibition of layoffs were leading to long years of consistent losses for the company. At the same time, Agnelli was being drawn ever more deeply into the thralldom of an unholy alliance with the most notorious dictator of the age. In 1969, the Agnelli group had begun construction of a $332 million FIAT plant in Russia. (Stavropol, the name of the Volga town where the plant was located, was duly changed by the Soviet government to Togliatti, in honor of the late Italian Communist Party boss.) Modeled after the Fiat 124, the first of the plant's VAT cars rolled off the assembly line in September 1970. In the meantime, however, additional capital had been needed. That capital was provided by Colonel Muammar al-Qaddafi, the twenty-nine-year-old junta leader who had seized power in Libya on September 1, 1969. In accordance with an agreement reached at a Moscow meeting between Agnelli, Qaddafi, and Kremlin representatives, a $200 million loan from Qaddafi to FIAT was transformed into a loan, at reasonable rates over a fifteen-year period, from FIAT to the Russian government. Subsequently, Qaddafi came to acquire $400 million in FIAT convertible obligations. Eventually, the Qaddafi regime would hold more than 13 percent of FIAT, and would gain two seats on its board. In January 1974, after the FIAT-owned newspaper, *La Stampa*, published an unflattering mention of Qaddafi in a humor piece, the Arab Boycott Committee would nearly bring about the firing of *La Stampa*'s managing editor, Arrigo Levi. Later, Carlo De Benedetti, the newly appointed managing director of FIAT, would be abruptly dismissed after only a hundred days in office—as long as it took Qaddafi to learn that De Benedetti's father was a Jew.

No, Sindona could not deny the truth of Giovanni Agnelli's words. Times were bad, and times were strange.

A month after the takeover of La Centrale, Sindona turned his attention to the Società Italiana per le Strade Ferrate Meridionali, the financial company that was commonly known as Bastogi. Though somnambulant for some time, the hundred-and-nine-year-old Bastogi was still a large and important concern. Carrying a book value of approximately $124 million, Bastogi owned considerable pieces of Montecatini Edison, Italcementi, Pirelli, and twenty-five other companies. Sindona was most interested in Beni Stabili, the real-estate firm Bastogi controlled, and in Cogeco, its construction company. His intention was to merge Bene Stabili and La Centrale's real-estate group, Habitat, with his already immense SGI, and to merge Cogeco with the construction companies of La Centrale and SGI (Cogefar and Sogene, respectively). The control of Bastogi itself would be transferred to La Centrale with the idea of merging the two companies into a new and grander financial corporation.

Sindona apprised Calvi and Hambros of his plan, having been assured by his friend Tullio Torchiani, the current president of Bastogi, that a takeover was possible. This takeover, however, would be like none their countrymen had ever known. Sindona was about to declare the first tender offer in Italy's history.

The September 8 issue of *Il Sole-24 Ore,* the financial daily of Milan, reported rumors of the odd scheme. In an official statement, Sindona denied the rumors. Meanwhile, he arranged for the tender offer to be declared the following Monday by the Westdeutsche Landesbank Girozentrale of Düsseldorf, West Germany, on behalf of an unnamed international group. Enrico Cuccia well knew who was at the center of that group. On the Friday afternoon before the offer was to be made, it was said in the upper halls of Mediobanca that Sindona would have but one way out on Monday: suicide.

It was officially announced on Monday morning, September 13, that the Westdeutsche Landesbank Girozentrale sought to buy 20 million Bastogi shares—33 percent of the company's stock—for the above-market price of 2,800 lire a share. On the following day, the Milan stock exchange reacted with rising excitement. The *Corriere della Sera* explained on its financial page that the tender offer (*offerta pubblica di acquisto*, or, as it came to be known in that acronym-loving tongue, OPA) was already common in "financial markets more advanced than ours," such as New York, London, and Paris, but was for Milan a *"novità assoluta."* And Enrico Cuccia scurried to Rome to meet with Prime Minister Colombo.

The prime minister notified Urbano Aletti, the president of Milan's executive committee of stockbrokers (the Comitato Direttivo degli Agenti di Cambio), that the Italian legal system contained no provisions for tender offers and that no tender offer should be allowed. But President Aletti answered that the tender offer violated no laws. In fact, Aletti said, this was the first time that the *parco buoi* and the *padroni del vapore* were being treated as equals. (*Parco buoi* was, and is, a condescending term for minority shareholders as a group, translatable as "cattle drove." The big speculators and controlling stockholders are *padroni del vapore*—"bosses of the steam.")

Contrary to the wishes of the government's most powerful official, the Bastogi OPA was approved and supported by the stockbrokers' committee. This support was echoed in *La Stampa,* the influential paper controlled by the Agnelli group.

Enrico Cuccia turned to André Meyer and Guido Carli. Together, Meyer and Carli pressed Bastogi's main stockholders not to sell, insinuating that they would otherwise risk the enmity of the Italian monetary authorities. There was protest by some banks that the governor of a central bank, Carli, should not become involved in private affairs. But that protest vanished in the breeze—soon to be followed, as the days grew cool, by the Bastogi OPA.

When Anna Bolchini Bonomi, one of the celebrated matrons of the Milanese financial world, had gone to Banco Ambrosiano to obtain funds for Beni Immobili Italia, the family holding company she had inherited from her father in 1940, she had handed over as security considerable stock in the Lombardy bank Credito Varesino. The troubled Bonomi group had not been able to repay the loan, and the Credito Varesino stock had been sold off to Sindona through the office of Roberto Calvi. Sindona had also acquired through Calvi the financial company known as Invest. Both these companies were now, through an option, part of Manifattura Carlo Pacchetti, a leather-tanning company Sindona had bought from the Credito Lombardo. Sindona had appointed Massimo Spada the president of Pacchetti, and together they were rapidly transforming it into a boldly diversified conglomerate.

Bishop Marcinkus had asked Sindona if he might be interested in taking over the Banca Cattolica del Veneto, an IOR holding centered in Venice. Sindona had discussed the idea with Massimo Spada, and they had decided that the Banca Cattolica could be acquired by Pacchetti then merged with La Centrale, Banca Privata Finanziaria, and Banca Unione, on the boards of which Spada sat with the title of vice-president. Without revealing to Calvi precisely how the acquisition was to be executed, Sindona had invited him to become involved in the deal. Calvi had eagerly accepted, seizing the opportunity to develop a closer relationship with Bishop Marcinkus.

While planning the Bastogi offer and preparing to negotiate the purchase of the Banca Cattolica, Sindona was approached by Graham Martin, the American ambassador to Italy. Martin told Sindona that Italy's English-language newspaper, *The Rome Daily American,* was in danger of being taken over by the socialist PSI, which published *Avanti!* The ambassador said that if Sindona should prevent this from happening, he would be doing a fine deed for the United States and for his old pal President Nixon. Sindona arranged to buy the paper in concert with his American friend Mark Antinucci and with General Sory Smith, the retired air-force major general who was the chief of the American military-assistance advisory group in Italy. On the eve of the Bastogi announcement, Sindona hosted a reception at the Grand Hotel in Rome to celebrate the acquisition of *The Rome Daily American.* (The Grand, where Sindona maintained a suite year-round—and where the restaurant's menu offered a variant of *spaghetti alla carbonara* called *spaghetti Sindona*—was a part of the CIGA group, which he owned through SGI.) At that September reception, Marcinkus told Sindona that he would like to conclude the Banca Cattolica deal as soon as possible.

When Sindona next spoke with Marcinkus, after returning from the International Monetary Fund meeting in Washington during the last week of September, the bishop told him that the Banca Cattolica negotiations would have to be suspended.

Marcinkus did not tell him why. He did not tell him that Enrico Cuccia's cohort Eugenio Cefis, who was now the president of Montecatini Edison, had once again paid a call on his friend Archbishop Giovanni Benelli, and that Secretary of State Benelli had done as Cefis had bidden him.

The days of the fall grew shorter and darker. John McCaffery, who had long talked of retiring to Ireland, had now left the Milan office of the Hambros Bank, where he was replaced by his son, John McCaffery, Jr. In Bishopsgate, London, there was a more momentous change. Jocelyn Hambro, the Hambros Bank chairman who had aligned his bank with Sindona in some of the biggest deals of the past decade, was moving aside to become the chairman of Hambros, P.L.C., the bank's holding company. It was known that Jocelyn would be replaced by his younger cousin Charles; and between Charles Hambro and Michele Sindona, whose natures were as day and night, no love was lost.

Sindona had gotten along well with Pietro Antonelli, the Roman count who was now the director of the Hambros office in Milan. But in November 1971, the count became the wicked messenger of Charles Hambro's will: All associations between the Hambros Bank and Sindona, beginning with La Centrale and SGI, then the banks, were to be sundered. When John McCaffery, Jr., persisted in doing business with Sindona, he was fired. Sindona gave him a job at Banca Privata.

Sindona's enemies in Italy did their best to fill the rift between Hambros and Sindona with calumny. The British bankers, it was said, had discovered Sindona *in flagrante delicto.* Sindona, it was said, had been caught cozening Hambros with his wily Mafia ways. The Hambros Bank, it was said, had suffered terrible losses.

"We never lost a penny with Sindona. In fact, we made a great deal of money together," Count Antonelli, now a Hambros director in London, later recalled. "He was very correct with us in that respect. The disagreement was over Sindona's failure to report to us concerning the companies in which we were involved with him. He would make decisions without letting us know. It must be said that, as the proxy holder of our company, he was perfectly entitled to make those commitments. But he should have kept Hambros informed. He made it very hard for us to explain things to the board.

"A close friend of mine once asked me, 'Tell me the truth now. Why in hell did you give up this relationship with Sindona?' And I said, 'Well, you know, when you get in a car, sometimes the person drives too fast for your comfort. It is not that he drives badly, it is just that you do not enjoy going that fast.'

"You see, this was the problem. Sindona was a very brilliant man. But his mind moved too fast for any back office or any board to follow. Sometimes, I think, even he lost track of what was going on. He had too many companies, too many deals going on at the same time. There was no one who could follow him. He made some acquisitions that made no sense. Why in hell did he buy this, or that? Because he had it in his mind that it could be resold to someone. But then, maybe, he forgot because something else came up. In the meantime, he had no chance to see if the management was right. It was too much for any man, even him.

"We found ourselves riding a tiger and not knowing how to get off. The deals were becoming too big, and he was moving much too fast.

"There were some very fierce discussions, but in the end he paid what he had to pay. I certainly couldn't complain of his behavior. The one thing that was not very much appreciated was, about six or seven months after we had quit him, he had bought some shares of Hambros and was threatening to come and make a row at the shareholders' meeting."

It seems that Sindona, roused by Charles Hambro's avowed concern for his board's enlightenment, was set on reporting more than Charlie might care to have known.

"Many of the deals Hambros had transacted in Italy had not been registered with accounting," Sindona said. "The deal for the control of Italcementi was an example of this. In relinquishing the stock Hambros and I had accumulated, I was able to turn a net profit of about $10 million. Hambros was my seventy-percent partner in the deal, which we carried out through Distributor Holding, S.A., of Luxembourg. So, after taking my cut, I credited a little more than $6,390,000 to Hambros. The money was transferred from the Rüegg Bank in Zürich through the Irving Trust Company of New York. This, and other deals, had not been carried on the bank's books. Banking laws were violated, and Hambros stockholders were left in the dark. Of course"—he laughed—"these were not the sort of disclosures that Charlie had in mind."

By this time, Sindona and Calvi had agreed on a ghost-company mechanism by which every transaction in their respective banking and financial operations would be realized in equal partnership. In late November 1971, the Hambros Bank's interest in La Centrale was acquired by Calvi for Banco Ambrosiano; and it was agreed that Sindona's interest in La Centrale, the Pacchetti group, and Credito Varesino (both now controlled through a Fasco-owned company called Zitropo Holding), along with the option to buy Invest, would pass to the Ambrosiano. This $119 million deal was concluded the following summer, in accord with their clandestine pact.

Meanwhile, the two men had begun to secretly take over the Ambrosiano itself. Their scheme was facilitated by the bank's charter, which restricted the amount of stock that could be held by any shareholder. Since no single person or group commanded more than a few percent of the stock, Calvi and Sindona, purchasing scattered shares through their multifarious ghost network, would need only to acquire some 15 percent of the bank's stock in order to gain effective, and secret, control. The money for this undertaking—Sindona contributed $18 million—was deposited in five numbered accounts, opened for this purpose, at the Union de Banques Suisses in Chiasso, the Crédit Suisse in Zürich, and the Banca del Gottardo (itself an Ambrosiano holding) in Lausanne. The accounts were maintained in the names of two Vaduz-registered bearer-share companies, Radowal Financial Etablissement and Ehrenkreuz Anstalt, for which Calvi and his wife, Clara, had the power of attorney.

The 37-percent interest in the Banca Cattolica del Veneto that the IOR had declined to sell to Sindona was sold to Calvi for $45 million in March 1972. Sindona, who in the past had thought that Bishop Marcinkus's vanity and dishonesty were equaled only by his stupidity, now thought worse.

A month earlier, in February, the Banca d'Italia, under Guido Carli, had filed two complaints against Sindona, charging possible wrongdoing at Banca Privata Finanziaria. The nature of the alleged wrongdoing was not publicly made known, nor were the complaints acted upon. In fact, a year later, in exchange for Sindona's forsaking a takeover of Italy's most important private credit institution, the Banca Nazionale dell'Agricoltura, Governor Carli himself, with the words "just quit busting my balls," authorized a merger of Banca Privata and Banca Unione, allowing Sindona to form a $1.6 billion bank called Banca Privata Italiana.

But Sindona well understood the message of those vague February complaints. They had been accompanied, Calvi said, by warnings from Rome that the Ambrosiano should end all dealings with Sindona. By the spring of 1972, Sindona made up his mind to leave Italy.

Roberto Calvi, all the while, lived in fear that his secret

partnerships with Sindona might be found out. Whenever they needed to meet, Calvi chose an obscure, modest restaurant or café where no one was likely to recognize them. Sindona savored the little man's lack of courage.

"I had a lot of fun embarrassing him," Sindona recalled. "I would always suggest we go to Biffi Scala, the restaurant owned by Cuccia's friend Carlo Pesenti."

That same year—the year of *The Godfather*—the Mafia rumors were stirred anew. In a broadcast called "Hot Dollars," one Jack L. Begon—not a newsman but a sixty-two-year-old employee of the Rome ABC bureau who occasionally filed radio stringer reports—told of a fabled November 1957 meeting at the Hôtel des Palmes in Palermo. At this meeting, Begon said, an international Mafia committee had appointed a young Sicilian businessman to become its financier. Lucky Luciano, who in reality had been regarded by the Sicilian Mafia as a *scorreggia di poca importanza,* was said to have attended; and, of course, Michele Sindona was implied to have been the chosen financier. Though the fable was laughed at by those with eyes to see, the fanciful Hôtel des Palmes meeting became apocryphal history. Later, in the summer of 1973, Begon claimed to have received a call from someone who possessed documentary evidence of the Hôtel des Palmes meeting. On July 22 of that year, hours before he supposedly was to have met that person, Begon vanished. He reappeared in Rome on August 20, claiming that he had been kidnapped by the Mafia and taken to America, where he was subjected to interrogations by mysterious Mafiosi in St. Louis, New Orleans, and Las Vegas. Even this farcical tale was not without its believers. The New York weekly *The Village Voice,* quoting profusely from a volume of Sicilian adages, gave it credence; so, too, did a couple of shoddy books. But, as a matter of record, Jack Begon was jailed the day after his reappearance in Rome and charged with simulating a crime and stealing $5,000 that had been found missing from the ABC office there. He spent fourteen days in jail, and he was later acquitted because of insufficient evidence.

During August of 1972, twenty-six years to the month after his arrival in that city of his fortune, Michele Sindona left Milan. With Rina, he moved to Geneva, to the lavish pied-à-terre above his Finabank headquarters at 2 Rue de la Bourse.

By 1973, the year Finabank took over Bankhaus Wolff of Hamburg, Sindona had literally lost count of his wealth. In May 1972, the International Monetary Market, the first exchange designed exclusively to trade financial futures contracts, had been opened as a division of the Chicago Mercantile Exchange. After the devaluation of the dollar nine months later, the world's monetary movement rose to exceed $2 trillion in 1973. Through Moneyrex alone that year, Sindona handled transactions of more than $40 billion, mostly in Eurocurrency. His overhead was low—one office, ten employees, ten Telexes, and twenty telephones—and he was able to pocket a net profit of more than $10 million for the year.

Through Moneyrex, his private window on the oceanic flux of the world's wealth, he had come to see, as few quite could, the maleficent powers that moved beneath the waves. Early in 1970, he had sold a 10-percent interest in Moneyrex to the central bank of Hungary. He had denied the bank any representation on the board of Moneyrex, and thus any knowledge of his dealings. At the same time, however, the Hungarian government's involvement in Moneyrex allowed him to monitor the speculative and destabilizing operations carried out by the Soviet government through this most important of its Eastern-bloc banks.

In July 1972, the United States had concluded a deal to sell enormous amounts of wheat and other grains to the Soviet Union at favorable terms. The U.S. Department of Agriculture estimated that the USSR would spend close to $1 billion for American farm products over the next year. Later that year, after the grain contracts were signed, the central bank of Hungary, acting on behalf of the Soviet government, placed an order through Moneyrex to sell short $20 billion. Sindona realized that Moscow, having closely followed the decline and instability of the dollar since the Smithsonian Agreement of August 1971, was betting that a greater, sudden decline was imminent—a decline that could be abetted by the massive short-sale order it was now placing. If Moscow succeeded, it should realize both a purely speculative profit and an indirect profit on the grain contracts, which had been stipulated in terms of more valuable dollars. Sindona—whose commission was to be the same, win or lose—notified President Nixon and David Kennedy, who had resigned as the secretary of the treasury and was now an ambassador at large. But the strange Quaker with the second-class clients seemed at this time—January 1973—to have on his mind more pressing concerns: Five Republican hirelings had just pleased guilty of trying to bug the Democratic National Committee headquarters at Watergate during the Quaker's reelection campaign the previous June. (Sindona, whose SGI counted the Watergate complex among its holdings, had subsequently tried to anonymously donate $1 million to Nixon's campaign. With great regret, Nixon's aide Maurice Stans told Sindona that anonymous donations of such size were forbidden by law. Sindona, who feared that a donation of public record would only add to the enmity his pro-American image had long aroused in Italy, told Stans that such donations were the norm where he came from.) Sindona's reports of the Soviet plot were not acted upon by Nixon's economic advisors. In fact, as if orchestrated by the Kremlin itself, Secretary of the Treasury John Connally devalued the dollar by 10 percent on February 12.

Thus, in a few weeks' time, the Soviet Union realized a $4 billion profit: $2 billion in the selling short of the $20 billion (which had been bought largely by the Bundesbank, the central bank of Germany) and $2 billion in the 10-percent devaluation of their grain-deal dollars. Sindona had never witnessed anything like it before.

"In its fathomless naïveté," he observed, "the United States provided the Soviet Union with $4 billion, money that has since doubtless been invested in the destruction of its gracious benefactors. I began then to see that America was the consort of her own ruin. I tell you, in all of history, no power has so blindly armed and succored its enemies as she."

It was also in late 1972 that Moneyrex had been approached by representatives of an international consortium looking to sell short the equivalent of $6 billion in lire. At the time, the lira was veering toward a fall under strong speculative pressures; and Sindona saw that the proposed short sale would likely have catastrophic results.

"They did not so much want to make money," he recalled. "They wanted to destroy the lira. They told me that there was $300 million in it for me."

After giving the matter some thought, Sindona decided to call his friend Prime Minister Andreotti and to explain the situation. He told Andreotti that there was a way for the hunter to be captured by the game, and Andreotti told him to go forward as he saw fit.

"I did not accept the consortium's order, and it was given to others. At the same time, I contacted a number of foreign banks and told them in confidence that the prime minister had authorized me to seek temporary support for the lira. Many of them agreed to cover the short sale. After about 400 billion lire had been sold short, the consortium abandoned its venture. The lira was being defended too strongly."

Later, in June 1973, Prime Minister Andreotti—who once had privately commented to Sindona, "I can't even draw a drink of water without first asking the communists"—resigned from office. Two days later, the lira plummeted.

In discussing the plot to destroy the lira, Sindona seemed reluctant to reveal the identity of the consortium. "It sounds bad," he told me, waving his hand. "I already have enough enemies." Finally, he waved his hand in the opposite direction. "They were Jews," he said. "The people who handled the money and did the talking were from Geneva, but the money was from Israel." He shrugged, then he looked away. "Many strange things I learned, many very strange things."

Strange things, strange times. The shadow play of Italian politics had become, in 1973, a nightmare. Deadly bombings, attributed to the left, shook Milan on the fifteenth day of the New Year. In March, Giangiacomo Feltrinelli, the forty-six-year-old communist millionaire from whom Sindona had acquired Banca Unione, was killed in another explosion near Milan. There were more bombings in April; in May, hand-grenade assaults. In July, the month after Giulio Andreotti resigned as prime minister, the Milan offices of the Mondadori publishing group were bombed. The press blamed all this bloodshed and destruction on, variously, Arab guerrilla organizations, communists, neo-fascist fringe groups, and the CIA.

At about eleven o'clock one night in the spring of that year, a young woman of Sindona's acquaintance called at his top-floor apartments above Finabank. This woman was a paid agent of the Italian Communist Party and a friend of the party's general secretary Enrico Berlinguer; but she was also the daughter of a man Sindona had greatly helped in life.

"Michele," she said, "we must go somewhere else."

"Why?" he laughed.

"Because at midnight someone will come to kill you," she said.

Sindona accompanied the young woman to her hotel across the Rhône. In the morning, he returned home to find that the locks on his door had been expertly broken. He had never known the young woman to lie to him; and, in any case, she knew that he kept no cash about.

Not long after this incident, Sindona moved once more. This time he chose America, where, the summer before, he had bought a bank called Franklin National.

VIII.
L'America

THE FRANKLIN NATIONAL BANK of Long Island had been in existence for less than eight years when Arthur T. Roth came to it in the spring of 1934. The bank was insolvent then, with deposits of less than half a million dollars and a staff of only five persons. Roth was twenty-nine years old, a former administrator of Manufacturers Trust Company, where he had started out as a messenger at the age of seventeen. He came to the little Long Island bank because his wife was pregnant and they wanted to get out of the city.

Roth managed the bank well, and fortune aided him, as Long Island became one of the fastest-growing market areas in the country. By 1962, Franklin's assets surpassed $1 billion. Two years later, Roth decided to branch out, to challenge the big Manhattan banks on their own ground. To the minds of many, this was a mistake. As Franklin's vice-chairman Michael Merkin would later say: "What business had Roth coming to New York? He didn't even know the way to '21.' "

In the summer of 1968, the president of Franklin, Harold V. Gleason, supplanted Roth as the bank's chief executive officer, and in early 1970, Roth was removed altogether from the board of directors. He contended that his overthrow was brought about through the conspiracy of Gleason and two directors (one of them was Merkin), following his declaration that Gleason was unfit to succeed him and that the two directors should be banished from the bank.

At the time of his retirement, Roth held 70,000 shares of

the Franklin New York Corporation, the bank's parent company. In November 1971, he wrote a letter to Laurence Tisch, the head of the Loews Corporation, which held the controlling interest in the Franklin New York Corporation. "You must be seeing what is happening at Franklin National Bank," he wrote. "The earnings of the bank are declining. You are a substantial stockholder and I am looking to you to take the necessary corrective action."

About eight weeks later, in January 1972, the investment-banking firm of Kuhn, Loeb & Co. approached Sindona with the news that Tisch might be willing to sell all or part of the Loews Corporation's 1.1-million-share stake in Franklin New York. It was said that the desire to sell had been prompted by Tisch's fear that the Board of Governors of the Federal Reserve was about to declare Loews a bank-holding company because of its 21.6-percent interest in Franklin. Such a declaration, in turn, would force Loews to divest itself of its many nonbanking interests—a circumstance that Loews dearly wanted to avoid.

On February 17, *The Wall Street Journal*, beneath a headline that described him as "Italy's 'Howard Hughes,'" reported that "Michele Sindona, one of Italy's richest and most respected financiers, is preparing to make a substantial increase in his American investments." Through the spring, speculation continued. "Italy's most successful and feared financier," observed *Business Week* in late April, "apparently has settled on the U.S. as his next major field of operations." A month later, on the afternoon of May 23, Sindona hosted a luncheon of bankers and investment managers at the Recess Club on Broad Street. It then became known—though Sindona revealed no details—that an outsider was about to enter the New York banking community at a level never before dared.

Sindona's acquisition of the Loews Corporation's controlling interest in Franklin New York was finalized on July 12. The purchase, at a price of $40 million, was made in the name of

Fasco International Holding, S.A., of Luxembourg, a wholly owned entity of his Fasco, A.G., of Liechtenstein.

At the time, the Franklin National Bank had assets of $3.4 billion, making it the twentieth largest bank in America. Sindona was aware of the bank's considerable credit losses, and he knew that *The Bank Stock Quarterly,* issued by the brokerage house of M. A. Schapiro, recently had declared Franklin to have the worst record of the more than one hundred banks it surveyed. But the bank's balance sheets, the auditors' certificate, and the report of the comptroller of the currency convinced him that Franklin was basically healthy and that its reserves were sufficient to cover further possible losses on its dubious credits. It was his desire that Franklin National should become a great international bank.

Sindona and Carlo Bordoni were elected to the board of directors of the Franklin New York Corporation in August. Ambassador David Kennedy, Sindona's longtime friend and associate, accepted board membership in the controlling company, Fasco International Holding.

The general manager of Credito Italiano at this time was forty-year-old Lucio Rondelli. "He was a man," Sindona said with a grin, "known in the banking community more for his looking like the head porter at the Grand Hotel than for his professional abilities." Immediately after Sindona's appointment to the Franklin New York board, Rondelli announced the cancellation of a line of credit that had been extended by his bank to Franklin.

Meanwhile, in New York, André Meyer warned all who listened that Sindona's arrival at Franklin was a dark and dangerous thing. "As long as Sindona is at Franklin," he announced at a society gathering hosted by Mary Lasker, "the bank will get none of my clients, and I'll advise the firms I do business with to keep their distance as well."

Late in October, Arthur Roth called on Sindona at the St. Regis, where Michele and Rina had taken up residence. (Soon, after discovering holes in the bedsheets, he would acquire a cooperative suite at the Hotel Pierre.) Roth advised Sindona to get rid of Gleason.

"Every business is the length and shadow of one man," Roth said, "and Gleason's length and shadow are bad."

After the meeting, Roth made notations in his diary. "Sindona," he scrawled, "is good for bank—is straightforward—appears honest, intelligent, knows where he is going."

Years later, in prison, Sindona nodded. "It was a mistake, keeping Gleason as president," he said. "He was a good public-relations man, but absolutely incompetent otherwise. Roth was right, but I was told by other people, 'Don't change Gleason. He is known by important men. He is known by Rockefeller.' I found out why: He gave Rockefeller $5,000 for his campaign. And when Rockefeller wanted to meet me—not the political one, but David, the financial one, of Chase Manhattan—he said, 'Ah, Mr. Sindona! It is a pleasure to meet you! Blah, blah. Remember that this man Gleason is under our protection. He is a good man.'

"It was a joke. Franklin gave money to everybody. You need money, go to Franklin, because they take money at Franklin under the table." He waved his hand. "It was ridiculous."

In early 1973, Sindona brought Peter Shaddick from the Bank of Montreal to head the international department of Franklin. Sindona then turned his eyes elsewhere. Through Fasco International, he began buying shares of the Talcott National Corporation, a factoring and commercial-finance conglomerate that was currently the target of a takeover by the Loews Corporation. While Talcott's chairman, Herbert Silverman, prepared to announce the acceptance of Laurence Tisch's offer, it became known that Sindona by then had quietly acquired nearly half of Talcott's outstanding common stock; and at the end of March, it was announced that Fasco, not Loews, was taking over Talcott. It was Sindona's idea to merge Talcott with Franklin to form a new, stronger institution. But the government turned its thumbs down to the scheme.

The Mafia rumors shadowed him. In an article about him, published in the August 1973 issue of *Fortune*, Dan Cordtz called the rumors "outright fiction" and said that "no one has ever produced any evidence to back up such gossip." Cordtz reported that "American officials in regular contact with the Italian police say that they have absolutely no suspicions about Sindona." But the shadows grew.

This, 1973, was the year that Moneyrex handled more business—the sum of transactions surpassed $40 billion—than the biggest bank in the world. And, as the year neared its end, Sindona narrowed his eyes toward that bank itself.

The Bank of America had been founded by Amodeo Giannini, an Italian immigrant to San Francisco. Now, at the suggestion of the head of the Bank of America's Italian subsidiary, Banca d'America e d'Italia, Sindona proposed to Giannini's daughter, Claire, that the Bank of America refresh its Italian roots. This refreshment, of course, should take the form of Michele Sindona's acquisition of 10, perhaps 15, percent of the bank's stock. The founder's daughter responded to the notion with charmed approval, and Sindona undertook a formal presentation to the bank's administration, headed by Tom Clausen. While Sindona's talks with Clausen progressed, David Kennedy informally approached the Federal Reserve on Sindona's behalf. He reported to Sindona that no one in Washington would deny his Bank of America plans as long as he simultaneously sold his interest in Franklin.

Sindona smiled. But—the New Year came; he saw the snow fall in New York, the snow fall in Milan—it was not meant to be.

The International Money Market, the first exchange to open to financial-instruments trading, was established, as a division of the Chicago Mercantile Exchange, in May 1972. The first contracts offered for trade were foreign-exchange futures;

and they rushed like a gust through the financial world.

That gust was in part responsible for the more than $40 billion handled by Moneyrex the following year. It was also in part responsible for the downfall of Michele Sindona.

Carlo Bordoni, now the *amministratore delegato* of Sindona's Banca Unione, had been true to his word. Since joining Sindona, he had not gambled. By the end of 1972, however, his left hand had once again begun to shake.

That winter, Bordoni called Sindona in New York to tell him that he was entering into some interesting relations with the National Westminster Bank of London and that he was executing exchange deals on that bank's behalf. Sindona, fully aware of National Westminster's prestige and power, congratulated Bordoni. At the same time, he was not surprised, as Moneyrex by then counted nearly all of the world's most important banks—close to 1,000 of them—among its clients.

Bordoni did not tell Sindona of the numbers involved, but only that the deals were based on a belief that the United States dollar would have to be revaluated in the medium term. In early 1973, however, the dollar ran into trouble and lost in value. Sindona and Bordoni received Telexes from the National Westminster's director, Harold Hitchcock, stating that he urgently needed to meet with them in Milan. It was then that Sindona discovered that the exchange transactions amounted to a position of more than $4 billion. Staring at the sum, he concluded that National Westminster, no matter how strong it was, could not be operating at its own risk at such high numbers.

"We are looking," he told Bordoni, "at a masked deal, at a transaction executed for the Bank of England, and almost certainly in agreement with other central banks."

According to Sindona, Bordoni claimed that wasn't the case. He said that a Mr. Joslin, supposedly the head of Westminster's exchange office in Frankfurt, asked him not to make the deal official. He said Westminster was operating without registering the contracts.

"You cannot play that kind of game with such numbers," Sindona said angrily.

Hitchcock arrived in Milan the next day with his London exchange dealer. He expressed his worries and asked Sindona to guarantee the losses that had matured to date for Westminster—about $800 million. Sindona told him he saw no reason why he should do anything of the kind. Hitchcock, flustered, returned to London, then flew back to Milan.

"We assume the responsibility to move the deal forward," he told Sindona. "Joslin, though we've fired him, will continue as our consultant in the transaction." He asked Sindona to keep the matter a secret.

In the end, the dollar took a jump, and Westminster was able to conclude the deal without harm. But the deal had resuscitated Bordoni's demon.

"He was drunk on the big numbers," Sindona later said. "I saw that. But there were other things I did not see."

During the early days of the Westminster deal, Virginia Cornelio, the forty-two-year-old woman with whom Bordoni was having an adulterous affair, told him that Sindona had tried to rape her. In September 1973, Bordoni's marriage to his wife, Eliana, was annulled, and in December, he married Virginia.

"Bordoni had always been crazy," Sindona recalled, "but he had never been a thief. Virginia changed him. She fed him ideas, started saying things. 'Why should Sindona grow rich from your work?' Then the accusations that I tried to rape her." Sindona sneered, then laughed. "You ever see this woman? She was a pig. She had been a dancer at the Astoria Club in Milan. This was a *balera,* a dance hall, where it was understood that the dancers would go to bed with the patrons for the right price." He laughed again. "His virgin bride."

On January 11, weeks after his marriage to Virginia, Bordoni opened a secret account, Number 634.612 C.B., at the Union de Banques Suisses in Chiasso. On the next day, $820,-000 were transferred to that account from Amincor, the Zürich bank through which Sindona's money often flowed and of which Bordoni was a director. Six days later, $1.15 million more were transferred from the Amincor Bank to Bordoni's numbered account in Chiasso. By the end of the year, more than $8.44 million had passed from Sindona's holdings to Bordoni's account, through Amincor, Finabank, and other institutions. The transferals increased through 1974. On July 5 of that year, a second account, Number 636.503 Newport, was opened in the name of Bordoni's wife, Virginia—an account into which further millions found their way.

In November 1972, the month Franklin moved to new headquarters at 450 Park Avenue, Sindona had given a lecture at the Harvard Business School. Other lectures followed: at Carnegie-Mellon University in February, at Adelphi University in June, at the University of Chicago in December. (In Chicago, where he spoke on "Capitalism Today," Sindona encountered Milton Friedman, soon to be awarded the Nobel Prize for economics. At a luncheon in Sindona's honor, the two men argued amicably about the gravity of inflation.) One lecture, delivered before the Bankers Factor and Finance Division of the Federation of Jewish Philanthropists and United Jewish Appeal of Greater New York, on December 13, stirred the enmity of the banking community. Speaking on the growing dangers of Third World debt, he predicted that the debtor nations would never repay their loans, and he damned bankers for not seeking methods of Third World assistance other than the mutually destructive usury, which could only serve to further enslave developing nations while dragging those who made the loans to bankruptcy's edge. Though Sindona's predictions were later proven true, and federal tax money later used to save the bankers he damned, he was, in 1973 and 1974, denounced as a paranoiac alarmist. When he confronted Walter Wriston, the chairman of Citibank, on the matter of Citibank's immense unpaid loans, Wriston defended himself by citing Warren Nutter's remark, "Good judgment comes from experience, and experience comes from bad judgment." Sindona smiled and shook his head, and he looked into Wriston's eyes, and he gave him words that were two thousand years older: *"Errare humanum est, perseverare diabolicum."* But while Sindona pontificated on the errors of others, the Franklin National Bank was tumbling down.

In January 1974, U.S. Ambassador John Volpe presented Sindona with the Man of the Year award at an American Club luncheon in Rome. Returning to New York, Sindona met with Norman Schreiber, the new chairman of the executive committee of Franklin. Schreiber told him that he wanted a free hand in every division of the bank and that he had a specific program to deal with all of Franklin's liquidity problems.

"I told Schreiber that I wasn't interested in the details of management. I explained that I had other business to attend to in Europe, regarding SGI, that was more important and profitable. I then left America for two months.

"Later, a director of Walter Heller, where Schreiber had been CEO before coming to Franklin, told a friend, 'We're grateful to Sindona for taking the biggest ballbuster ever known off our hands.' By then, I knew what he meant. Schreiber was out to dispose of everyone else at Franklin. He wanted to push aside Harold Gleason. He wanted to get rid of the president, Paul Luftig. He wanted to exile Peter Shaddick. He wanted to set himself up as the chairman and CEO. He went around New York telling other bankers that Franklin was in terrible shape and that only he could save it.

"In April, not only was I away from New York, but Gleason, Shaddick, and Kennedy were, too. Schreiber had a clear field. Instead of working to help the bank, he spent all his time searching out the bank's past mistakes and improper dealings, which he then shared with the financial community. Instead of a banker, we'd hired a none-too-bright cop.

"While I was in London, I received a call from a bank director. He told me that deplorable things were going on at Franklin. It turned out that Schreiber, aided by one of his personal lawyers—whose bills were charged to Franklin—was conducting an investigation of the international division. He claimed to have found formal irregularities in a deal Shaddick had executed with the Italian government agency Crediop.

"Shaddick returned to New York immediately and had a violent confrontation with Schreiber, who all the while threatened to send him to prison. Shaddick had a nervous breakdown and was unable to work for a long time. During his absence, employees at Franklin, realizing that Schreiber had no real grasp of foreign-exchange matters, executed exchange contracts without referring them to accounting. This led to Franklin's severest losses.

"In Italy, I received a call from Harold Gleason, who told me to come to New York. He said there had been losses of $6 million in the fixed-rate sector. When I arrived, I asked Schreiber and Luftig, who were supposed to oversee that division, why such sloppy operations had been allowed. Both of them denied any knowledge of the transactions. I told them that, even if that were true, they were still directly responsible."

While Sindona was studying the situation at a meeting with Harold Gleason, Norman Schreiber, and the attorney Randolph Guthrie, Peter Shaddick, not much improved after his long rest, rushed into the room and announced in a frenzy that he'd discovered, in the drawers of dealers at the World Trade Center offices of Franklin, exchange contracts that neither he nor the accounting department had been aware of.

"He told us three or four contracts were involved, amounting to a loss of about $4 million. We told him to go back and keep looking. A few hours later, he told us that there were many more unrecorded contracts, but that he couldn't interpret them all."

By this time, an evaluation report on Franklin, solicited from the Lesta Research consulting firm, had been received. Dated May 1, it stated that "we must advise you that the Bank is in *immediate danger of becoming insolvent.*" In reference to Franklin's foreign-exchange operations, the report advised,

"We strongly recommend that this activity be terminated forthwith." There was more advice: "It is not apparent whether the Board of Directors has been fully and currently informed of the Bank's financial difficulties. We urge that the Board be immediately informed and be kept informed on a day to day basis until the situation is rectified."

On May 8—Sindona's fifty-fourth birthday—the Franklin National Bank borrowed $110 million from the discount window of the Federal Reserve Bank of New York, the lender of last resort. The Federal Reserve Board, which had raised the discount rate the previous month to an unprecedented 8 percent, was aware that the world economy was sick. Several months before, the Board had witnessed America's first billion-dollar bank failure, when the U.S. National Bank of San Diego was declared insolvent and merged with Crocker National Bank; and the Board sensed greater dangers in the wind. The world, as the *Annual Report, 1974–1975* of the Bank for International Settlements later observed, was nearing the brink of the "deepest and most pervasive recession" since World War II.

But these were not, for Sindona, days of lemons and grain. Franklin National would find itself at the Federal Reserve's discount window every day hence, borrowing more and more, as the Fed funds rate soared eventually beyond 13 percent, as the outflows from Franklin escalated into a run.

Carlo Bordoni was called in to New York from Milan. He arrived on May 10, and met the next morning with Shaddick and other members of the foreign-exchange division. At ten o'clock that night, Bordoni reported that he was able to trace about forty unrecorded contracts, constituting undeclared losses of about $30 million.

That same Friday evening, Comptroller of the Currency James E. Smith called to say that he did not welcome Bordoni's presence at Franklin and that he was sending over his own man to put things in order.

"This was," Sindona said, "First National City Bank's long-awaited chance to avenge themselves on their former employee, Bordoni, and on me. It was a matter of actions motivated by vulgar vendettas. The New York establishment, perhaps under the guidance of Walter Wriston and André Meyer themselves, was set on eliminating Franklin, and me with it. It did not matter that Citicorp itself would soon find itself on the comptroller's list of problem banks."

On Saturday and Sunday, May 12 and 13, Sindona went with Carlo Bordoni, Harold Gleason, and Randolph Guthrie to meet with representatives of the Federal Reserve, the comptroller's staff, and the Securities and Exchange Commission at the Federal Reserve Bank of New York, on Liberty Street. It was a matter of deciding whether to open Franklin for business the following Monday. "Of this group," *Fortune* magazine later observed, "the only one who could conceivably claim a nodding acquaintance with Franklin's operating problems was Gleason."

It was decided, as Sindona wanted it to be, that the bank should remain open. Calling from Washington, Comptroller Smith asked Sindona to guarantee, through Fasco, a recapitalization of $50 million. Sindona agreed. Smith then told him that he wanted him to appoint a fiduciary to take over the voting power of his Franklin shares.

"I expressed my disappointment in learning of this intention to push me aside at the very moment when I was undertaking a huge financial sacrifice," Sindona later recalled. "Smith justified himself by saying that he really had nothing against me, but that gossip coming from Europe had rendered such measures advisable in the interest of Franklin. Schreiber, I knew, had become the crier of this gossip, and I was not surprised when Smith proposed Schreiber as the fiduciary of my shares. I told Smith that such a notion could not be entertained. Smith then proposed that Harold Gleason should resign and be replaced as chief executive officer and chairman by Schreiber. This also would be impossible, we said. Finally, it was agreed that David Kennedy should become the voting fiduciary of my stock for the period of one year and that, as soon as Kennedy returned from the Far East, where he was at the time, he would convene with Smith to decide on a proper replacement for Gleason."

On Sunday night, a press release was prepared. Intended as a calmative, it stated that Franklin's future seemed promising and that "the Federal Reserve System stands prepared to advance funds to this bank as needed." As the release was being signed by Gleason, one of the bank's vice-presidents, H. Erich Heinemann, formerly an assistant to the financial editor of *The New York Times* (where in July 1972 he had written about the Franklin takeover), rushed to *The Wall Street Journal* to denounce the release as inaccurate and misleading.

On Monday, Heinemann and President Paul Luftig, who had hired him, were dismissed by the Franklin board; Peter Shaddick resigned.

On the following day, newspapers throughout Italy carried alarming stories of Franklin National Bank's foreign-exchange losses. Immediately, the value of SGI stock began to fall, and there were massive withdrawals from Sindona's Banca Privata and Banca Unione. By the end of the month, Sindona had to inform the Banca d'Italia that his Italian banks were facing a liquidity crisis.

On June 5, Comptroller James Smith issued a statement that Franklin's outflow had "definitely stabilized" and that the bank remained solvent. In truth, however, deposits were rapidly being withdrawn.

After David Kennedy returned to America, it was decided by him and Smith that Joseph Barr, a former chairman of the FDIC, should take over as chairman and chief executive officer of Franklin. By the time Barr assumed his position, on June 20, Franklin had been forced to borrow more than $1.2 billion from the Federal Reserve.

On July 2, Comptroller Smith, prodded by Chairman Arthur Burns of the Board of Governors of the Federal Reserve, wrote to Chairman Frank Wille of the FDIC, asking that agency to solicit possible buyers for Franklin. In the months to come, the FDIC worked closely with Franklin, as Joseph Barr tried to convince that agency, and congressional leaders in Washington, of a plan that would allow Franklin to remain alive and independent as a bank on Long Island, where it had been founded.

Meanwhile, in Europe, withdrawals from Banca Privata, Banca Unione, and now Finabank were increasing as fear grew —a self-fulfilling prophecy—that Sindona's looming insolvency at Franklin might sweep in a sudden wave across the Atlantic. In July, Sindona went to the Banco di Roma to obtain a loan of $100 million, secured by 100 million shares of SGI and 51 percent of Banca Unione (which by now held all of Banca Privata's stock and the controlling shares of both Finabank and Banca di Messina). At this time, Sindona's plan for the merger of Banca Privata Finanziaria and Banca Unione, proposed the previous year, was approved by the Banca d'Italia, and on August 5—three days before the resignation of that strange and now-trembling Quaker, Nixon—Banca Privata Italiana came into being, under the tutelage of the Banco di Roma.

"It was," Sindona recalled, "one of the largest private banks in Italy. But, as I soon saw, it was already dead at birth."

There were other things that escaped Sindona's eyes as the days of that hot summer passed. The SEC had discovered, among the billions of dollars' worth of foreign-exchange trans-actions recorded by Franklin, evidence of several exchange deals between the bank and Amincor of Switzerland that were obviously rigged, through contracts bearing fanciful exchange rates, to ensure profits for Franklin, and thus to bolster the bank's poor earnings. On July 10, while Sindona was in Italy, Carlo Bordoni was interrogated at length by the SEC. At a quarter to nine that night, he telephoned Peter Shaddick, and he tape-recorded the conversation.

"I must be very frank with you," Bordoni said. "Today I was at the SEC, and I was questioned for something like five hours, and all of a sudden I was told that you testified that I have been arranging as far as amounts and rates were concerned—"

"I can't hear you, Carlo."

"I said I was told that you testified that all the transactions which went through Amincor Bank in Zürich were arranged, as far as amounts and rates were concerned, by myself. You understand?"

"Why, you didn't put the rates on those at all."

"Well, I didn't do anything, as a matter of fact. In fact, I told them that I wasn't involved in those transactions at all for two simple reasons: First, because I have no powers, as you very well know, as a Franklin director, and, in the second place, because, as you know again, I resigned as a vice-president and managing director of Amincor Bank on the 18th of September 1972."

"That's correct. Listen, where are you now?"

"Well, I'm calling from outside."

"Do you have a number there?"

"I beg your pardon?"

"Give me a number where I can call you back."

"Listen, can't you tell me what happened? I was really surprised."

"Not on this line, Carlo."

" 'Not on this line'—well, why not? What's wrong? I'm calling you from the outside because I'm not even at the hotel, you see?"

"Yeah, but it's this one."

"I beg your pardon?"

"It is this one."

"Which one?"

"Mine."

"Yeah, but it doesn't matter. I mean, once you say what it is exactly, you see, I mean, that's all. I mean, I was really shocked when I was told all this, you know?"

"No. I had a conversation with Michele, oh, I don't know, I guess a couple of months back, and we talked about the

Amincor deals, and Michele said that they were done at your instigation because you were a consultant to Amincor—"

"I have never been a consultant to Amincor, my dear friend. If Michele told you that I was instigating this operation because I was a consultant to Amincor, that was wrong, false altogether. You see what I mean?"

"You and I better talk pretty serious, then."

"No, it is not a question of talking seriously. What I am saying is just that I was told that you very clearly declared and testified that I arranged amounts, rates, and everything else between Franklin National Bank and Amincor Bank."

"So, you had nothing to do with the rate structure at all."

"I had nothing to do with anything because I was in no position to do that. This is what really surprised me no end."

"How did the Amincor deal take place?"

"Well, I don't know, my dear friend. Look, you see, now, if you had been in there you would find out that they were practically comparing your declaration with what I said."

"I don't like talking on this line, Carlo. Where can I reach you?"

"Well, I'll call you from somewhere else, because at this very moment I cannot—"

"Yeah, but I don't want to use this phone."

"You don't want to use that phone."

"Right."

"Well, wait a minute, I'll try to get hold of the telephone line." There was silence. "Hello, call on this number: 212-986-2434."

". . . 2434—in five minutes."

The minutes passed.

"Yes, Peter."

"Listen now, just a minute. When this thing first came up, right, I went up to see Michele and I said to Michele, 'Look, they're going to ask me a lot of questions about the Amincor deals of last September and the $2 million that came in at the bank, and how the hell am I going to explain that away?' And he said, 'Look, Carlo has already testified,' and I don't know who you testified to, but—I was sitting in his suite at the St. Regis—he said, 'Carlo is an adviser to'—yeah, Maureen was there—'Carlo is an adviser to Amincor. They want to do business in the United States, they want a connection with a large international bank in the hopes of getting a line of credit, and they are paying this $2 million as some sort of a commission or whatever,' and I said, 'OK, I'll say that.' There is no way that I can say that the contracts are contrived; we're both in trouble."

On that same July day, $150,000 was transferred from Bordoni's numbered account at the Union de Banques Suisses in Chiasso to an account, Number 41626288, at the Bankers Trust Company branch at 605 Third Avenue, in New York City. Eight days later, $500,000 more was transferred; $2 million more on July 24. In the months to come, an additional $12,-243,822.57, in checks drawn against the numbered account of Virginia Bordoni, would be sent to New York. The recipient of these millions was Assemblyman Anthony G. Di Falco of Manhattan, to whom Sindona had introduced Bordoni as a potential client some time ago, as a favor to the young lawyer's father, his friend Judge Sam Di Falco.

By the end of August, more than $12 million had been deposited in Virginia's account, Number 636.503 Newport, at the Union de Banques Suisses in Chiasso—and all of it had been passed along, in a series of nineteen checks, to Assemblyman Di Falco.

Sindona was then in Italy, trying to obtain more money from the Banco di Roma. The governor of the Banca d'Italia, Guido Carli, agreed to intervene on his behalf—or so he said. During the first week of September, Sindona was called to the Banco di Roma. He was told that additional funds would be granted, but on the condition that the management of his Italian banks be handed over to the Banco di Roma, along with another 120 million shares of SGI as a surety. Sindona then entered into negotiations to sell SGI and the newborn Banca

Privata Italiana outright. The Banco di Roma obtained Governor Carli's preliminary approval to buy Banca Privata, and agreed to work with Sindona to find the best buyer for SGI.

On September 10, the Banco di Roma offered Sindona 45 billion lire for his Banca Privata Italiana stock. He countered that, as the bank's total value on the Borsa had been about 200 billion lire prior to its collapse, a price of 100 billion for his 51-percent interest would seem more just.

At sundown, the meeting was adjourned until the next day. When the next day came, Sindona was told that the negotiations were suspended. For the first time in its history, the state leviathan IRI had moved to violently interfere in the affairs of the venerable, ninety-four-year-old Banco di Roma.

"This," Sindona reflected, "was the day, September 11, 1974, when I saw the end coming. It was the verdict of Enrico Cuccia expressed through the president of IRI: 'The banks of Sindona must disappear.'"

It was pronounced in Rome that the three IRI banks—the Banca Commerciale Italiana, Credito Italiano, and the Banco di Roma—would take over Banca Privata together. The management of the Banco di Roma threatened to resign in protest, but in the end bowed to the plan of Governor Carli: Forty percent of Banca Privata would be assigned to the Banco di Roma, 20 percent to Credito Italiano, 20 percent to the Banca Commerciale Italiana, and 20 percent to IMI. There was no mention of any compensation to Sindona.

At the same time, the Banca d'Italia filed complaints against Sindona, charging him with wrongdoing that had been brought to light during an examination of his bank's books.

"The irregularities they claimed to have found," Sindona said, "were common to nearly every credit bank in Italy. They had to do with a 'double-accounting' system notoriously referred to as 'reserved with the Banca d'Italia's knowledge.' They also claimed to have found falsified Banca Unione balance sheets from 1970 and 1971. But everyone at Banca Unione knew that I never drew up the bank's *bilanci* and that I never handled the books. During those two years, in fact, I went to the bank only to attend a few board meetings. And they came up with some passbooks that had been used to make withdrawals in imaginary names. It seemed that Ugo De Luca, the bank's manager, had rendered the signatures. At least that is what the Banca d'Italia auditors first told me. At the time, they invited me and others to denounce De Luca. Then they invited De Luca and others to denounce me.

"The Banca d'Italia, presiding over a system that was awash in black funds, was feigning shock at the possible commonplace manipulation of balance sheets."

Next, Credito Italiano, under Lucio Rondelli, withdrew from the Banca Privata consortium, providing the Banca d'Italia with justification for placing Banca Privata into forced liquidation. This measure was duly approved by Treasury Minister Colombo in the third week of September. "There seems little doubt," said *Business Week* of the liquidation, "that this spells the end of Sindona in Italian banking and, most probably, in world banking, too."

"Cuccia, Colombo, and the others had succeeded," Sindona said. "The value of my holdings and credits, along with my reputation, had been annulled. It was a matter of pillage sanctioned by the state. The Banco di Roma, which had a real interest in developing Banca Privata, was also hurt, as were others. But there is an ancient Roman expression: *'Muoiano gli amici, purchè insieme muoiano anche i nemichi'*—'Let friends die, so long as enemies die with them.'"

And in that September breeze, Sindona received a call from New York. It was Carlo Bordoni's lawyer, newly re-elected Assemblyman Di Falco, informing Sindona that Bordoni had left for parts unknown and that he wished to break off relations with everyone, including Sindona.

Sindona flew to New York. On October 3, the Board of Governors of the Federal Reserve formally rejected Joseph Barr's proposed plan to save the Franklin National Bank. On the next day, a Friday, the Italian Ministry of Justice in Rome issued two orders for Sindona's arrest. On the following Monday, October 8, Comptroller of the Currency James E. Smith declared the Franklin National Bank insolvent and appointed the FDIC receiver. It was, as headlines the next day would announce it to be, the biggest bank failure in American history. Waiting troops of auditors under the command of FDIC Chairman Frank Wille descended on the bank and its branches. By midafternoon, the FDIC had auctioned off the bank to the European-American Bank and Trust Company, whose winning bid of $125 million beat out the bid of Manufacturers Hanover by $2 million. Overnight, the signs were changed, and the Franklin National Bank became a bad memory.

A few days later, at the Palace of Justice in Milan, Sindona was legally declared to be in a state of forced bankruptcy, and his holdings were ordered to be seized and liquidated. At the end of the month, the control of SGI was sold, through the Banco di Roma, to a cartel of Rome construction firms. On November 7, Treasury Minister Emilio Colombo told a parliamentary commission in Rome that Banca Privata and Banca Unione had been run fraudulently since 1970.

And this was the November that Assemblyman Anthony Di Falco introduced the vanished Carlo Bordoni to a Venezuelan lawyer named Carlos Martinez, who represented Bordoni in a petition for citizenship in that South American country. In time, there were many Venezuelan lawyers under Bordoni's retainer: Sosa and Castillo, Arias and Gonzalez, Montero and more. And there came to be a company in Caracas, in that country near the sea, called Inversiones Marfal, whose founders' names were hidden in its own: Martinez and Di Falco. And the Venezuelan lawyers were paid by Marfal, and Carlo Bordoni was paid by Marfal; and Marfal owned the Caracas estate where Bordoni dwelt, which he had named in fealty to his loving bride: Villa Virginia.

On the seventh day of the New Year, the last of Sindona's banks, Finabank, was ordered shut by the Swiss authorities. A

160

few weeks later, as U.S. Treasury Secretary William E. Simon publicly blamed the current weakness of the dollar on the fall of Michele Sindona's banking interests, a request for Sindona's extradition was forwarded from Milan.

He shed his skin, and he flew to the end of the world.

IX.
The Last Days

SINDONA LET THE TEACUP WARM HIS HANDS, and he drank, watching the slow, spidery movements of the hands, thinner and knotted with age, of the man who sat by him. The eyes and smile of the old man were those of one awaiting death in the form of a shadow. He was Chiang Kai-shek; and the shadow would arrive in the April-tide breeze he had always loved.

They spoke of Ambassador Kennedy, who had, on a happier day, introduced them. They spoke of the weather and of their wives. Then Chiang Kai-shek, laying down his porcelain cup, spoke of the ways of the world he knew.

Forty-seven years ago, young Chiang and the Kuomintang had wrested China from the warlords. Mao Tse-tung, twenty years later, had wrested it from them. Chiang had come then to this island, Formosa, and he proclaimed it to be Taiwan, the Republic of China, and himself its president.

The Americans, who had first aided then deserted him, embraced him once again, swearing to protect his nation and to forever bar Mao's communist People's Republic of China from admission into the United Nations. And he had believed them. There were many of his Kuomintang army who did not believe. He watched them go south, to Thailand, where they came to be known as the Third Army of the Kuomintang. Supported and shielded by the Thai government, which turned to them in its fight against communist insurgents, these men had become the lords of the world's heroin trade. In their control of that ever growing trade, they had created an empire, sunless but as powerful and unconquerable as any on earth. They lived now—Koh Bak Kin and others—on the outskirts of Bangkok in villas more fabulous by far than Chiang's own presidential estate here in Shinlin.

And, in October 1971, Mao's communist China had been given Taiwan's seat in the United Nations; and four months later, President Nixon journeyed to Peking to embrace his enemies. It was then sworn, in a florid Sino-American communiqué, that the goal of America was to completely withdraw its forces from Taiwan.

"It had been decided by certain agencies in Washington," Chiang said, "that our struggle against communism should be entrusted to the heroin lords who were the descendants of the Kuomintang. So it came to pass that they inherited the East."

The two men spoke of President Nixon, who six months before had been driven from office in shame. Chiang expressed bewilderment that the Quaker had not destroyed the incriminating tapes.

"It was greed," Sindona said. "He wanted to make a big-selling book of them someday."

They spoke then of Sindona's troubles, and of what the future might hold.

"Stay here," Chiang Kai-shek told him. "Remain as a consultant of the Bank of Taiwan in Taipei. Be the guest of my family. You can live here, Michele, like a king."

"I did nothing that Walter Wriston did not do," Sindona said. "I want to go back and clear my name."

In the moments of silence that followed, Sindona found himself once again watching the old man's hands. Then Chiang Kai-shek's eyes drew Sindona's to them, and the old man held his gaze as he spoke.

"Don't go back," was all he said. "They betrayed me, they'll betray you, too."

Two years before, Sindona had been told by friends that General Vito Miceli, the head of the Italian military secret service, desired an introduction to him. Not long after that, General Miceli called on him at his suite at the Grand Hotel in Rome.

The *generale* was aware of Sindona's closeness to the U.S. ambassador in Rome, Graham Martin. He knew also of a report on the PCI that Sindona had prepared with Giorgio Almirante, the secretary of the right-wing MSI, and that Ambassador Martin had personally delivered to the White House. He told Sindona that he was editing an anticommunist magazine for the military, and that this propaganda tool—whose viewpoint, Miceli stressed, was similar to Sindona's own—could use some financial assistance.

"I must confess," Sindona later said, "that I shared General Miceli's fears of an Italian communist dictatorship. In Miceli, though, those fears seemed to have become so deeply rooted that he was very nearly paranoid, in the clinical sense.

"I told him that I couldn't help him with money from the companies I controlled because their budgets were handled by others. He said he knew all about the triple-bookkeeping systems of Italian corporations, and he complained that I was merely fabricating an excuse. I ended up giving him money out of my own pocket—a lot of money, throughout the year.

"Early in 1974, he came to see me at the Grand Hotel. He said he would like me to meet a man named Licio Gelli, who he said was a great friend of his. When I told him I didn't know who Gelli was, General Miceli was very surprised. He explained that Gelli was the *famoso* leader of the P-2 Masonic lodge, the members of which were the most important political, judicial, financial, and cultural figures in Italy. I shrugged and told him that I had never been one for group activities, but that I would be happy to meet this friend of his. He made a telephone call, and thirty minutes later, Gelli arrived at my suite."

Gelli, born and raised in the Tuscan city of Pistoia, was a year older than Sindona. In the late thirties, he had fought for Franco in the Spanish Civil War. Returning to northern Italy, he had gone into the mattress business, then the clothing business. In 1963—by which time he had become a man of great wealth—Gelli joined one of the lodges of the Grande Oriente d'Italia.

Spread by the British throughout the Western world in the early eighteenth century, Freemasonry was seen by many as an order dedicated to revolution. In America—where in 1734 Benjamin Franklin published the Masonic *Constitution of the Grand Lodge in England;* where, to this day, dollar bills bear the Masonic symbol of the all-seeing eye atop a pyramid of ashlar—twenty-two of the thirty-nine signers of the Declaration of Independence were Masons. In Italy, where Lord Sackville established the first Masonic lodge in Florence in 1733, the secret society was opposed by both state and church, beginning with the 1738 condemnation of it by Pope Clement XII. But by 1861, the year the united kingdom of Italy came into being, there were three powerful Masonic groups, centered in Turin, Naples, and Palermo. The grand master of the Palermo group was Giuseppe Garibaldi, under whom the three groups were united in 1864 as the Grande Oriente d'Italia. Under Mussolini, who declared Freemasonry to be "a danger to the peace and quietude of the state," the secret society was proscribed by the Anti-Masonic Law of 1925. After World War II, the society resurfaced, and in time there were more than 500 lodges active under the aegis of the Grande Oriente d'Italia.

Licio Gelli's was not one of them. Unacknowledged by the Masonic hierarchy, Propaganda-2 was essentially an underground group dedicated to the overthrow of the Communist Party and the trade unions. (The name of the lodge was chosen to invoke the patriotic aura of an earlier Propaganda lodge, headed by Giuseppe Mazzini during the revolution of 1848.) Gelli, who was a great lover of intrigue, maintained files on most of Italy's prominent citizens—the more scandalous the datum, the more savorously he filed it, whether he believed it or not—and he often did not hesitate to inscribe in the P-2 membership log the names of men he barely knew, or knew not at all.

"Gelli began the conversation," Sindona recalled, "by thanking me for having come to the aid of 'a dear and important fellow Mason.' Until then I hadn't known that General Miceli was a Mason. Gelli kept me for about an hour, telling me about the aims and ideologies of his lodge. He said that he fully shared my ideas on economics and free trade.

"While the Franklin and Banca Privata problems were brewing, I called Miceli and asked him to set up a meeting for me with Gelli. I went to Gelli's home, Villa Wanda, on the hillside of Santa Maria delle Grazie in Arezzo. Gelli's wife, Wanda, was there, as were their two daughters and two sons. I recall being struck by the brightness and manners of the children, and by the respect they showed for their father. Also present was Carmelo Spagnuolo, who was the president of the fifth session of the supreme court. It turned out that he was also a Mason.

"I laid out the facts of my situation, and I asked Gelli to intercede on my behalf with the help of his Masonic friends in government. He was optimistic.

"In October, after Franklin had fallen, he came to see me in New York. He told me he had run into a lot of difficulties. He said Enrico Cuccia had said, 'Sindona should not only be destroyed, but his ashes scattered to the winds.'

"Gelli came to New York again around Christmas, then several times more during 1975. On two occasions, he brought Carmelo Spagnuolo with him. Spagnuolo had prepared an eighty-page report on the illegalities of the warrant that had been issued against me in Italy. Later, President Spagnuolo issued an affidavit saying that I was political prey. As a result, his government pension was denied him.

"During our meetings in New York, Gelli talked a great deal about politics. He explained that the main goals of P-2 were to reinforce the democratic strengths of Italy and to avert the destabilizing chaos created by those who took naïve workers into the streets on any pretext to show that the unions and paramilitary wings of the Communist Party could, if so desired, take power at will.

"Gelli, I believe, operated in good faith for the ideals of democracy. His fault—and I told him this—was that he was steered by his emotions rather than by his intellect. He had seen his own brother killed in Spain by the communists; and I don't think he had ever gotten past that. There were many who ascribed enormous powers to Gelli and believed that he had the means to carry out large-scale revolutionary actions. It was said that he was backed, *sub rosa,* by the CIA. Gelli never refuted such talk. He wanted people to perceive him as a man with important connections, as a man of secret powers —the Masonic title he'd bestowed on himself was *supremo regolatore dell'universo* (supreme regulator of the universe). But it was all fanciful nonsense that could be believed only by people who did not know him, or by people given to belief like children to the breast.

"As an indication of his presumed powers and connections, I can tell you that when he wanted to open a bank account in the United States, he was unable to do so. In the end, I introduced him to my friend Phil Guarino, the chairman of the Italian-American Division of the Republican National Committee and a *cavaliere ufficiale* of the Republic of Italy. Guarino was a director of the D.C. National Bank in Washington, and it was he who, at my request, helped Gelli open a simple bank account.

"During one of our conversations, Gelli asked me to prepare a proposal for the recovery of the Italian economy and for the reclamation of Italy's credit abroad, which had badly deteriorated in the seventies. I gladly drew up several reports for him to present to his P-2 friends. These reports, along with Spagnuolo's political and juridical reports, were later confiscated with the rest of Gelli's papers. But the parliamentary commission assigned to investigate P-2 made no mention of those reports, which showed P-2, contrary to the calumnies of the communists, to be primarily concerned with the resuscitation of democracy in Italy.

"Along with a letter of thanks for my work, Gelli sent me a P-2 membership card. Without signing the card, I wrote back to him saying that I was grateful for the honor but that, as in the past, I did not wish to join any organization or political party. On his next trip to New York, he told me that he understood and respected my decision and that nothing would change between us.

"It was then that Gelli told me that his Masonic ties to South America, to Argentina especially, were very strong. He said that these ties had been established when he befriended the exiled Juan Perón in 1971 and helped him to regain power two years later. In gratitude, Perón had brought Gelli as a guest of honor to his inauguration in Buenos Aires, and he had appointed him an Argentine diplomat, naming him a special counselor to the embassy in Rome. I remembered that, at Gelli's villa in Arezzo, I had seen some inscribed photographs of General Perón. Now they made sense to me.

"I told him what I thought was happening in South America: Fidel Castro, backed by Russian advisers, was exploiting the discontent caused by obtuse right-wing dictators to lure South American countries into seeking communist protection. I told him that the regimes of repression, torture, and murder maintained by the rulers of Argentina—now nominally General Perón's widow, Isabelita, but in truth José López Réga— and bordering countries were unthinkable for nations that wished to be considered civilized in this day and age. Such regimes were playing right into the hands of Castro and his allies. By raising the South American peoples' standard of living, I said, both the right and the left wings would be stripped of vantage ground.

"Argentina didn't have the funds to develop its immense natural resources. The creation of a solid financial entity, such as a bank, with both investment and ordinary-credit operations could serve to gather funds on the local and international levels and then reassign them to sound private ventures. It could also serve to attract and to negotiate investments in local industrial concerns from abroad.

"I told Gelli that I would welcome the involvement of Banco Ambrosiano in South America. I assured him Archbishop Marcinkus would be able to secure the support of the Vatican for such a project, as South America had the highest percentage of Catholics in the world, and the church's fear of losing those Catholics to communism was very real.

"By this time, though we were still partners under our pact, Roberto Calvi had shifted before my eyes from Cincinnatus to Pontius Pilate, washing his hands of my fate as far as he was able.

"My wife and I had joined his family in the Bahamas for Christmas of 1972. He had shown me then both the headquarters of Banco Ambrosiano Holding, which he referred to as 'our group,' and his ever so virile abilities as a tuna fisherman. It seemed like a century had passed since I first encountered him, a timid little functionary at the door of my office in Via Turati.

"I remember that Christmas also because he then asked me to buy on his account a huge number of shares in the Bonomi group's SAFFA. The Bonomis were heavily backed by the Ambrosiano, and he wanted to hurt them so that he could acquire one of their holdings, the Banca Prealpina di Lugano, at better terms.

"Two months later, in February 1973, I had asked Calvi if we might meet again in the Bahamas, this time to reorganize some business. He declined, saying that he was preoccupied in Milan.

"After the Franklin troubles had begun, I went to Calvi and confronted him. The network of companies I had set up for the acquisition of the Ambrosiano's control, toward which I had invested $18 million, was proceeding with a series of confidential transactions executed in concert with the Vatican and other groups abroad. Why, I asked him, had he not kept me informed?

"He answered with great embarrassment—I could tell by his sudden nervous tic: an uncontrollable twitching of his moustache—that, due to his position at the Ambrosiano, he had to maintain total secrecy. I asked him if he had forgotten that I was the one who was responsible for his having achieved that position. Then, in a very harsh manner, I told him that he had better give me an accounting for the ways my money was being used.

"On my last trip to Italy, I had tried to arrange a meeting with him, only to be told by his secretary that he was unavailable. The truth of the matter, as I well knew, was that Calvi was frightened by my plight. He was afraid that he, as my partner, might be dragged down as well.

"In 1975, while Gelli was with me in New York, I called Calvi in Milan and introduced the two of them over the telephone. They set up a meeting in Rome for the following week. I asked Gelli to see what he could do about getting Calvi to return my money to me, for by now I had nothing. My credit was destroyed, and I was living on the profits of small commodity-futures transactions and the benevolence of a few friends.

"Calvi, who in his worldly impotence was ever eager to believe in the occult powers of others, was quite swept away by Gelli at their first meeting. He believed that Gelli and P-2 could be of inestimable help to him in Italy and abroad. Keen on joining the forces of Gelli's *sottogoverno,* Calvi soon became a member of P-2.

"When Gelli returned to New York, he told me that Calvi was enthusiastic about our South American scheme. He also told me that Calvi would reimburse what he owed me a bit at a time, so as not to disrupt the market by selling off a huge number of bank shares at one time. In addition, Calvi would take care of the legal expenses that were looming before me. As he was afraid that any payments made directly to me might prompt charges against himself, he wished to send the money to New York through Gelli's accounts in Switzerland. I later confirmed all this with Calvi himself.

"I then got in touch with Archbishop Marcinkus. He, like Calvi, had run scared, washing his hands of me. On his visits to New York, he didn't even telephone to ask after my well-being.

"It was true that when Finabank and Banca Privata Italiana were forced into liquidation, the IOR lost the value of its shareholdings in those banks. But it was also true that, soon before their liquidation, both banks had increased their capital, at which time the IOR had not underwritten the new issue but instead had sold its option rights. Thus the IOR had greatly reduced its share in the two banks and, with the sale of its rights, had earned income that was not only sufficient to cover the cost of its shareholdings, but to show a decent profit in its budget as well.

"I had complained about the archbishop's recent behavior to our mutual friend Mark Antinucci, who spoke to him. He told Antinucci that he had avoided contact with me because he didn't want to sully his and the IOR's reputations. So much for Christianity.

"Anyway, I talked to Marcinkus. He said that he was wholly in accord with our ideas for South America. It was agreed that the IOR would act as a fiduciary bank for the Ambrosiano's transactions on that continent. I then drew up an organizational outline that provided for the establishment of offshore companies in countries where we would be able to operate in the international money market without being constricted by national fiscal authorities. The establishment of these companies would be aided on the diplomatic and political levels by Licio Gelli. I myself would eventually take full charge.

"I told Marcinkus to get in touch with the lawyers in Costa Rica who had organized similar operations for Citicorp of New York or Barclays Bank of London, and to have Banco Ambrosiano Holding of Nassau underwrite the member companies' funds. As it turned out, he enlisted the same professionals who had worked for Citicorp."

Sindona's friend Lewis H. Young, the editor of *Business Week,* had proposed to him that he compose a weekly or monthly financial-advisory newsletter. Such newsletters, which carried exorbitant subscription rates, were a lucrative racket.

"Most of them," Sindona said, "are the work of men who don't know what they're doing. They are like the men who make their living handicapping races or predicting the winners of football matches for the newspapers. If they knew what they were talking about, they wouldn't need their jobs. Mr. Young was convinced that a newsletter written by me and published under the aegis of *Business Week* would be a grand success."

While the newsletter never came about, Sindona and Young remained close. In March 1975, *Business Week* published an interview with Sindona. "I acted morally, ethically, and in a correct way," were his closing words. "I'm fighting for the principle and for my family. I want to show my friends that they were right when they placed their trust in me."

A month later, on April 6—the day after Chiang Kai-shek died—another interview with Sindona appeared, in *La Stampa* of Turin. In that interview, Sindona threatened that he would write a book on "a decade of Italian shame—with all the names."

He resumed lecturing, starting on April 15 with a speech on "The Phantom Petrodollar" at the Wharton School of the University of Pennsylvania. Other lectures followed, at Columbia, the University of Minnesota, and UCLA. In an article entitled "An Unlikely Lecturer," *Time* reported, "He denounces the evils of socialism and expounds at length on the evolution of multinational companies into 'cosmo-corporations.'"

* * *

In August, Peter Shaddick was formally indicted by the U.S. Attorney's Office in New York for fraud in the matter of the Franklin National Bank. Carlo Bordoni, whereabouts unknown, was indicted in September. The government also indicted the foreign-exchange traders Donald Emrich, Andrew Garofalo, Martin Keroes, Michael Romersa, Paul Sabatella, and Arthur Slutzky.

Charged with conspiracy, they were accused by the government of falsifying documents, of misapplying funds and credits in excess of $30 million, and of defrauding the FDIC, the Board of Governors of the Federal Reserve System, the comptroller of the currency, and the Franklin New York Corporation. The final indictment, a thirty-two-page document filed on September 29, comprised eighty-seven counts, ranging from individual charges of perjury to wire fraud involving the execution of "illusory" foreign-exchange deals.

What lay in store was one of the most bewildering entanglements in American judicial history.

"It all started with the insurers," recalled a lawyer who was involved with the case from the beginning. "By law, banks are required to hold blanket fidelity bonds, which insure them against losses due to employee dishonesty. At Franklin, as at most large banks, there were several layers of coverage, totaling to $15 million. There was a $100,000 deductible, after which the first $5 million in coverage was maintained by a policy with the National Surety Company. The next layer of $5 million was covered by Aetna. The last $5 million in coverage was provided by INA, the Insurance Company of North America, which was represented by Shea & Gould.

"The foreign-exchange losses at Franklin were so big that all three layers of coverage would be exhausted. Furthermore, both the FDIC, as Franklin's receiver, and the trustee of the holding company were suing, each claiming to be entitled to recovery under the bond.

"There was an unwieldy number of lawyers involved. The FDIC was represented by Casey, Lane & Mittendorf. The

174

three insurance carriers, the holding-company trustee, and the various defendants all had their own lawyers. Then more lawsuits cropped up. The FDIC decided to sue the directors of Franklin for negligence. The stockholders of the Franklin New York Corporation brought a class-action suit against those same directors. Then came a lawsuit against the bank's auditors, Ernst & Ernst, who brought in the firm of Davis, Polk & Wardwell to defend them.

"The depositions began in the library of the Metropolitan Correctional Center, the prison behind the federal courthouse in downtown Manhattan. There were a dozen or so of us sitting around a cluster of Formica card tables we'd bunched together. We started with the foreign-exchange traders—Slutzky and the rest—and we worked up to the directors. Each of them was deposed for days on end. In the meantime, there were tremendous depositions from the comptroller of the currency. The Ernst & Ernst depositions went on for months. Casey, Lane & Mittendorf had a whole team of paralegals that maintained a warehouse on East 45th Street. Everything relating to the case was stored there. Eventually, there were some 40 million documents. For many of us, this was also the first case during which we stored depositions in computers and used the computerized legal-research system called LEXIS.

"There were a number of meetings between the insurance companies and the FDIC in an attempt to settle the matter out of court. Everyone's greatest fear, I think, was that we might actually have to try the case. Nobody had ever tried a case this big. No one knew how to try a case this big. How would we even squeeze all the attorneys into one room?

"What happened is what should have happened: We settled. The insurance carriers—National Surety, Aetna, INA—each kicked in a piece of change; Ernst & Ernst kicked in a piece of change; and that was that. For there was really no way that the judicial system, as it is, could have arrived at true justice in this case.

"Out of all this came the case against Sindona. All along, the insurance companies' defense was based on the language of the bond. We asserted that the dishonest acts committed at Franklin were not, in fact, committed merely by employees, and thus were not covered within the terms of the bond. It was the insurance companies' contention that the bank itself had, in effect, acted as a dishonest entity. The bond was meant to insure an honest bank against being defrauded by dishonest employees. If the bank itself was the criminal party, the insurance carriers were not liable. To establish that this was the case, they had to show that Franklin's chief managers and directors were culpable.

"For a while, we thought of aiming higher. As a matter of law, someone suggested that we might have a shot at establishing that the United States government, in failing to fulfill its supervisory obligations, was responsible for the whole mess. But that remained more or less just an interesting legal theory. The carriers decided to show that everything had been done at the behest of Michele Sindona, through his henchmen.

"A great deal of time and work then went into extricating the details of Franklin's foreign-exchange deals, and of the many recondite transactions between Franklin and banks in Switzerland and Italy."

"Did you ever actually figure it out?" I asked the lawyer.

"No," he said. "To this day, I don't think anybody really understands what was going on. Sometimes I wonder to what extent Sindona himself knew what he was doing."

On November 19, in Milan, Roberto Calvi was elected *presidente* of Banco Ambrosiano. There was now no one above him—at least at the bank.

A few days later, the *pubblico ministero* of Milan, Guido Viola, flew to New York with an investigating magistrate, Ovilio Urbisci. The young, bearded Viola, a communist, had earlier been known as "the magistrate with a gun," a nickname derived from his practice of accompanying police on raids. He would wait outside until danger had passed, then enter brandishing his *pistola*. It was Viola who, as Milan's public prosecutor, had initiated the first request for Sindona's extradition, ten months before, and it was Viola who would stalk Sindona's shadow for ten years to come and more.

After meeting with representatives of the U.S. Department of Justice and the SEC, Viola held a press conference in New York. A reporter asked him if he had any idea how Sindona was presently supporting himself.

"We know," Viola replied, "that in Italy there is a lot of money missing, but we don't know where his money comes from."

On the following morning, Thanksgiving Day, *The New York Times* carried a brief interview with Sindona. "They want to put me in prison and brainwash me and maintain me there for twenty years," he was quoted as saying. He spoke also of receiving strange letters, stranger calls: "They talk to me about suicide as the best thing."

On the morning of December 3, Peter Shaddick pleaded guilty before Judge Thomas P. Griesa at the U.S. District Court in Foley Square. Accepting the deal offered him by Assistant U.S. Attorney John J. Kenney, Shaddick agreed to turn evidence against Sindona in exchange for leniency.

The foreign-exchange traders also pleaded guilty following proposals by Kenney, and were sentenced by Judge Griesa to spend several weeks in the Metropolitan Correctional Center.

"It's all your fault, with that stupid damned movie!" he yelled at Charlie Bludhorn.

"Blame your friend here," Bludhorn said with a laugh, gesturing to Dino De Laurentiis. "He makes the damned things; I just own a company."

"Never mind him." Sindona waved at Bludhorn. "I know

Dino a long time. He's bad enough. But you! *The Godfather* is yours, Charlie."

The three of them laughed together then; but Sindona's laughter was not so deep.

He and De Laurentiis were old friends. In 1972, the year after he sold his Italian studio, De Laurentiis had needed more money. Sindona arranged for Franklin to lend him $1 million, guaranteed by Banca Commerciale Italiana (which had been the actual buyer, through the SAINDA real-estate firm, of his studio). He had moved the following year to New York, where he lived on Central Park South, not far from Sindona's home at the Hotel Pierre or from the offices of his Dino De Laurentiis Corporation in Bludhorn's Gulf & Western building. He and his wife, the actress Silvana Mangano, dined frequently with Michele and Rina at one or the other of Sindona's favorite New York restaurants, Nanni al Valletto and La Caravelle, or at Sindona's suite at the Pierre, where one or more of them would cook. "Dino was very good with *calamari*," Sindona said, "and with *melanzane*." Charlie Bludhorn often joined them. He couldn't cook, but he could eat.

"I mean it," Sindona said. "Every Italian who is sent to jail in this country is going to get an extra five years on account of that stupid fairy tale." He had seen the movie, which had so enriched Paramount and thus Bludhorn, at its charity premiere in New York, in March 1972. "Ever since that damned picture, prosecutors have been seeing ghosts. Everybody is a *capo*, everybody is a *padrone*. You've got wet-behind-the-ears kids from Harvard Law School talking as if they grew up in the shadows of the Ucciardone in Palermo."

"I wish I had produced the damned thing," Dino said with a smile.

Sindona looked at his friend, then tossed his head back and his right hand into the air. Again, they laughed.

"That's entertainment," Bludhorn said.

* * *

The new managers of SGI, looking for hidden assets, had commissioned an independent investigation into the occult financial machinations that had preceded the downfall of Sindona's empire. In charge of the investigation was a Lugano lawyer named Luciano Cattaneo, who entrusted the most technically complex aspects of the detection work to a Swiss accountant by the name of J. A. Hilton. The results of his research, which came to be known as "The Hilton Report," was delivered to Avvocato Cattaneo on April 2, 1976. This lengthy document, which was in French and which bore on every page the stamped seal of the *juge d'instruction* (examining magistrate) of the canton of Geneva, provided a detailed account of Carlo Bordoni's plunderings. Hilton included copies of ledger sheets from the Union de Banques Suisses in Chiasso, fiduciary-contract notifications signed by Bordoni, and the endorsed and canceled checks to Di Falco, along with Di Falco's signed confirmations of receipt.

Before his noon Sunday blessing of April 4, Pope Paul VI publicly proclaimed that he was not queer.

On May 3, in New York, Sindona and Aviva Najar, the wife of the Israeli ambassador to Rome, founded the International Anti-Drug-Abuse Foundation. A clinic was built in Tel Aviv.

On September 8, Sindona surrendered at the federal courthouse in Manhattan on a warrant for his extradition to Italy. Accompanied by his attorneys Robert Kasanof of Baer & McGoldrick and John J. Kirby, Jr., of Mudge, Rose, Guthrie & Alexander, he was asked to take the stand and swear to the truth of his statement that his current assets now amounted to only $800,000. Judge Thomas Griesa adjourned the extradition hearing to a later date, and Sindona, after posting $150,000 in cash and T-bills, along with the Hotel Pierre cooperative

179

shares held in his wife's name, was released on a personal-recognizance bond of $3 million.

As Sindona was now unable to travel to South America, Licio Gelli turned to his P-2 brother Umberto Ortolani, a Roman businessman formerly associated with SISMI, the Italian military-intelligence organization. Ortolani had spent much time in Uruguay, where he owned the Banco Financiero Sudamericano of Montevideo. He also had excellent relations with the hierarchy of the Vatican. His friendship with Giacomo Cardinal Lercaro, one of the moderators of the Second Vatican Council, was long-standing and well-known. On the recommendation of the cardinal, Pope Paul VI had made Ortolani a Gentleman of Honor of His Holiness. Surely, Gelli explained to Calvi, Ortolani's involvement would be welcomed by Marcinkus, whose hunger for the purple cloth grew daily.

"Ortolani," Sindona later said, "was an excellent lawyer, but not much of a banker. When I was told that Gelli and Calvi had decided to work with Ortolani on our South American plans, I let them both know what I thought. I told them that I believed in his honesty, but not in his ability."

Nevertheless, the alliance was inaugurated. In the fall of 1976, Banco Amrosiano Holding purchased 5.5 percent of Ortolani's little bank in Montevideo.

On September 24, Carlo Bordoni was jailed in Venezuela on orders from the U.S. Department of Justice.

A few weeks later, Bordoni's chief Venezuelan lawyer, Carlos Martinez, sent a Telex to Anthony Di Falco in New York. The message was that the credit of their company, Inversiones Marfal, was collapsing in the wake of Bordoni's arrest. Martinez suggested that Di Falco loan the company the equivalent of $700,000 in bolivars. Martinez concluded that the money should be made payable to his personal account at the Banca Mercantil d'Agricola in Caracas.

From his cell, Bordoni brought criminal charges against

Martinez in December. He accused the lawyer of mortgaging his home, Villa Virginia, without his knowledge, and of stealing $360,600 in hundred-dollar bills from a safe in that home.

Sindona watched, dumbfounded, as Jimmy Carter was elected president. In a country where a man such as this could be chosen to rule, he reflected, all things were possible.

On December 13—the day on which Milton Friedman delivered his Nobel lecture at Stockholm University's School of Economics—Sindona appeared at the federal courthouse to file a parcel of documents intended to help block his extradition. To a seventy-two-page defense of his stance against the extradition, Sindona appended affidavits from Anna Bonomi, Licio Gelli, Phil Guarino, John McCaffery, Carmelo Spagnuolo, and others attesting to his integrity and to the belief that he was the prey of political persecution in Italy. There were also photographs, taken at the Università degli Studi in Milan, showing a group of students carrying placards that bore the words *"Morte a Sindona."*

"Wealth," the Bible says, "maketh many friends; but . . ."
—Sindona now discovered how the verse ended.

In the cold days of that winter, he was invited as a guest of honor to a dinner for the mayor of San Remo at the exclusive Tiro a Segno club on MacDougal Street, in the Italian end of Greenwich Village. Among those whom Sindona recognized from across the sea that evening was Mario Salinelli, a reporter who frequently worked for RAI, the state-run broadcasting corporation of Italy. Salinelli, Sindona remembered, had been one of the first Westerners to interview Mao Tse-tung.

Salinelli told him of plans that were under way to launch a newspaper. The ostensible purpose of this newspaper would be to apprise Italians abroad of the dangerous political developments in Italy. Its primary purpose would be to influence public opinion to grant suffrage in Italy's elections to Italians who resided overseas. This newspaper, Salinelli explained, was to be published in English and Italian editions in New York and Australia, and in Spanish and Italian editions in Argentina and Venezuela. Salinelli had already visited the countries involved to lay the groundwork, and claimed to have procured advertising guarantees from Alitalia, FIAT, and others. He described to Sindona the logo—two clasped hands and the legend *"Ho bisogno di te"* ("I need you")—designed for the publication by an Italian artisan. He said that this logo would be cast in images of silver and gold, to be given to those who participated in the gala celebration of the paper's maiden issue. This big event, to be held at Madison Square Garden, would be a grand and glamorous evening, featuring Frank Sinatra and a score of other celebrities.

Then, moving past the milling, dark-suited figures at the Tiro a Segno bar, Salinelli introduced Sindona to the man he said would help to organize the big event at Madison Square Garden. "I have known him a long time," Salinelli said, "a very long time."

The man to whom Salinelli introduced him was thirty-six-year-old John Gambino of Brooklyn. The name, which was a common one in Italy, meant nothing to Sindona. The only Gambino he had ever known was his Italian lawyer, a university professor in Venice. John Gambino was, however, the nephew of Carlo Gambino, a man who had been regarded by many as the most powerful Mafioso in America. Carlo, at the age of seventy-four, had passed away peacefully in his Brooklyn apartment that October. Though his nephew John's name remained unsullied by the media, it would soon be placed on one of those charts of which the government is so fond. According to that chart, John Gambino was a Mafia *caporegime*, third in power to his uncle's successor, Paul Constantine Castellano (FBI Number 824437), and underboss Agnello Joseph Dellacroce (FBI Number 327320). If there was truth in this chart, John Gambino, who had no FBI number and whose name had never appeared in a newspaper, must have been doing something right.

"I know that you are a businessman," Gambino said to Sindona. "Tell me, what do you think of the venture your friend has told you about? You see, I don't want to be involved in anything that might lose money."

"I think that the idea is a noble one," Sindona replied. "I think also that, if Signor Salinelli has got the advertising commitments he says he has, it is a relatively sound gamble."

Sindona found Gambino to be dignified, polite, and well mannered, but unlettered. They conversed that night in Italian. Sindona, as was his wont when talking to a stranger, used the formal second-person singular, *Lei.* With a smile—"Please, give me the *'tu,'* " he said—Gambino asked him to use the more familiar and friendly form of address.

"But," Sindona said, smiling in return, "I don't know you."

Soon, there were dinners at Valentino's Supper Club in Cherry Hill, New Jersey, where John introduced him to his younger brother, Rosario, who lived in that town. Rosario, age thirty-four, was one of the twenty-two "South Jersey soldiers" the government's chart placed beneath John. The food at Valentino's was nothing special.

In his attempts to stay in business, Sindona could no longer say that his associates were the most prestigious in the world or that his undertakings were so grand. He became involved in some small-time real-estate and construction deals with a new friend named Joe Macaluso. Born and raised in Racalmuto, Sicily, Macaluso, who was fifty-two, had come to New York in 1950. He had settled on Staten Island, where he now owned a motel called the Conca d'Oro, at 2232 Forest Avenue.

The man who managed the Conca d'Oro for Macaluso was also a Sicilian: Antonio Caruso, a forty-four-year-old former officer of Barclays Bank of New York.

Macaluso showed Sindona the swimming pool he had built with pride, and Caruso told him, likewise, of his brother, who was vice-prefect of Catania, on the island of their birth, and

Sindona recalled for them the times of the lemons and the grain.

In February, Luigi Cavallo, a fifty-seven-year-old former UN translator and longtime free-lance *provocateur* for both the government and private industry, published an arraignment of Roberto Calvi in his Turin newsletter, *Agenzia A.* In time, further assaults on Calvi appeared in Cavallo's *Agenzia A.* These assaults, accusing the banker of fraud, embezzlement, and much else, were reproduced on posters that appeared mysteriously all over Milan, especially in the vicinity of Banco Ambrosiano.

According to a future warrant, Cavallo first claimed that this campaign was carried out on behalf of Sindona, who was seeking to extort money from Calvi.

"This," Sindona said, "was absurd. Luigi Cavallo, no stranger to the state's payroll, was most likely working for those same government elements who later compelled him to implicate me. In the first place, Calvi had already agreed to pay me what he owed me. In the second place, what good could Calvi's ruin possibly do me?"

Cavallo later declared to the Court of Assize that he had acted on his own initiative and against Sindona's will.

Sindona's attorney in Rome, retained by him in the dark days of October 1974, was a man named Rodolfo Guzzi. Now, on March 23, 1977, Guzzi went to Enrico Cuccia with Sindona's conciliatory proposal for the restoration of Banca Privata Italiana as a satellite of the national-interest-banking consortium. Guzzi also went that spring to seek the intercession of Prime Minister Andreotti. But no stones were moved. On June 25, in Milan, Sindona was sentenced *in absentia* to three and a half years in prison on charges relating to the downfall of Banca Privata.

That same week, in New York, another Franklin National

Bank officer was indicted: Howard Dillistin Crosse, an elderly vice-chairman who, before coming to Franklin, had worked for many years at the Federal Reserve. Like the others, Crosse agreed to become a government witness in return for leniency.

On July 7, Sindona's son-in-law, Piersandro Magnoni, met with Enrico Cuccia in London. "I went to London," Cuccia would later testify, "because it had been rumored to me that Sindona, holding me responsible for his troubles, had intentions of abducting my daughter. Magnoni showed me a plan of settlement for Banca Privata Italiana. I stressed to him right away that the plan had no chance of being realized."

Later that month, it was revealed that Sindona's friend Charlie Bludhorn was under investigation by the SEC. The investigation would lead to a civil complaint against Gulf & Western, Bludhorn, and his executive vice-president, Don Gaston. The government's pursuit, however, would end, years after, in a stalemate, with Bludhorn neither admitting nor denying any wrongdoing.

"His only crime," Sindona said with a laugh, "was to be my friend."

Roberto Calvi traveled several times that year to meet in Nicaragua with President Anastasio Somoza, the dictator who had imposed martial law on his country three years before, and whose campaign against the Sandinista guerrillas was escalating toward a reign of terror. An agreement was reached between Calvi and Somoza, and on September 29, the Ambrosiano Group Banco Commercial opened in Managua.

On January 11, 1978, in Milan, Mario Barone, a former managing director of the Banco di Roma, was arrested on charges of suppressing evidence relating to the investigation of Michele Sindona.

Carlo Bordoni, upon his incarceration in South America

more than a year before, had been advised by his Venezuelan attorneys to prepare a self-exculpating account of his years with Sindona. Now, in February 1978, that account, in which Bordoni portrayed himself as the reluctant and fearful vassal of Sindona's evil will, was published in two consecutive issues of the Italian business weekly *Il Mondo.*

"And *Il Mondo,*" Sindona said, "was controlled by Gemina, S.p.A., which was controlled by Enrico Cuccia."

On April 17, a team of inspectors from the Banca d'Italia, led by Giulio Padalino, converged at Roberto Calvi's office to begin a full-scale, though ostensibly routine, investigation of Banco Ambrosiano.

In Rome, on May 13, the body of the former prime minister and Christian Democratic leader Aldo Moro, killed by the communist Red Brigades, was borne into St. John in Lateran.

Five days later, in New York, Judge Thomas Griesa ruled to grant the extradition of Sindona to Italy. In a seventy-eight-page decision, the judge declared that "the evidence submitted by the Italian government was sufficient to establish probable cause that Sindona committed the crime of fraudulent bankruptcy as defined by Articles 216 and 223 of the Italian bankruptcy law."

On June 4, Carlo Bordoni was extradited to New York from Caracas.

Sindona was still not aware of "The Hilton Report," or of the blackness of the bond between Carlo Bordoni and the son of his old friend Judge Sam Di Falco. By the time he became aware of these things, it would be too late to call on the justice of that old friend. For the past six months, the retired judge had been the primary target of a grand-jury inquiry into State Supreme Court case fixing, and on the night of June 28, while dining with friends at the Columbus Club, he was felled by a heart attack. On the following Saturday morning, his coffin was brought to St. Patrick's Cathedral, where Sindona bade his friend of long-ago nights good-bye.

On July 10, Sindona filed a federal suit against the Loews Corporation and its chairman, Laurence Tisch, from whom he had acquired the controlling interest in Franklin New York. Charging breach of securities laws and fraud, he sought to recover the $40 million he had paid Tisch, along with $400,000 in fees and $80 million in punitive damages. Forty-eight hours later, the FDIC also filed suit against Tisch, for restitution of the damages suffered by Franklin. The FDIC held that Tisch's failure to investigate Sindona's background constituted a breach of fiduciary duties.

On the next day, July 13, an indictment on federal fraud charges was filed against the former Franklin chairman Harold Gleason, the former president Paul Luftig, and the former executive vice-president J. Michael Carter. Named "as co-conspirators but not as defendants" in the indictment were Peter Shaddick, Howard Crosse, and Carlo Bordoni. Of these three men, Bordoni, distraught but inscrutable, was the only one who refused to be bargained with by Assistant U.S. Attorney John J. Kenney.

In the papal summer estate of Castel Gandolfo, Giovanni Montini, the pope whose home was not this world, passed away on the Sunday night of August 6. Beside his bed, on a night table, lay the Bible his father had given him, seventy summers ago and more.

The appointed executor of Paul VI's handwritten will, dated July 30, 1965, was Monsignor Pasquale Macchi. According to a codicil of that will, all of the pope's personal papers were to be destroyed. While Vatican craftsmen wrought a triple papal coffin—bronze within cedar within cypress—Macchi watched the flames that devoured all that might ever be known of Montini's soul.

To hasten Bordoni's juridical enlightenment, the United States formally indicted him on September 5. He pleaded not guilty to all charges. But then, slowly, enlightenment came. Some weeks later, after many long meetings with the prosecution, Bordoni—represented by Anthony Di Falco and John Sprizzo (today a federal judge)—changed his plea to guilty on two counts of misapplication of bank funds and falsification of records, and agreed to work for the prosecution. As was the government's policy, his sentencing would be suspended, like a sword of Damocles, until after his work was done and appraised.

At dawn on October 9 and in the late night of October 10, Enrico Cuccia, at his home near the Palace of Justice, received two menacing telephone calls advising him to do what he could to have the Italian warrants for Sindona's capture revoked. The caller, Cuccia said, spoke in English with a distinctly *"broccolino"* (as in Brooklyn) accent.

Eight days later, in Zürich, Cuccia met again with Sindona's son-in-law, Piersandro Magnoni. On October 21 and 25, he met in Milan with Sindona's attorney Rodolfo Guzzi, who entreated him, in vain, to discuss Sindona's situation with Prime Minister Andreotti. During these meetings, as at later talks with Magnoni in Lugano, Cuccia repeated that there was nothing that could be done. On November 17, there was another call; then someone set a fire at his door.

A few days later, not far from the New York prison where Bordoni was being held, two men entered the office of Nicola Biase, a former employee of Sindona's Banca Unione and Banca Privata in Milan. They were thirty-seven-year-old Luigi Ronsisvalle, a Sicilian-born Brooklyn hoodlum who would later profess to be a Mafia killer and drug-runner, and a twenty-seven-year-old Manhattan man by the name of Bruce McDowall. They introduced themselves as Mr. Romano and Mr. Caruso—the name of Sindona's friend from Staten Island.

According to Biase, the two men told him that he must retract statements he had made in a deposition for Sindona's extradition proceeding and that he must not cooperate with the government against Sindona in any way.

"*Avevamo avuto istruzione di tagliare le gambe,*" Biase claimed he was told. "We've had orders to chop your legs."

Luigi Ronsisvalle, who, after being arrested for a Brooklyn stick-up the following year, would become one of the federal government's most familiar and cherished professional witnesses, later stated that a man who "said he was acting on behalf of Michele Sindona" had paid him $200 to threaten Biase. Ronsisvalle added that this same mysterious courier had told him that Sindona was willing to pay $10,000 for the murder of Assistant U.S. Attorney John J. Kenney.

"If this were one of Dino's pictures," Sindona said, "I would have laughed and walked out. But the men who were prosecuting me did not laugh—at least not in public. They proclaimed a very convenient belief in the truth of these things. I would think that a man such as Mr. Ronsisvalle, who has murdered many times, might also perhaps be capable of lying, especially when it could gain him favor. The government, however, seems to entertain no such doubts about the integrity of its trained rats.

"As for the calls to Cuccia"—he turned his palms upward and shrugged—"I know that one of them was made, without my knowledge, by my friend Antonio Caruso. He came to me one day and said, 'I don't think you'll be having any more problems with that Cuccia character you talk about so much.' I looked at him. 'What do you mean?' I said. And he told me then that he had telephoned Cuccia and thrown a good scare into him. I was infuriated. I went right away to his boss, Joseph Macaluso, and I told him, 'No more! Caruso has done the worst possible thing that can be done.' Macaluso was smart; he understood."

"Unsolicited favors can be of the greatest danger to a man. No one knows that better than I."

On December 7, Carlo Bordoni, the star witness for the prosecution, testified at the trial of Gleason, Luftig, and Carter. He told the court that Gleason had been aware of the wrongdoings at Franklin and that, as manager of Banca Unione in Milan, he had regularly followed Sindona's orders to falsify records.

As the trial progressed, there was concern that members of the jury were unable to grasp the technical aspects of the financial transactions at the heart of the case. Scott Edward Pardee, an economist and vice-president at the foreign department of the Federal Reserve Bank of New York, was called in as a witness to clarify matters.

"Well," Pardee said, "at the opening, by these various sheets, we will take the spot rate, which is easier to read."

"What is a spot rate?" Judge Griesa asked.

"That's the rate for delivery—two days, or for the first of April probably. We're talking in terms of 238.90 to 239, a ten-point spread. Not cents but hundredths of cents."

"You said 238.90. Is that $2.38 and then another cent divided into one hundred parts? Your referring to ninety— would that be one hundred mil equal one cent?"

"I don't know. That's from taxes rather than foreign exchange. We don't talk in terms of mil."

And so it went. In the end, Harold Gleason, Paul Luftig, and J. Michael Carter were found guilty of a conspiracy to falsify Franklin's earnings. Judge Griesa sentenced each of them to three years in prison.

"When someone is indicted federally," Harold Gleason's attorney, Stanley S. Arkin, would later say, "it is likely that he will be convicted. Only a relatively small percentage of federal trials end in acquittal. I think the figure wavers yearly between four and seven percent.

"In our case, there was no refuting that a crime had been committed. There were phony foreign-exchange transactions. It was a matter of convincing the jury that Gleason, Luftig, and Carter had no knowledge of the crime. To this day, I personally believe Gleason was innocent.

"But, as in many cases, the pursuit of justice turned into a ballgame. Federal prosecutors are almost always young and ambitious. Their decisions as to whom to indict and whom to bargain with are more than occasionally not based on a wealth of human experience and wisdom. There is no question that the two men, Bordoni and Shaddick, whom the prosecution recruited to its team, were the very men responsible for the phony transactions.

"Any witness who testifies for the government tailors his testimony to some extent. It's not called perjury." Arkin smiled. "It's called preparation. Bordoni, obviously, was as full of shit as a Christmas turkey. I shot both him and Shaddick full of holes as witnesses. But, in the end, the jury, I think, took the indictment as evidence of guilt—which, of course, it is never supposed to be taken as, but which, of course, it often is."

I asked Arkin if he had ever met Sindona. Yes, he said; one of Sindona's lawyers, Robert Kasanof—now the chief of corrections for New York City—was a good friend. I asked him then what his impression of Sindona had been.

"He struck me as a brilliant, immensely calculating, and tough individual."

Giorgio Ambrosoli, the Milanese lawyer appointed by the state to investigate and liquidate Banca Privata, had been immersed in his job for more than four years. On December 10, 1978, he was called to New York, where he convened with Assistant U.S. Attorney John Kenney and other government representatives. While he was away, his wife, Annalori, read once again the letter he had written on his first journey of the investigation. "I will pay a very dear price for this assignment," he had said in that letter of February 25, 1975. "I knew that before accepting it and I have absolutely no regrets. For me, it has been a unique occasion to do something for the country."

Four days later, in Milan, Giulio Padalino, the Banca d'Italia inspector who had been sent to investigate the Ambrosiano, submitted his report. It included revelations of the bank's cloaked dealings with the IOR and of its elusive connections to a multitude of ghost companies. On the basis of Padalino's report, an investigating magistrate, Emilio Alessandrini, was ordered to begin a formal inquiry into the Ambrosiano's affairs.

A well-known lioness of Italian business came to see Sindona in New York. "She had seen better days," he recalled. "Her jewels had been handed over to the Banca Nazionale del Lavoro as security for a loan. Her powers in the family corporations had been arrogated by her son. She was in trouble. She begged me to persuade Roberto Calvi to forgive a debt of $5 million, for which he had personally issued checks, in violation of Italian currency regulations. I was to relay to Calvi her promise that, in return, she would see to it that a relative, a prominent politician, interceded on his behalf at both the Banca d'Italia and the treasury ministry. She implored me not to tell her son about this—she was terrified of him. I agreed, and she told me that she would pay me a fee of $500,000 if I succeeded.

"I talked with Gelli on his next trip to New York. He, Calvi, and the woman met later in Rome. Calvi forgave the debt. The woman never again came to see me, nor did she pay me the money she'd promised. I notice, however, when I see her picture in the magazines, that her jewels have been returned to her neck, and she smiles in those pictures just as she smiled at me when she declared her thanks and eternal affection."

Giorgio Ambrosoli received the first call three days after Christmas. On the fifth day of the New Year, there was another; four more over the course of the next week. The last of them, which Ambrosoli taped, came on January 12. *"Devi morire come un cano,"* said the unknown voice. "You should die like a dog."

"Those calls," Sindona said, "were no more my doing than the calls to Cuccia. One of them, I know, was received while Guzzi was meeting with him. Surely, if I were behind those calls, I would not have wanted to supply Ambrosoli with a witness—my own lawyer, no less."

Later that month, *Business Week* published "The Dirty Game of Dumping the Dollar," Sindona's defense of the American dollar as the only true international reserve currency. On January 29—the cover date of the *Business Week* issue—Emilio Alessandrini, the Milan magistrate in charge of the Ambrosiano inquiry, was murdered by five terrorists identified as members of the left-wing Prima Linea group. The Ambrosiano case was transferred to another magistrate, Luca Mucci, who called the Guardia di Finanza to join in the inquiry.

Roberto Calvi, meanwhile, was in Peru. Civil war and the overthrow of Somoza in Nicaragua had driven him to seek a new base in South America. His meetings with the Peruvian finance minister, Javier Silva Ruete, led to the establishment in Lima of the Banco Ambrosiano Andino. Through Banco Andino, more than $150 million would be converted into irrecoverable "loans" to a Calvi-controlled, Luxembourg-registered ghost company called Manic Holding, S.A. These "loans" would be guaranteed by Banco Ambrosiano shares held by other ghost companies, in Liechtenstein and Panama, also controlled by Calvi, through Manic Holding.

"The IOR," Sindona explained, "was the fiduciary of many of the bearer-share companies where the Ambrosiano stock was being sheltered. When I discovered this, I told Calvi and Gelli that they were being imprudent; and I warned Archbishop Marcinkus to limit the IOR to its fiduciary role and to avoid any direct obligations.

"Calvi had become mesmerized by the designs of Gelli and Ortolani. A lust for publishing had always been one of Ortolani's follies. In 1960, he had lost all his money trying to resurrect the old Fascist news agency, Agenzia Stefani. Later, he had tried to buy out the Roman daily *Il Tempo* from Onorevole Angelillo. Now, with the Ambrosiano group's money, Ortolani was running around buying newspapers in South Amer-

ica. His dream, which Gelli and Calvi shared, was to comman-
deer the powers of the native press to undermine communism.

"I explained to them that this was a very serious mistake.
Such things should not be done in the light of day, I told them.
Castro's forces and the other leftists in these countries would
not forgive them. All our plans for quiet intervention would be
endangered—as, in fact, I told Calvi, would be his own life,
since he was the head of the trespassing group.

"I learned also that Gelli was indulging his South American political friends far too much. He was buying into real-
estate schemes on their self-serving advice. Underwritings in
dollars were being provided for companies that would never
meet their obligations because of wild inflation. I explained to
Gelli that the Ambrosiano must not make strong-currency
loans in these countries without first insuring through swaps
against the hazards of the exchange rates. I reminded him that
we were to concentrate on the collection of savings and their
distribution to sound local enterprises in the local currency.
Because the group's strong-currency deposits from abroad
would serve as security, the Ambrosiano could confidently col-
lect the native currency without assuming the graver risks of
local devaluation.

"After I expressed my complaints and dissatisfaction, Gelli
and Calvi gave me less and less news of the goings-on in South
America. I began to suspect that, instead of taking on new
backing, the two of them had decided to finance their further
acquisition of Ambrosiano stock by means of a deceitful loan
from the bank itself. Gelli didn't have the courage to confirm
my suspicion. He lied, telling me that Calvi no longer informed
him of what was happening.

"Though both men stood by me in my troubles—Calvi,
especially, helped me with money until the end—they slowly
divorced me from their South American plans. Gelli was con-
structing a complex, if unwise, network of links between financial and political entities in those countries he liked—Argentina, Peru, Paraguay, Uruguay. He was acting as a politician,

not as a financier, and he didn't want me to know the details because he feared, perhaps rightly, that I would object."

On March 19, the U.S. government indicted Michele Sindona, charging him with ninety-nine counts of fraud, perjury, and misappropriation of bank funds.

On the following day, as on every Tuesday, the Roman journalist Mino Pecorelli published a new issue of his political scandal sheet, *OP*. Pecorelli, a disgruntled P-2 member, had been calumniating against Gran Maestro Gelli in *OP* since the first week of January. The March 20 issue alleged that secret-service dossiers that were presumed to have been destroyed five years before had in fact been purloined by Gelli.

That evening, sitting behind the wheel of his parked car, Mino Pecorelli encountered the last man he would ever see. The barrel of a gun was shoved into Pecorelli's mouth, and the trigger pulled twice.

Pecorelli, through *OP*, had cultivated so many enemies, within the government and without, that the authorities did not know where to begin their search for the man who silenced him.

On April 9, Sindona retained Marvin E. Frankel of Proskauer, Rose, Goetz & Mendelsohn to represent him in his upcoming trial. Frankel, who would be assisted in his defense by John J. Kirby, Jr., of Mudge, Rose, Guthrie & Alexander, was a former Columbia University professor of law and a U.S. District Court judge. The author of *Criminal Sentences* and other books, Frankel had left the federal court six months before, at the age of fifty-eight. This would be his first important case since stepping down from the bench.

Two days later, on April 11, Enrico Cuccia met with Sindona at the Regency Hotel in New York. "Sindona," Cuccia would later say, "was evidently overstrung. He arrived at the point of saying that his sons would have me killed."

Sindona laughed angrily at Cuccia's account. "I would

never speak of my sons in such a manner. Besides, to even think of them as killers . . ." He laughed again, without anger. "No," he said. "That day, I confronted Cuccia with his decree that 'Sindona should not only be destroyed, but his ashes scattered to the winds.' It was he who then became overstrung. 'Let's stop talking about the past,' he said."

On July 6, Judge Henry F. Werker ruled to bar Sindona's previously granted extradition to Italy, on the grounds that Sindona was being prosecuted in America on a federal indictment involving offenses similar to those contained in the Italian charges against him.

Six nights later, the New York media reveled in blood. Sixty-seven-year-old Carmine Galante, whom many believed to have been the successor to the imperium of Carlo Gambino, was shot to death at a restaurant in the Bushwick section of Brooklyn. His dramatically gruesome corpse was a feast for photographers and reporters, and little notice was given in the next day's papers to the blood that had been spilled in a street in Milan hours before Galante's death.

For three days, Giorgio Ambrosoli had testified before Italian judicial authorities, representatives of the U.S. government, and Sindona's attorneys, divulging the results of his long investigation. On July 11, his deposition was done. It was very nearly midnight when he arrived at his home in Via Marozzo della Rocca. He heard the shadows before he saw them. One of them called to him softly, and he turned. Four bullets entered his chest, and he was dead.

His killer was William Joseph Arico, age forty-two, of Valley Stream, Long Island. A cockroach exterminator by trade and a paid killer of humans by calling, Arico had spent most of the past decade in the federal penitentiary at Lewisburg, Pennsylvania, serving time for bank robbery and murder. He had made at least six trips to Milan in the past eleven months, traveling with a false passport which bore the name Robert McGovern. He had checked into the Hotel Splendido on the afternoon of July 8, then rented a red Fiat 127, in which he and two others drove on July 11 to Ambrosoli's house. The next day, Arico returned to New York on TWA's afternoon flight 843.

Giorgio Ambrosoli had received half a dozen threats in the months before his death. Several of these—which, predictably, had been recorded—clearly invoked Sindona's shadow. Yet there was an inviolate precept by which men such as William Arico operated. "If you're going to do it," the saying went, "don't advertise it."

Light would fall; but before it did, Arico himself would perish.

A few weeks later, Sindona met with Calvi at the Hotel Carlyle in New York. He saw immediately that Calvi was not himself. There was darkness beneath his eyes, and his hands trembled.

"You were right, Michele," he said. "The situation in South America has become very strange. I don't know exactly what Ortolani and Gelli are doing, but they are giving me reason to fear. I use this when I travel down there"—he showed Sindona a fake passport—"and still I am followed, and still there are calls."

"You must sell the newspapers—to independents, if you can," Sindona told him.

Calvi nodded rapidly, but so abstractedly that Sindona wondered if he had even heard his words.

"It is too much, Michele," he said at last. "It has all become too much."

Sindona's trial was set to begin on September 10. Throughout July, he met with his lawyers to study the growing mass of documents obtained through rogatories from abroad—"The Hilton Report" among them—and to plan the course of his defense. The attorneys assured him that he was right in foreseeing victory.

On the afternoon of August 2, he was seen walking on Fifth Avenue near the Hotel Pierre. He was smiling in the

197

hazy summer sun, and the world was smiling back at him. Then the world lost sight of him.

The news of his disappearance broke the following week. Beneath his photograph and the headline "Sindona Missing," the front page of *The New York Times* of August 7 quoted Sindona's attorney Marvin Frankel as saying, "It appears to me that he has been kidnapped." The photograph in *The New York Post* that day, far larger, showed him bug-eyed and gesticulating. "Has this financier been kidnapped or is it just a scam?" asked the *Post* in forty-eight-point type.

At a few minutes after three o'clock on the Friday afternoon of August 10, a call was received at the New York bureau of ANSA, the Italian news agency. "This," an unidentified male voice said, "is Proletarian Justice. Michele Sindona will be executed by firing squad at dawn tomorrow."

On the following Tuesday, the FBI issued a public appeal requesting that "anyone in possession of information concerning the disappearance of Michele Sindona contact either the New York City Police Department or the Manhattan office of the FBI. All calls will be held in the strictest confidence."

He was still missing on September 10, the date his trial had been scheduled to begin. By then, his family had received more than twenty letters from him. These letters, postmarked in Brooklyn and Newark, told of interrogations at the hands of mysterious captors, but bade his wife and children not to worry. Now, on the morning of September 10, a threatening letter arrived at the Park Avenue home of Sindona's daughter and son-in-law. It was addressed to Piersandro. "If you value his life," it said of Sindona, "you will provide all the facts in your possession." The letter advised that further details were on their way to Sindona's lawyer Rodolfo Guzzi in Rome.

Guzzi had already received a call, seven days earlier, from a woman identifying herself as a member of the Comitato Proletario di Eversione per una Giustizia Migliore (the Proletarian Committee of Eversion for a Greater Justice). On September 21, Guzzi opened a fat envelope bearing a Brooklyn postmark. In it, there was a photograph of an emaciated Sindona. Upon his chest was a hand-lettered placard stating, *"Il giusto processo lo faremo noi"* ("The true trial will be handled by us"). In his report from Rome published three days later in *The New York Times,* Nicholas Gage would describe the picture as "strongly suggestive of the photographs of Aldo Moro sent by his kidnappers before they killed him."

A letter, signed "All written by me on precise orders, Sindona," accompanied the picture. The letter posed a series of vague, incriminatory questions, and asked for the names of politicians and industrialists who had been involved in certain crooked dealings with Sindona. The answers to these questions, observed *The Economist* the following week, "could embarrass major Italian political figures, the Vatican and some of the country's largest financial institutions."

On October 9, a thirty-one-year-old man was seized and taken into custody by Roman police as he attempted to deliver a message to the home of Rodolfo Guzzi. This message, according to the police, was a request from Sindona for a passport and "a large amount of money." The seized man was Vincenzo Spatola, the younger brother of Rosario Spatola of Palermo. The elder Spatola, age forty-two, was the owner of a large construction company, and a son-in-law of the brother of Rosario Di Maggio, who was considered to be one of the most powerful Mafiosi in Sicily. The Spatola brothers were cousins of the Gambino brothers in America. Rosario Gambino of New Jersey was, in fact, a partner in Montegrappa Costruzioni, a subsidiary of the Spatola construction company in Palermo.

A few days later, police converged to search the summer villa of Rosario Di Maggio in Torretta, near Palermo. Following their search, old Don Rosario suffered a heart attack and died. The next week, on October 16, Rosario Spatola was taken into custody. The police, who had discovered that Spatola had been in New York from the end of July until August 21, asked him why he had gone there. To take care of family business, he answered, and to visit a favorite aunt, Salvatrice Gambino.

While the Roman police were questioning Spatola that Tuesday, October 16, Michele Sindona suddenly appeared at the corner of Tenth Avenue and 42nd Street in New York. He called Marvin Frankel's office from a pay phone there a few minutes after eleven o'clock that morning. By noon, his son-in-law arrived to retrieve him.

There was a gunshot wound in his left thigh. He waved away his family's concern, but they telephoned his physician, Dr. Elliott Howard, who ordered them to take him to a hospital. By sundown, he was lying in a suite on the eleventh floor of Doctors Hospital, under arrest and heavy guard by federal marshals. The next morning, while Judge Thomas Griesa appointed a psychiatrist, Dr. Gustin Goldin, and a cardiologist, Dr. Meyer Texon, to examine Sindona to determine when he would be able to appear in court, FBI agents and New York detectives began a long series of bedside interrogations.

Over the course of the coming days, Sindona told them that, on the afternoon of August 2, he had received a call at the Hotel Pierre from a man who identified himself, in perfect Italian, as a friend of his lawyer Rodolfo Guzzi. The caller said he urgently needed to see him, and asked him to meet him later at the Hotel Tudor on East 42nd Street. That evening, as he neared the Tudor, he was overtaken by an armed man. He was ordered into a waiting car, blindfolded by another man, and taken away. After about three hours, they arrived at a quiet place. He was brought to a windowless room, where he was held for most of the time during the following ten weeks. He soon surmised that his captors, who spoke northern Italian, were leftists, as they excoriated him for his "economic crimes." About three weeks before his release, when a guard fell asleep, he rushed to escape; but the guard awoke and shot him in the leg. Someone who seemed to have had medical experience tended his wound, which bled profusely. Finally, early the previous Tuesday, he was again blindfolded, driven away, and released with no explanation.

Sindona repeated his account for Judge Griesa at the federal courthouse the following Wednesday afternoon. His weary eyes seemed to brighten now and then with this or that promising flicker of sudden remembrance: He had prepared two eggs for himself on the afternoon of his abduction; the man who overtook him in the street spoke Italian like a Greek; the car was a beige Fleetwood; the blindfold seemed elastic.

He lied wonderfully. The autumn wind was his to savor one last time.

X.

Sicilian Shadows

A YEAR BEFORE HIS DISAPPEARANCE, Sindona had come to know Rear Admiral Max K. Morris, who was then in New York as a Pentagon representative to the United Nations. Admiral Morris shared Sindona's belief that Sicily was an island of supreme strategic importance to the future of the world's democratic powers. On September 20 of that year, on stationery of the Royal Thames Yacht Club, the admiral wrote to tell Sindona that he had discussed his ideas with Admiral Stansfield Turner, the director of the CIA, who was with him then in England for the annual meeting of the Institute for Strategic Studies. On October 6, from his home in Jacksonville, Florida, Admiral Morris wrote again, to say that "the meetings of the Institute for Strategic Studies pointed up many of the acute problems we discussed." After a long telephone conversation, the admiral informed him, in a letter dated December 13, that "both a high military figure and a similar person in the intelligence field" were giving "interested attention" to "the information you gave me." He said that while there was "no way to determine if either of these people will carry the matter further, I certainly urged them to do so." He concluded by saying that "all of us, I know, appreciate your efforts in behalf of this country and of the West."

"At about this same time," Sindona recalled, "I had seen an article in *Panorama* that told of a strange meeting that had taken place aboard a yacht off the coast of Sicily. Presiding over this meeting, *Panorama* said, was a Masonic doctor named

Joseph Miceli Crimi. The purpose of the meeting was to help me. According to the article, Miceli Crimi often traveled back and forth between Italy and America, and was the person through whom Licio Gelli and myself communicated.

"Though I had never in my life heard of this man Crimi, the article did not surprise me, as I was long inured to seeing fiction about myself presented as truth in the Italian press.

"Sometime later, however, I received a call from this mysterious Dottor Crimi, who was in New York and who referred to the *Panorama* article by way of introducing himself. During our first meeting, he spoke of one of his little grandchildren, who was very ill. Then he began to tell me that he worked with another doctor, a Palermo gynecologist named Michele Barresi. He said that Dottor Barresi was the *gran maestro* of a very important Masonic lodge called the Camea. He also told me that the head of the Masonic women's alliance in Sicily, Francesca Paolo Longo, was his close friend and assistant. He said that it was his desire to merge the various Masonic lodges. He admitted that he had never met Licio Gelli, but professed great admiration and respect for him.

"After that meeting, I asked Gelli for information about Crimi. Gelli said that he did not think Crimi was an important man in Masonry, but was a serious professional with a good practice and many friends in Sicily. He was, Gelli said, Palermo's police doctor and the son-in-law of the former head of that police force.

"In later meetings, I discussed with Crimi many of the same matters I had talked about with Admiral Morris. Crimi, like myself, was aware that the communists in Sicily had welcomed the establishment of the American ICBM base at Comiso. Only the pacifists and the Autonomia Operaia, the Workers' Autonomy group, had protested against the coming of the missiles to Sicily. The communists, and other, more secret forces, embraced those missiles as weapons to be foreseeably seized and turned against those who brought them.

"After many meetings between Crimi and his friends, and

after I'd spoken to my own business friends on the island, it was decided that my taking a trip to Sicily could set forces in motion to effect a decisive political shift. It was believed that my reputation in the region was powerful enough to attract huge numbers of Sicilians to vote in favor of whatever political ideas I might lay out. It was agreed that I would go to Sicily in the summer of 1979, traveling incognito to avoid arrest under the warrants outstanding against me in Italy.

"Then the Franklin trial was scheduled. I asked Crimi and my friends to postpone my clandestine journey. They told me that meetings had already been organized and that many important bureaucrats and representatives of the Partito Separatista Siciliano had postponed or canceled their vacations. To put off my trip would be to jeopardize all support for our plans. Besides, I could be back in time for the trial in September.

"My friends Joseph Macaluso and Antonio Caruso knew of these plans. They shared enthusiasm for our proposed project, and they agreed to help me get away.

"So, on August 2, 1979, I left New York wearing a false beard and moustache and carrying a false passport in the name of Joseph Bonamico. Caruso and I took TWA flight 740 to Vienna, where a friend of Macaluso's was to meet us and take us by car through the Brenner Pass to Italy. The border guards, Crimi told me, were Masonic friends. In Rome, we were to change cars, according to further arrangements made by Macaluso, and then proceed to Sicily, where Crimi and his friends would be waiting.

"There was trouble from the start. The flight to Vienna that Caruso and I took arrived more than four hours late because of a storm in New York and another in Vienna. At the airport, we found Macaluso's friend, Gabrielle Irnesberger, and the driver, Guenter Blumauer. They told us that the border crossing would take at least six hours because of traffic problems on the Brennaro road. I feared that this would make the crossing dangerous, as Crimi's friends would probably no longer be on duty and because there might by now be an

Interpol alert concerning my disappearance. I decided then to stay in Austria for the night. We checked into the Hotel Berghof in Salzburg, and from there I called Crimi in Palermo and Macaluso in New York.

"Macaluso arrived in Austria the next day, and we moved to the Hotel Inter-Continental in Vienna. Two days later, I left alone for Athens on Austrian Airlines flight 381. I checked into the Hilton there, then, after telephoning Crimi, I moved on his advice to the Hotel Park. Caruso, meanwhile, returned to New York. He had begun to drink, and he had gotten cold feet. Macaluso went to Sicily, intending to help Crimi get me there safely.

"Crimi met me in Greece on August 9 and told me he'd arranged to bring me to Palermo on a boat owned by one of his Mason friends. On August 12, three of his friends came to Athens. They were Francesco Foderà, Giacomo Vitale, and Ignazio Puccio—more Masons. They said there would have to be another change of plans. The *guardacoste* had renewed its campaign to intercept cigarette smugglers. If our boat were to be searched, I might be discovered. It was decided that I should take the ferry that ran between Patras and Brindisi, across the Strait of Otranto. The five of us—Crimi, Foderà, Puccio, Vitale, and myself—left aboard the *San Andrea* on the night of August 14, and we arrived in Brindisi at four o'clock the next afternoon. The customs men there seemed to know my companions well, and there was no problem. Foderà, Vitale, and I rented a Fiat from Avis and headed right away for Sicily. Crimi and Puccio went to Rome, where they would later catch a train for the island.

"We came to Caltanissetta, in the center of the island, at two o'clock the next morning. I was greeted by Gaetano Piazza, another of Crimi's Mason friends. Francesca Paolo Longo was waiting for me at Piazza's home. Crimi joined us the next day, and we traveled finally to Palermo, where I moved into Signorina Longo's house, at Via Diodoro Siculo 4. From there, I contacted the people, many of them unknown to me, whom Crimi had enlisted for our project. They were, for the most part, members of the Partito Separatista Siciliano, and of the Masonic hierarchy through whose network the *separatisti* operated. These people shared my conviction that the secession of Sicily from Italy and the decimation of the island's communist forces could be brought about in one great swoop.

"There was trouble in Palermo, however. Three weeks before I arrived, Boris Giuliano, the head of the Palermo anti-Mafia police, the Squadra Mobile, was shot to death in the Bar Lux. Roadblocks were still set up, and many people who were supposed to meet me were afraid they might inadvertently be found consorting with me, a fugitive from Italian justice. In fact, the circumstances in Palermo made it very difficult for me to move around. To cover my tracks, I devised letters to my family and lawyers saying that I'd been kidnapped—letters to be posted from within the United States.

"At the end of the month, Dottor Crimi decided to go to America to meet with Johnny Gambino. Crimi not only, like myself, knew Gambino, but had also known his father, who had given him, among other gifts, a Cadillac. Gambino, until then, did not know where I was. He knew only what he read in the papers. After Crimi's visit, he agreed to come see me. He arrived in Palermo on September 6 and met me at Signorina Longo's house. He told me that my stay in Palermo could prove dangerous for many people. He proposed that I move from the city, and he offered to bring me to a villa in the hamlet of Torretta. This villa, not too far from Palermo, was owned by the in-laws of his cousin Rosario Spatola.

"Gambino had introduced me to Spatola in New York, to see if I might be able to help him get on the list of contractors authorized by the Ministry of Public Works to participate in the government-run bidding on construction projects valued above 6 billion lire. At the time, Spatola's company was authorized to bid only on the jobs in the lower price categories. I had told Spatola that I would be happy to introduce him to friends in Rome, but that he would first need to prepare a portfolio of banking references. The two biggest banks in Sicily, the Banco di Sicilia and the Cassa di Risparmio delle Province Siciliane, supplied perfect references. They said that he was a serious builder with banking credits of several billion lire. I was then able to send him to Rome with an introduction to my lawyer Rodolfo Guzzi.

"At Torretta, Gambino, Crimi, and Signorina Longo stayed with me. Macaluso came to see me, bringing with him an American typewriter he'd had Caruso buy. I used this machine to type the letters to my family and lawyers, to add further credence to the U.S. postmarks.

"Meanwhile, there was another terrible killing in Palermo: Cesare Terranova, a judge who had taken part in the Parliamentary Anti-Mafia Commission, was shot down. Police control over the region was tightened, and our meetings with the Masons and *separatisti* became even more difficult.

"At that point, I saw that it would be impossible to carry out our plans. I decided to return to New York, and then, after the trial, come back to Sicily, as I was sure I'd be acquitted.

"Crimi's Sicilian friends, however, did not accept my decision. They were afraid that the U.S. authorities would somehow force me, by means of judicial extortion, to reveal the names of those involved in our plans, which, in turn, would lead to their prosecution in Italy. I told them not to worry, but they were still fearful. It was then that I decided to have myself shot in the leg. They agreed with me that this would likely banish any doubts the authorities might have concerning my tale of being kidnapped.

"So, on September 25, Dottor Miceli Crimi, assisted by John Gambino and Signorina Longo, shot me in the left leg. Six days later, the wound was threatening to become infected, and I returned to Palermo, where it could be tended to. On October 8, when I was feeling better, John Gambino and I flew to Milan. From there, in a car driven by one of Gambino's friends, we went to Austria. A few days later, on Saturday, October 13,

I flew back to New York from Frankfurt on TWA flight 741. At Kennedy Airport, a lady friend of Gambino's helped me through customs and led me to a van, which took me to a house in New Jersey, where I stayed, recuperating, until the next Tuesday morning, when John's brother Rosario drove me into Manhattan.

"And that was that."

At the prison in Voghera, and again in a letter, I told Sindona that there seemed to be light lacking in his account. "About my 'disappearance' in Sicily," he wrote, "I told you everything. Only the names of the high-ranking bureaucrats, military officials, and industrialists who shared our scheme have been omitted. Revealing these names could serve only to destroy people who trusted in me and believed in me." He sent me an excerpt from a suppressed FBI report that said, "The U.S. government was . . . completely aware of the plans for a Sicilian revolution, of Sindona's role in it, and encouraged it."

But, Sindona told me, there was more to that Sicilian summer than a dream of revolution. The plans for Middle Eastern economic strategy that he had once prepared for the shah and prime minister of Iran had, after Ayatollah Khomeini's takeover earlier in 1979, been carried to the attention of the royal family of Saudi Arabia. From there, Sindona's plans had traveled to the hands of Colonel Muammar al-Qaddafi, who sought a way to recycle his so-called petrodollars in a manner that would, perhaps through the acquisition of strategic commodities, give him dangerous economic powers to use in his dealings with America. During that summer on the island of his birth, Sindona was contacted by Qaddafi's emissaries. In exchange for his consultancy, the young dictator would give Sindona money, asylum, and the intercession of the Libyan sword in his problems with the Italian government.

Sindona was already aware of Qaddafi's considerable powers in Italy, where Libya maintained large industrial and real-estate interests. But he came that summer to be aware of things he had not imagined.

209

"I learned about Karl Hansch, the man known, to those few who know him, as el-Hanesch," Sindona said.

"In recent years, the best intelligence on Libya has been gathered by the French secret services, the Israeli Mossad, the Algerians, the Egyptians, and the Turks—in that order. All of them collaborate with the CIA and the DIA. The best-informed of all, though, are the Soviet secret services—the KGB and GRU—and the intelligence arm of the East German Republic directed in Tripoli by Karl Hansch.

"For more than a decade now, Hansch has acted as Qaddafi's ideological adviser. It was Hansch—rather, in his Islamic incarnation, el-Hanesch—who secretly guided the writing of the infamous 'Green Book' and devised the theory of the Three Circles that has been promulgated by the Historical Research Center in Tripoli. The circles are Arabism, Panislamism, and Panafricanism. The theory is that, in our time, an unstoppable historic destiny will unite three great powers under Allah. From the Magreb—that is, North Africa from the Red Sea to the Atlantic—the uniting wave will extend to Makhrek, the Arab nations beyond the Red Sea; then finally to the Islamic lands in Asia and to black Africa.

"Hansch also serves as the commander of Qaddafi's guard, and oversees his personal security. The secrecy with which Hansch directs Qaddafi's movements is so strong that, in March 1978, when a group of apostate Libyan officers launched a rocket to destroy the helicopter in which Qaddafi was supposedly conducting surveillance over Tripoli, it turned out that Werner Lamberz, an East German agent, was killed instead. Later, in 1980, a similar attack was also foiled. Qaddafi's official plane was shot down upon returning from his visit to Moscow. But Hansch had seen to it that the colonel was following in a less conspicuous plane.

"In all his security and counterespionage work, Hansch is supported by forces of about two hundred, drawn from the East German SED, as well as from the Libyan military and police hierarchies. It was these forces, under Hansch, which later overcame the mutiny of the Tobruk garrison that had been organized with the help of the French and Egyptian secret services in the spring of 1981.

"And it is Karl Hansch, this little-known German Islamist, who is in direct command of those terrorist operations and guerrilla training camps that have brought down the world's wrath upon Qaddafi and Libya."

But—Sindona smiled and his dark eyes narrowed—Libya was merely a shadowland, a fire in the desert maintained to divert the eyes of the world from the truth.

"Libya today is really only the violent whore of Russia's will—an organizational center through which East Germany, under Soviet command, carries out deeds designed to effect the scattering and withdrawal of American, French, and other NATO forces in the Middle East, and ultimately to destabilize, and disrupt the alliances of, Western powers. Toward this end, Islam blindly supplies countless men willing to sacrifice themselves for what they perceive to be a holy cause—especially the Hezballah and other Shiite sects that behold martyrdom as the gate to an ever-green garden of sacred, infinite orgasm. What they do not realize is that the voice of Allah and the voice of the Kremlin, through el-Hanesch and his cohorts, have become one.

"El-Hanesch operates closely with Markus 'Mischa' Wolf, the head of the HVA, the East German intelligence agency. Wolf, who was a personal friend of Yuri Andropov's, is the only Jew to direct an espionage agency for the East. In the past, when Andropov was in charge of the KGB, Wolf had been entrusted with reorganizing the secret services of both Bulgaria and Czechoslovakia. Under Wolf, secret agents from the Middle East as well as from the Eastern bloc came to be trained in Potsdam.

"In Tripoli, Wolf's confidant Hansch serves to implement plans calculated to multiply conflicts and increase terrorism throughout the Arab and Islamic regions. The training of the Libyan armed forces—now about seventy thousand men—is handled principally by a cadre of twelve hundred Soviet and eight hundred Cuban military experts. The MiG pilots are trained by North Koreans and Pakistanis. Above the German and the Jew, Hansch and Wolf, all clandestine strategies in the Middle East are overseen by Geidar Ali Aliyev, the former head of the Azerbaidzhan KGB and now a full Politburo member.

"Because of things I learned in Sicily, and later through certain persons at the Compagnie Française des Pétroles who had been my associates at CTIP, it was no surprise to me that the Italian troops alone were spared during terrorist attacks in Lebanon. It was no surprise to me that Prime Minister Bettino Craxi's denunciation of Israel's retaliatory attack against the Palestine Liberation Organization command in Tunisia in the fall of 1985 was more vehement than the reaction of Tunisia's own government. And it was also no surprise to me that Italy released Abul Abbas, the PLO leader, after the *Achille Lauro* incident. I knew of what bound Italy and the Libyan terrorist network.

"On February 6, 1984, in Tripoli, representatives of the Italian and Libyan governments signed a secret accord. Under the terms of this accord, which had been in negotiation for more than a year, Italy agreed to supply Libya with the strategic matériel which was now forbidden by the United States to be exported to Libya.

"Like Tecnopetrol, controlled by the Compagnie Française des Pétroles, SNAM Progetti of Italy was to furnish Libya with equipment for irrigation, drilling, and offshore refining. SAIPEM would make available the *Saipem II* for exploratory research in Libyan waters, at depths exceeding a thousand meters. Spurious contracts would be contrived to indicate activities within the bounds of both NATO sanctions and the entreaties of the Reagan administration.

"Through SNAM Progetti, AGIP Nucleare would bring Western nuclear technology to the Qaddafi regime.

"All these companies—SNAM Progetti, SAIPEM, AGIP Nucleare—are controlled by ENI; and ENI is completely controlled by the Italian government."

In 1985, after Sindona had told me these things, *Euromoney,* the nine-dollars-a-shot monthly magazine of international finance, reported that ENI's losses had fallen from a grim 1.37 trillion lire in 1983 to a much rosier 100 billion lire in 1984. An initial public offering of SAIPEM stock had been very successful, the magazine reported, and Mario Gabbrielli, the chief financial officer at ENI, was looking to gain a listing for the stock in New York in 1986. "We'll go for the Big Board," Gabbrielli was quoted as saying, "because it will be the first Italian stock to be listed in America, and because we regard the SAIPEM listing as an introduction to the ENI group in the U.S." This meant, if what Sindona said was true, that America might soon be able to invest in its own downfall.

"It was in Sicily, where I was approached by Qaddafi's emissaries, that I began to learn of these things," Sindona said. "Because Sicily is where the guardians of Qaddafi's secret interests live. From an office in Catania, a lawyer named Michele Papa and his assistant, Signor Novello, protect their benefactor well. All that is held by Qaddafi through the Libyan Arab Bank —the 13.5 percent interest in FIAT, second only to that of the Agnelli family itself; the control of the giant Tamoil company —is guarded and manipulated from his strongholds in Sicily and the small island of Pantelleria, halfway between there and Tunisia. The future takeover of the American missile bases in Sicily will be accomplished by the communists in concert with a Libyan terrorist group of about three hundred men, which has already been established on the island—the counterpart of the larger underground Libyan group that lies waiting in America. It is all part of the time bomb that has been activated by the exploitation of the deep hatred—human perhaps more than religious—between Arabs and Jews.

"You see"—he smiled—"it is Qaddafi's belief and hope

that the island of Sicily will be restored to Islam, that Palermo will become al-Madinah once again."

In January 1986, amid the arrival in Libya of Russian SAM-5 surface-to-air missiles and the maneuvering off her coast of the American Sixth Fleet, Colonel Qaddafi sent a message, through his embassy in Rome, to President Rino Nicolosi of Sicily. It spoke warmly of the *"mare di pace e amore"* ("sea of peace and love") that "our Mediterranean" would someday become.

Sindona told his wife and children that the kidnapping had been a lie; but he did not tell his lawyers. Judge Griesa rescheduled the trial, and he permitted Sindona to remain at liberty as long as he paid to have himself guarded by a court-approved security firm.

The world press, long-circling, descended on him while he was awaiting trial. In its November 4 issue, the Italian weekly *L'Espresso* published an article that described former judge Marvin Frankel as a "debatable" lawyer who had been "forced on" Sindona. It was stated that Frankel had known that a Mafia convocation had been "scheduled by Sindona for August 2," the date of his disappearance. From January 6 to February 3, *The Sunday Times* of London, which now lay under the control of scandal-mongering Rupert Murdoch, ran a five-part series called "The Man Who Swindled the World." The final installment, entitled "Sindona and the Mafia," closed with an account of his return to New York in October: "He had a bullet wound in his thigh. Since then, he has steadfastly observed *omerta,* the rule of silence." Concerning John Gambino, the article quoted Paul Rao, Jr., a New York lawyer who has represented numerous Mafiosi. Asked about Gambino, "Rao brushes the question aside. 'Gambino is a nobody,' he says."

I called Paul Rao, Jr., and I read him the quotation attributed to him.

"I never said it," he told me. "First of all, I do not say such things about anyone. I have never seen that article, but I can assure you that those are not my words. They are not even a misrepresentation of any words of mine."

Rao told me that he had met Sindona in 1975, while serving as the national president of Americans for a Democratic Italy. "I have never," he said, "in all my years, in all the trials and investigations I have taken part in, in all the wiretaps I have listened to—and they have been considerable—heard Michele Sindona's name mentioned by any member of organized crime. I have represented many of them in court, and not one of them has ever referred in any way to him or claimed to have known him."

In the third week of January, while the *Sunday Times* series was running, *The Village Voice*, another Rupert Murdoch acquisition, published its version of the Sindona story, "A Chapter from the Godfather?" Though this investigative report quoted from but one new source—Marvin Frankel's secretary: "Mr. Frankel has nothing to say to you"—it did manage to employ the phrase "as in a Pirandello play."

Sindona, meanwhile, had heard again from Calvi, who called him one day from Zürich. He sounded much calmer then he had been when they last met; but his words, Sindona thought, were those of a madman.

"Not only had he not sold off the South American newspapers, but he was talking about completely taking over the Rizzoli group. The Ambrosiano, at the urging of Gelli and Ortolani, had already loaned a great deal of money to Rizzoli, and Ortolani had been granted a place on the Rizzoli board. I told Calvi that he was on the road to destruction. Never, I told him, would he be allowed to control a publishing group as important as Rizzoli, and certainly never Italy's most prestigious paper, the *Corriere della Sera*, which Rizzoli had owned since 1974."

"With the *Corriere della Sera* under my control," Calvi resolutely answered, "no one in Italy will dare touch me. It is my last chance to defeat the men who seek to bury me alive, as they have buried you."

"Calvi, I knew, was under the influence of Gelli and Ortolani," Sindona said. "This takeover of Rizzoli and the *Corriere* was born of Ortolani's dream of revenge on the world of publishing, which had repeatedly snubbed him."

Calvi, Gelli, and Ortolani proceeded with their plans. Gelli enrolled new names in his P-2 membership ledgers: Angelo Rizzoli; the Rizzoli group's director, Bruno Tassan Din; and Franco Di Bella, the new editor of the *Corriere*. Calvi opened another South American bank, Banco Ambrosiano de America del Sud, with headquarters in Buenos Aires. The opening was hailed in the Argentine newspapers published by the Avril group, recently acquired by Rizzoli. Later in 1980, Gelli had himself interviewed by the *Corriere della Sera* on the subject of his political philosophy. The time had come, he declaimed, to end the parliamentary system and raise a presidential republic in its place.

Gelli visited Sindona frequently in New York. At one of their meetings, when Gelli was en route to Buenos Aires, Sindona asked him to deliver a message to Jorge Videla, the Argentine dictator who had led the 1976 coup to depose Isabelita Perón.

"The Carter administration had appointed my lawyer Marvin Frankel to a commission investigating human-rights violations in Argentina," Sindona said. "He knew of my relations with Gelli, and he asked me if Gelli might be able to persuade his friend Videla to end the torture and killings that were widespread under his regime. I told Gelli to explain to President Videla that the Ambrosiano's millions could be withdrawn from his country as easily as they had been placed there. A few days later, on his return from South America, Gelli said that he had spoken with Videla. There was nothing to be done about torture in Argentina. It was a political fact of life. But, Gelli said, Videla had assured him that there would be fewer 'disappearances' in the future. And, in fact, there were only about seventy vanishings in the year that followed, as opposed to more than seventeen hundred the year before."

Videla's friendship, however, would soon be of little value to Gelli, or to anyone. He relinquished his presidency in 1981. Four years later, he was sentenced to life imprisonment for his "dirty war" against the Argentine people, nearly 9,000 of whom had disappeared during his reign of terror.

A new, sixty-nine-count indictment was filed against Sindona on January 11, 1980, superseding the original indictment of ninety-nine counts. The trial was scheduled by Judge Griesa to begin on February 6.

God's man decided that it was time to call in the favors. What finer way was there, after all, for a man to convince a court of his righteousness than by having the church itself attest to it?

He telephoned his cousin Anna Rosa, who was the sister-in-law of the late Monsignor Amleto Tondini and a close friend of Cardinal Guerri's. He asked her to find out if the cardinal was willing to testify on his behalf. It was not long before he heard from Guerri, who told him that both he and Cardinal Caprio would be happy to testify. Sindona then asked his friend Mark Antinucci to procure the cooperation of Archbishop Marcinkus. After a meeting with Guerri and Caprio, the archbishop told Antinucci to have Sindona send him a letter outlining the statements he wanted him to make.

On January 24, Marvin Frankel impressed Judge Griesa with the news that three Vatican holy men would be testifying as character witnesses for the defense. As it would be impossible, under Vatican policy, for the prelates to appear personally in the courtroom, it was agreed that their testimony would be videotaped at the American embassy in Rome, where they would also be questioned by Frankel and Assistant U.S. Attorney John Kenney.

The jury-selection process proved troublesome. Ms. Winkler said she could not bear the pressure, while Mrs. Stallworth dreaded confinement in a hotel. "I don't know too much English," Ms. Martinez fretted. Another Ms. did not want to miss her daughter's seventh-birthday party; yet another had a sickly mother. There was still no jury when Frankel and Kenney left for Rome.

While Kenney waited at the embassy, Frankel went to meet Guerri, Caprio, and Marcinkus at the Vatican. He immediately sensed that something was wrong. Guerri and Caprio were visibly disconcerted. Marcinkus, speaking for them as well as for himself, told Frankel, in a firm, detached voice, that the new Vatican secretary of state, Agostino Cardinal Casaroli—appointed six months before by Pope John Paul II—had forbidden them to testify. Cardinal Casaroli, Marcinkus said, wished to avoid setting a precedent.

Frankel pleaded that if the promised testimony were not delivered in court, Sindona's credibility would suffer a tremendous blow. Marcinkus was unwavering, and refused to discuss the matter again with Casaroli.

"It is my suspicion," Sindona later stated, "that Cardinal Casaroli had asked the advice of Marcinkus and that Marcinkus had told him that the testimony would not be received kindly by the governments of Italy and the United States. He perhaps reminded Secretary of State Cardinal Casaroli that only weeks before, in November, Italy had declared that Catholicism was no longer to be considered the state religion. In any event, I am quite sure that it was Marcinkus, not Casaroli, who helped to seal my fate.

"Thus, finally, I discovered the value of being God's man. I know now that the power of the Vatican is the system of time. We die, but it does not. A lifetime is nothing to the centuries that are the slow beat of the Vatican's pulse. They condemn Galileo, and they are still trying the case three hundred years later. It is the system of time. Men such as Marcinkus are the cogs, replaced as they wear out, every half century or so. It is terrible.

"I'm convinced that Guerri and Caprio wanted to help me. But these were men of the old ways, who lived according to the Vatican code of obedience."

A few years later, not long before his eightieth birthday, I asked Cardinal Guerri about Sindona, seeking to find what his forbidden testimony might have been. In a signed statement, handwritten in the semicursive style of another time, the cardinal told of the SGI and the Condotte d'Acqua deals.

"I must attest," Cardinal Guerri said, "that in all negotiations Avvocato Sindona behaved in an extremely correct manner and with the greatest fairness."

On February 11, 1980, after learning that Sindona's promises from the Vatican had been rescinded, his friend in Washington, Phil Guarino, wrote a letter to Licio Gelli in Italy: "Caro, carissimo Gelli, how I'd like to see you. Things are getting worse for our friend. Even the church has abandoned him. Two weeks ago, everything looked good when the cardinals said they would testify in Michele's favor. Then suddenly the Vatican secretary of state, S. E. Casaroli, forbade S. E. Caprio and Guerri to testify for him."

"My experience," Gelli answered on April 8, "tells me that for certain classes of humanity it is a natural law to help the strongest and wound the weakest. Thus not even the church could keep from denying the man it once called 'the one sent from God.' "

In his report to Judge Griesa, Frankel described his trip to the Vatican as a "catastrophe." But it was only a prelude to what awaited him on the morning of the trial.

Judge Thomas Poole Griesa—born in Kansas City in 1930, graduated *cum laude* from Harvard in 1952, raised to the federal bench in 1972—had a reputation for diligence and prudence. He had been involved in all the criminal proceedings relating to the Franklin collapse, from the first indictments, five years earlier. This, the last of them, loomed the largest. The months leading up to this trial certainly had been the most arduous. There had been numerous delays, the defendant had vanished amid a storm of publicity, and the jury-selection process had dragged on until the very eve of the court date. This is perhaps why, on the Wednesday morning of February 6, as

Judge Griesa prepared to robe, he did not bother to open the folded note that had been slipped under the door of his chambers, but only placed it in his pocket and proceeded down to court.

Stepping to the bench, he saw that the eyes of the prosecution—John J. Kenney and his assistant government attorneys, Walter S. Mack and Charles M. Carberry—were like those of children on Christmas morning. He stared back at them, nonplussed. Kenney and the others realized then that he had not read the note they had left for him. After a few words from Kenney, Judge Griesa called the defense—Marvin E. Frankel, John J. Kirby, Jr., and adjutant counsel, Stephen E. Tisman and Steven Stein—to join him and the prosecution in a closed meeting in his robing room. Sindona, in a dark gray suit, watched inquisitively as they left.

In Judge Griesa's robing room, John Kenney revealed that the government possessed incontrovertible proof that Sindona's disappearance had been a hoax. In addition to the airline tickets bearing the name of Joseph Bonamico, the FBI had brought to light that the Kennedy Airport customs-declaration form signed in the name of Bonamico bore both the handwriting and the fingerprints of Michele Sindona.

Marvin Frankel was aghast. It was, he would later say, "the blackest day of my life in a courthouse." He requested, and was granted, permission to confer with his client in private. He took Sindona to a room down the hall, and they stayed in there for a long, long time.

When the court convened that afternoon, Judge Griesa announced the revocation of Sindona's $3 million bail, without revealing to the jury the details of the morning's closed session. He remanded Sindona to be confined in the federal prison at all times except for his attendance in court; and, in that stuffy, overwarm courtroom, while winter light and the gavel fell, Sindona breathed his last, stale breath of freedom.

XI.
Gun, Rope and Gavel

JOHN KENNEY FACED THE JURY. "This," he said, "is a case about the Franklin National Bank. It is a case about fraudulent conduct, subtle corruption, and the criminal use of power."

He said the government sought to prove to them that Sindona had bought control of Franklin with money illegally removed from his Italian banks, that Sindona had embezzled and misapplied Franklin's funds and had falsified the bank's earnings.

Kenney said that Sindona, through Carlo Bordoni, had caused the Franklin National Bank to make what appeared to be a $15 million time deposit at Interbanca in Milan. This money, he said, had in fact then been passed from Interbanca to the Amincor Bank in Zürich, and from there to Sindona's Banca Unione, back in Milan. He said that similar fiduciary procedures had been used to provide the $40 million with which Sindona had bought Franklin in the first place.

He said that Sindona, again through Bordoni, had concealed $30 million in foreign-exchange losses by inventing illusory profits from other, fabricated foreign-exchange transactions. In subsequent accounting periods, after the fictitious earnings had served their purpose, the transactions would be reversed at the same artificial rate of exchange, washing out the effect of the original false transactions.

Marvin Frankel faced the jury. "It is," he said, "the privilege and the duty of those of us at this table to appear in defense of Mr. Michele Sindona."

He told them of "a man with whose name you will become very familiar in the weeks that you sit and work with us, a man named Carlo Bordoni, a man, by his own admission, who is a villain, a liar, a cheat, a man with strange and grand ambitions, a man so wedded to his own ambition and his own imagination about himself that you will wonder—I think you will wonder—about the degree of his balance in general."

He suggested to the jury, "You will want to think very long about Carlo Bordoni" and about "the songs he will sing" and "the promises he must deliver." The former judge wondered aloud "whether there has come a time here when perhaps the government's servants, our servants, should apologize for bringing liars and deal-makers before you in an effort to convict and condemn other people."

He said Sindona had lost millions upon millions, while Carlo Bordoni and Peter Shaddick were "lining their own pockets and accumulating wealth."

Sindona, *The New York Times* reported the next day, "appeared thin and tired as he listened to the opening statements, occasionally writing notes on a yellow legal pad at the defense table."

On February 12, Frankel cross-examined Bordoni. He asked him about the testimony he had given under oath to the SEC some years earlier.

"How long did that session of testimony under oath before the SEC continue?" he asked.

"Let me see," Bordoni mumbled. "I would say about seven, eight hours."

"And during that long session, Mr. Bordoni, is it not fair to say that you lied over and over again?"

"Yes, Mr. Frankel."

Perhaps Frankel should have stopped there. Later, as the evening recess approached, he questioned Bordoni about the allegations that Sindona had tried to rape his wife.

"My wife for about two or three months was behaving in

a very unusual way. What I mean to say is that all day she was crying, day and night, and I didn't know why. I knew that I had done nothing wrong to her, because I am very proud to say that since I met my wife I never even thought of another woman. And so I had no explanation whatsoever, because I knew that she was corresponding my love, my affection, fully.

"So, one afternoon, I think it was February 1973, I couldn't stand that situation any longer, and I told my wife, for the first time in my life, what was the matter with her? And I am sorry to say that I did that in a very rough way—in words, naturally. She started crying, and I just couldn't get her to stop. Then she recovered some and said, 'Well, I have a terrible thing to tell you.'

"So, she told me what had happened—and I don't think it's the case of telling the court all the details that she told me. In any case, as soon as I was aware of what had happened, the first thing I did was to call by phone Piersandro Magnoni and Nino Pedroni, who was an associate of Mr. Sindona; and I told both of them that it was a very serious thing, and that I wanted them to be there. They rushed to my flat in Milan, and I was waiting for them. My wife, Virginia, was sitting in the living room, where I introduced both Piersandro Magnoni and Nino Pedroni. In front of them, I again asked my wife to repeat exactly what she had told me.

"When she finished, the first words that Magnoni pronounced were, exactly, 'I cannot believe it, because if it were true, I wouldn't hesitate one second in abandoning Sindona, and I would ask you to go around with me and work together.' The comment of Nino Pedroni was entirely different. He said, 'I'm not surprised at all, because things like this have involved Mr. Sindona on a number of occasions.' Then I told Piersandro Magnoni to inform Sindona, Mr. Sindona, that he had better not to meet me, at least until I got calmer, because in that very moment I could have done something irresponsible, and—well, more or less, that's all."

"Mr. Bordoni, do you recall, in a series of questions leading to this subject, I began by asking you whether you hated Michele Sindona, and you said, 'No'?"

"Yes."

"You recall I asked you whether, in the last couple of years, you have publicly and to officials reiterated that you hate Mr. Sindona? And what is your answer to that?"

"Well, as far as I recall, I may have said so."

"Within the last couple of years, yes?"

"Well, last couple of years exactly I can't say, Mr. Frankel."

"As late as the end of 19—"

"Don't interrupt him," Judge Griesa said. "You phrased this; you must let him finish."

"I'm sorry, Your Honor," Bordoni said.

"You may complete your answer," said Judge Griesa.

"I'm sorry, I thought he completed," Frankel said.

"What is the last question?" Bordoni asked, and the record was read.

"Well, Your Honor," said Frankel, "I'm at the court's pleasure."

"Well," Judge Griesa turned to the witness. "In the course of those last few questions, was there anything that you did not complete that you wanted to state?"

"Well, I just—"

"If there isn't, then there is no problem."

"Your Honor," Bordoni said, "I happen to be a little upset emotionally in this very moment."

"All right." Judge Griesa lifted his gavel. "We will take our evening recess. Ten o'clock tomorrow, ladies and gentlemen."

There was little doubt that the plans of the defense had backfired. The jury had both believed and been moved by Bordoni's performance.

"Frankel and I had rehearsed examinations and cross-examinations for months," Sindona later told me. "All the defense attorneys present at those rehearsals thought I did extremely well and that I would prove my points in court. But after the details of my disappearance became known, Frankel was very upset with me. He forbade me to take the stand."

Judge Frankel, who is today a partner of the firm Kramer, Levin, Nessen, Kamin & Frankel, gave me his own account: "I think we never recovered, either physically or spiritually, from the government's unloading its evidence concerning Sindona's disappearance. A lawyer, however, cannot forbid a client to testify. Both Kirby and I advised him that, on the whole, it was probably just as well he did not take the stand. But that decision, in the end, rested with him. He made it. I gather he has had second thoughts about it from time to time. Even then he was very uncertain as to what was the wisest course."

In a closed session on February 28, John Kenney argued that the facts of Sindona's disappearance should be permitted as evidence establishing conscious guilt.

"There is," countered Marvin Frankel, "a rather substantial roster of men once very wealthy indicted for pecuniary crimes who have gone away, and the characteristic thing that those men have done is that they have not come back, at least they have not come back willingly."

Judge Griesa eventually decided in favor of the prosecution. On March 6, the suppressed evidence was presented in court.

Complicated financial documents, and the tortuous transactions they presumably represented, proved, as in the earlier Franklin trials, to be troublesome. There was also some confusion caused by the fact that fiduciary deals, while illegal in America, are lawful and proper abroad.

"Under my understanding," defense attorney Stephen Tisman said to the court on March 11, "the fiduciary contract such as Government's Exhibit 12 provides for the creation at Amincor of fiduciary accounts, and these Exhibits 14, 15, and 16, I believe, are statements of those fiduciary accounts."

"The first column," Judge Griesa said, "is headed by some —you work from the left. You have the entry date, and I will

225

pass the next one, and then you have this column headed '*Soll.*' Is that right?"

"Yes."

"What does that mean?"

"I'm afraid I don't know."

" 'Debit,' Your Honor," interjected the attorney Walter Mack of the prosecution.

"The next one says '*Haben,*' " the judge continued.

"That means 'credit,' Your Honor," Mack explained.

"If you are right, Mr. Mack, that under the debit column all you have is a date—"

"There are a lot of questions about these documents. One thing, for instance, that has not been addressed is, the column on the right says Swiss francs, and I assume everybody is thinking that those amounts are dollars. It says '*franc,*' or '*franca.*' I am sure the defense has considered that, and they think it is wrong, but if they are talking about that, they are going to have Swiss francs. Whether Swiss francs are relevant in this case or not is a question the government is entitled to ask."

"I think a good deal of this may be evidence, but this kind of document could be very important and I don't have the faintest idea what it means," Judge Griesa said at last, sensing the jury's bewilderment. "I just sit here and I don't understand. I am sure the jury does not. So you work on this over lunch."

As the days of March passed, the atmosphere in the courtroom grew volatile. Frankel was reprimanded by Judge Griesa for misleading the jury. Frankel demurred, and the judge apologized.

"Your Honor," Frankel said, "this may be, and I believe it is, and I have been very lucky, the first time that I have sat or stood in any courtroom in the United States—and I have been in many of them—where I have been subjected to abuse; and this is not the first time in this case. I remember an occasion, Your Honor, that I will not forget, when I tried to make an objection for the record to protect the interests of my client and was treated like some shyster lawyer who had just been disbarred, and hollered at and interrupted and sat down, and I took no comfort, Your Honor, and I want the court to know that fact, that sometime later, after a recess, for reasons that I don't know, the court saw fit to apologize.

"I want you to know that I never accepted that apology, and I do not now. And I want the court to know that the record of this case will show, in my judgment, and I say this advisedly, such contrasts between the treatment of the government counsel and the treatment of defense counsel as should upset anybody interested in the administration of justice.

"It is the first time in my life as a litigator, and I haven't repeated this ever, but both of us know that I was a judge in this court for a long time, and it is the first time in my life as a lawyer and a judge that I have felt degraded in the performance of my professional duty.

"It has not always been joyous, but I have never felt demeaned and put down and personally attacked the way I have constantly felt in the effort to do my job in this case. And I am sorry about that, Your Honor. But, for those reasons, I move for a mistrial."

"The motion is denied," Judge Griesa said. "The occasion which gave rise to the apology is a situation where I had made a ruling, if I remember, after a long argument, and I was concerned that the defense lawyer was simply continuing to argue without accepting the ruling. And I did interrupt that argument, and I was somewhat heated, and I very quickly regretted giving in to heat, because I don't like to do that from the bench or any other way.

"I think that the record ought to also reflect, and we can be reminded, that there were efforts and steps taken by this court to assist in the difficult process of discovery in Europe which I am reasonably sure another judge in another court might not have engaged in.

"There is no real occasion for personal remarks back and forth. But there is a problem which I must face in doing my duty. It has nothing to do with personalities. But I have a jury trial going. I have a responsibility to protect this process, and I have my role to play. Each lawyer has his role to play, and at times we will be in sharp disagreement."

On that same day, March 19, across the Hudson River, Rosario Gambino and his thirty-four-year-old brother, Giuseppe, were arrested by federal agents at Valentino's Supper Club in Cherry Hill, New Jersey. They were brought to Newark, where they were charged with running a $10 million heroin-smuggling ring operating between the Middle East and America via Milan.

The jury deliberated for six days. At eleven o'clock on the Thursday morning of March 27, the forelady of the jury, Mrs. Nehrbauer, printed the words "Your Honour, We are ready with our verdict" very neatly on a small piece of graph paper and put it in the brown envelope that had been supplied by the court.

Sindona was found guilty of all but one of the counts charged against him. (He was acquitted on one of the lesser wire-transfer charges.) He was remanded to the Metropolitan Correctional Center to await his sentencing.

"Before the trial began," Sindona later claimed, "the government offered me a deal. They said that if I pleaded guilty to one count, all the other counts against me would be dismissed. They assured me of getting off with a maximum sentence of two years. They also suggested that if I were willing to testify against David Kennedy, all charges against me would be dropped.

"But I wanted the trial. The charges were wrong. The money used to buy Franklin was mine. I had proof also that the Franklin deposits with Interbanca were not fiduciary in nature, and that, in any case—even Ambrosoli, the state investigator admitted this in his report—Amincor had already begun to repay the funds. I thought also that no one would believe the lies of a man, Bordoni, who himself admits that he is a liar. And I thought that people, with common sense, might wonder why a man with $500 million, a man who could walk into the Bank of America and get hundreds of millions more on credit —I thought they might wonder why such a man would waste so much time and energy bothering to steal a few paltry million. But I was wrong. I believed then, to some degree, in justice. Now, in my old age, I know a little more, and I believe only in injustice."

"I think," Judge Frankel told me, looking back on the trial, "that a losing lawyer is a poor person to get an objective view from. With that cautionary note, I will say that I felt at the time that an injustice was done to Sindona. I had a sense that there was a widespread belief, probably shared by the judge, that Sindona was a villain and that his connections were evil. Obviously, I think, the judge decided that Michele was a very evil person."

I asked Frankel if he had been convinced of his client's innocence.

"That's not a statement a lawyer ever should make or can make," he said after halting a moment. "I didn't make it there, and I guess I shouldn't make it here."

As I stood to leave his office, Frankel asked me how Sindona was faring.

"They've got him in a women's prison in northern Italy," I told him. Judge Frankel grinned slightly.

"He always was a ladies' man," he said.

On the first morning of the trial, before remanding Sindona to jail, Judge Griesa had ordered that certain government documents—dirt against Sindona—be placed under seal. Now, at the end of March, that dirt was unsealed and brought to light. On the day after the verdict, it was revealed that Luigi Ronsisvalle and Bruce McDowall, the two men who had threatened Nicola Biase in November 1978, had been indicted the previous May 30, had pleaded guilty in June, and had been sentenced in September to, respectively, five and three years in prison. U.S. Attorney William M. Tendy was quoted as saying that "it was the government's position that these two men acted on Mr. Sindona's behalf." Also unsealed, three days later, was a three-page affidavit signed by the prosecutor John J. Kenney before the start of the trial. In it, Kenney declared that Luigi Ronsisvalle had stated that "the same person who asked him to threaten Biase" had "asked whether he or someone he knew would agree for a price to kill the assistant United States attorney in this district then handling the extradition proceeding against Sindona"—that is, Kenney himself. "This proceeded to the point of Ronsisvalle and others locating a paid assassin who was willing to perform this task for $100,000 before the plan was dropped." Kenney's affidavit also told of threatening letters received the previous December 7 by Virginia Bordoni and Anthony Di Falco. The letters, printed in Italian and signed with the name of the fictitious Proletarian Committee to which Sindona's "kidnapping" had been attributed, told Bordoni's wife and lawyer that they would die if Carlo did not keep quiet. Kenney added that Giorgio Ambrosoli had been "brutally shot down in front of his home in Milan, Italy, after giving testimony unfavorable to Sindona in a deposition." Though, as the *New York Law Journal* noted, on the front page of its April 1 issue, "there was nothing in the affidavit that directly connected Mr. Ronsisvalle to Mr. Sindona," the darkness that fell then upon him seemed to bring with it a certain finality.

"Can you imagine," Sindona said, "that I would send such letters as the trial was getting under way? That I should be that stupid? And who was this man who they say approached Mr. Ronsisvalle in my name? Where is the evidence that any such man existed—other than the word of Mr. Ronsisvalle, who at the time wanted to make a deal with the government, who in turn at the time had no greater desire than to convict and destroy Michele Sindona?

"The government—this is the real Mafia. They are the

true criminal Mafia. My partners, I told them, were a respected part of the world's establishment when the FDIC did not exist. My partners, I told them, were establishment when the Federal Reserve System did not exist. My partners were establishment when the United States did not exist! But they say that I am Mafia. Why? Because their friend Mr. Ronsisvalle, who brags of murdering thirteen people but whom we must believe to be above lying, says so."

The Federal Witness Protection Program had been established by the Organized Crime Control Act of 1970. By 1980, the U.S. Department of Justice was spending some $25 million a year in tax money to care for and harbor the 4,000 and several hundred informers who had been granted the protection of the state in return for their continued cooperation. Luigi Ronsisvalle, through his services, beginning with his accusations against Sindona, was to become one of the Witness Protection Program's most prized performers.

Carlo Bordoni, after successfully testifying against Sindona, was sentenced with the leniency he had been promised: five years and a fine of $20,000. He was also given protected-witness status. Under the program, all prisoners who join it are segregated from the general prison population and placed in one of the few, classified locations reserved for them by the federal government. One such location is the Witness Protection Unit on the third floor of the Metropolitan Correctional Center in downtown Manhattan. It was there that Carlo Bordoni and Luigi Ronsisvalle came to know each other.

Six floors above them, in the high-security unit called Nine-South, Sindona sat in his cell and thought the worst things a man can think. One day, he removed the blade from the disposable plastic safety razor that had been issued to him. At three o'clock on the morning of May 13—five days after his sixtieth birthday, and the day before he was scheduled to be sentenced—he drew the blade across his left wrist. A passing guard glanced in to see him sitting at the edge of his bed holding out his arm and watching his own blood spill into a wastebasket. He was taken to the prison infirmary, then to New York Infirmary–Beekman Downtown Hospital, where he was admitted in critical condition. Physicians dismissed his wound as a "simple laceration," but expressed some concern for what appeared to be cardiac problems.

"Before I cut my wrist," Sindona later explained, "I took four bottles of digitalis and ninety Librax."

On May 16, a hospital spokesman announced that his condition had worsened and that he refused to reveal the nature of the drugs he had taken. "He remains critical," the spokesman said, "but is now considered unstable."

"Then my family came to me," Sindona said. " 'Papa, you must fight,' my children said." He turned his palm and shrugged, then uttered a low, confounding guttural sound. "And so I fight."

On Friday morning, June 13, Judge Thomas Griesa sentenced him to three twenty-five-year terms and one twenty-four-year term, to be served concurrently, and a fine of $207,-000. In addition, the court imposed on him the costs of the prosecution.

Before the sentencing, Judge Griesa had met in private with Sindona. He had asked him if he had any desire or willingness to make restitution. Sindona would not be moved. "No," he told him. Now, in meting out the maximum sentence and fine for each count of fraud, Judge Griesa spoke before the crowded courtroom of Sindona's lack of remorse.

Here, he said, was "a man who achieved a very high position in the business community, indeed in the international business community, and he used that position for criminal purposes."

Sindona showed no emotion as he received the sentence. He stood. He turned to smile briefly at his daughter, Maria Elisa. Then he was led away.

Speaking to the press afterward, the prosecutor John Kenney and his boss, John S. Martin, the U.S. Attorney for the

Southern District of New York, said they believed this to be the harshest sentence ever handed down for any so-called white-collar crime. The sentence, Martin declared, would "demonstrate that the rich and powerful who commit crimes will be vigorously prosecuted and, if found guilty, appropriately dealt with." Sindona's attorney Marvin Frankel described the sentence as "Draconian and uniquely harsh." *The New York Times,* in an editorial of June 19, found in that harshness "a suitable expression of justice."

"I was not part of their Mafia, and I paid for it," Sindona said five springtimes later. "Walter Wriston takes all his depositors' money and throws it away in Latin America. They put a wreath on his head. E. F. Hutton is indicted on two thousand counts of fraud involving billions of dollars, and nobody does a day in jail. Robert Foman, the president of Hutton, still has lunch with his friend William Smith, the attorney general. And here I am."

William Gabler had three felony convictions for dealing in property stolen from trucks when he was sentenced to nine years in prison by a Brooklyn judge in 1977. While serving his sentence at the Metropolitan Correctional Center, he had joined the Witness Protection Program.

"Once I was accepted into the Witness Protection Program," Gabler recalled after his term was done, "I was incarcerated in the Witness Protection Unit on the third floor of the MCC. There were never more than twenty inmates housed in the Witness Protection Unit, therefore we all knew one another fairly well. During the time that I was housed in the protective-custody unit, I met and talked with Carlo Bordoni and Luigi Ronsisvalle.

"I became particularly friendly with Luigi Ronsisvalle, since we discovered that we had grown up in the same neighborhood and knew many of the same people from the Knickerbocker Avenue area of Ridgewood, Queens.

"During the course of one of my conversations with Luigi Ronsisvalle, I asked him what he was doing on the third floor of the MCC. He told me that he had been 'hired to kill a couple of people.' I asked him if I knew any of the intended victims, and Ronsisvalle told me that I did not know the individuals but that one of them, Michele Sindona, had been in the newspapers often. Ronsisvalle told me that he had been hired to kill Michele Sindona and somebody in Italy. Ronsisvalle told me the name of the man in Italy to be killed, but I am not certain of that name today. I do recall specifically that it sounded very similar to the name of the Italian opera star Enrico Caruso. I distinctly remember that the first name was Enrico and the last name was an Italian name that began with a *C.* Ronsisvalle never told me who it was that paid him to kill these two individuals.

"Ronsisvalle told me that Bordoni was involved in the Sindona case. I had no substantive discussions with Carlo Bordoni, who for the most part kept to himself. I did observe Ronsisvalle and him talking on several occasions. While both of them spoke English, on those occasions when I observed them and was close enough to hear what was being said, they spoke in Italian, which I could not understand."

Sindona was transferred to the federal prison in Springfield, Missouri. In the first week of October, seventy-five-year-old Massimo Spada was arrested in Rome on a warrant charging him with complicity in Sindona's alleged banking crimes.

"Spada was old and weak," Sindona said, "and, in his weakness, he was fearful of the magistrates' threats. He went along with their lies against me, having let me know through a *deputato* of our mutual acquaintance that he was afraid. He seemed to have forgotten certain hard times we had gone through together. He seemed to have forgotten that, when he left the IOR, when Enrico Cuccia told me to abandon him to the dogs, I took him in. I told myself that Spada's betrayal had to do with his old age and infirmity. But it was a painful thing."

Hours after Spada's arrest, Carlo Bordoni was extradited to Milan on a five-year-old warrant charging him, like Spada, with conspiracy. It was the first step toward his getaway.

A few days later, on October 7, Sindona was indicted by a federal grand jury in New York on charges of conspiracy, bail-jumping, and perjury relating to his fraudulent kidnapping. His friends Joseph Macaluso and Antonio Caruso were also indicted.

Throughout the first months of his imprisonment, Sindona had remained in contact with Licio Gelli, who was one of the few who still stood by him. Toward the end of the year, after Ronald Reagan's victory in the November election, Gelli told Sindona he would like to attend the inaugural ball in Washington on January 20. Through Phil Guarino, the Republican Party National Committee chairman he knew, Sindona arranged for Gelli to receive an invitation. After the inauguration, the Italian press, Sindona was amused to see, reported that Gelli had attended the ceremony through the kind offices of unnamed friends in the CIA and secret services.

It was a small world—at least that part of it that lay in shadows. Michele Papa, the Sicilian lawyer who guarded Muammar al-Qaddafi's interests, had come to play an obscure role in that 1980 presidential race. Three years before, Mario Laenza, an Atlanta businessman and acquaintance of President Jimmy Carter's family, had vacationed in Catania. He had met Michele Papa there. The next summer, Billy Carter, the president's brother, had gone to Libya on an invitation extended by Papa through Laenza. During that September 1978 visit, the president's brother received $50,000 in expense money and a $220,000 "loan" from Qaddafi's regime. He promised in return to "do something" about getting Qaddafi the eight C-130 military-transport planes he had ordered from America but that had been embargoed in reaction to Qaddafi's support of terrorism.

Billy Carter's Libyan dealings remained concealed for

more than a year—until Francesco Pazienza, an aide to the head of the Italian military-intelligence agency SISMI, approached Michael Ledeen, an American journalist and state servant who sometimes also worked for SISMI. (His coded identification at SISMI, according to Pazienza, was Z-3, and all payments to him—$120,000 in 1980—were paid into a Bermuda account.) Pazienza arranged a meeting between Papa and Ledeen, then helped wire the American with a hidden recording device. Based on what Papa told him, Ledeen wrote an article called "Qaddafi, Arafat, and Billy Carter," which was published in *The New Republic* in late October. The scandal it created grew steadily until Election Day, leaving newspapers to wonder in the aftermath of Jimmy Carter's defeat how much "Billygate," as they called it, had contributed to the Republican triumph.

Michael Ledeen went on to become a consultant to the State and Defense departments under the Reagan administration, as well as a fellow at the Georgetown Center for Strategic and International Studies. And, in January 1981, Francesco Pazienza became a special consultant to Roberto Calvi and the Ambrosiano group.

On February 5, 1981, the Italian authorities drew ominously closer to the Vatican. Old Luigi Mennini of the IOR, who, like Spada, had sat on the boards of Sindona's European banks, was arrested in Rome on charges of conspiracy.

Eight days later, Joseph Macaluso, after a two-week trial, was convicted on charges of conspiracy and aiding and abetting bail-jumping. At a subsequent trial, Sindona and Antonio Caruso were also convicted. Judge Pierre N. Leval imposed on Sindona a two-and-a-half-year sentence, to be served concurrently with his prison term, and a fine of $25,000. Macaluso and Caruso were released on probation.

"Judge Leval conducted this trial in fairness," Sindona said. "But my new lawyer, Joseph Oteri, was no good. He wanted to defend me by saying I was crazy. 'I don't need to be crazy,' I told him. 'I've got enough trouble as I am.' "

Having been turned down, the previous December, by the U.S. Court of Appeals, which affirmed his Franklin conviction on all counts, Sindona decided to take his case to the Supreme Court. His petition was filed on March 18, 1981. In an attempt to haul in the big guns, subpoenas were issued for the testimonies of the former president Richard Nixon, the former U.S. ambassador Graham Martin, and the director of the CIA, Admiral Stansfield Turner.

"Phil Guarino in Washington told me that Senator Laxalt of Nevada had assured him that I would be freed. I don't know what happened—I have never been able to find out—but, within one week of that, Laxalt changed his line to Guarino: 'Forget it.' He must have been threatened with scandal from above. But, as I say, I don't really know. Guarino told me nothing more."

The Supreme Court of the United States denied his petition on April 20, little more than a month after it was filed. Once again, Sindona blamed his lawyer—now it was Ivan S. Fisher, a well-known New York attorney who specialized in defending drug dealers. (One of his more celebrated clients had been Vincent Papa, a central figure in the so-called French Connection case.) Sindona later tried to sue Fisher for the return of his legal fees, but he was unsuccessful.

"Fisher took my money and he didn't do a damned thing for me," Sindona claimed. "This is what I tell people when they say I am the big Mafioso I have been painted to be: It was a joke without end—a joke and a nightmare both."

The situation in Italy was darkening. Two magistrates from Milan had gone to Sicily to question Joseph Miceli Crimi, the Masonic doctor who had been the instigator of Sindona's ruinous disappearance. The magistrates wanted to know why Crimi had traveled 600 miles to Arezzo during the time Sindona was hiding in Palermo. Crimi told them that his dentist lived in Arezzo, and he had been stricken with a toothache. The magistrates did not relent, and, on March 14, 1981, Crimi gave in, telling them that "I went to Arezzo because Licio Gelli is there."

Three days later, on March 17, the Guardia di Finanza raided Gelli's home in Arezzo and his office in nearby Castiglion Fibocchi. In his office, along with photocopies of various state documents, the finance police found what appeared to be the P-2 membership list. It included the names of cabinet ministers, military and secret-service officers (among them the head of SISMI, Francesco Pazienza's boss, General Giuseppe Santovito), industrialists, bankers (such as Roberto Calvi), journalists, and foreign political figures (such as Phil Guarino of the Republican Party in Washington).

The list was given to Prime Minister Arnaldo Forlani, who decided to suppress it while appointing a three-member commission to investigate P-2. On May 21, however, through Socialist politicians in Rome, the secret list of 962 P-2 members became public, and with it the tale of Gelli's lodge, seen as the heart of a vast and maleficent conspiracy to take Italy from within. Days later, the Forlani government collapsed amid what had become one of the greatest scandals since the birth of the Republic. The new prime minister, Giovanni Spadolini, declared that Italy was in a state of "moral emergency."

And on the day before that list was made public, Roberto Calvi was arrested at his home in Via Giuseppe Frua by a Guardia di Finanza captain. On June 10, while Italy wondered to which end of the earth Licio Gelli had vanished, Roberto Calvi was brought to the Palace of Justice, there to be duly tried for fraud, illegal export of capital, and—though it was not said in so many words—grasping beyond his place.

On the evening of July 2, Calvi sent a message from the Lodi prison to the three Milan magistrates who were investigating the P-2 affair: He was willing to talk. The magistrates—one of them was Sindona's nemesis Guido Viola—arrived at the prison within a matter of hours. During the long interrogation that followed, Calvi said that Gelli and Umberto Ortolani had exercised considerable power over him. He had, he said, been led by them to believe that "in my position, I had particular need of protection and support," which they could provide. The magistrates pressed him to tell all he knew about Gelli and Sindona.

"I'm just the last wheel on the cart," Calvi pleaded wearily. "Try to understand. Banco Ambrosiano is not mine. I'm simply in the service of someone else."

"But who controls you?"

"I cannot tell you any more." It was three o'clock in the morning.

In the course of that night at Lodi, Calvi told the magistrates that he had paid $30 million in black-money bribes to the Socialist Party in an attempt to buy political protection. When the magistrates returned to question him again three days later, Calvi recanted what he had said about his *bustarelle* to the socialists. In the course of those three days, his wife, Clara, had received threatening calls from politicians in Rome. Did Roberto so love prison, these callers wondered, that he wanted to spend the rest of his life there?

On July 9, in the hours between midnight and dawn, Calvi, once again drawing inspiration from his mentor, took an overdose of barbiturates and opened the veins of one wrist. On the following day, in Parliament, Bettino Craxi, the head of the Socialist Party, stood to declare that Calvi's trial was being conducted in an ambience of "intimidatory violence" and that the court authorities were making "political use of judicial papers."

But what Calvi's *bustarelle* had bought him, if anything, was not enough. Toward dusk on July 20, he was found guilty. The three judges sentenced him to a term of four years in prison and imposed a fine on him of 16 billion lire (the equivalent at the time of about $10 million). He was released pending an appeal. His wife came to take him home in their custom-armored Mercedes SEL. A yellow Alfetta carrying two bodyguards preceded the Mercedes through the streets; a white Alfetta with two more bodyguards followed close behind.

Through the rest of the year, Calvi maneuvered desperately to salvage his life and fortune. By the end of the summer, he succeeded in obtaining what are known as "comfort letters" from the Vatican. In statements typed on IOR stationery and dated September 1, 1981, it was admitted that the IOR "directly or indirectly controls" eleven ghost companies indebted to the Banco Ambrosiano Andino of Peru and the Ambrosiano Group Banco Commercial of Nicaragua, and that the IOR was "aware of" that indebtedness. These comfort letters looked good. But, to procure them, Calvi had secretly given Archbishop Marcinkus a letter of his own in exchange. This secret letter absolved the IOR of any responsibility for those debts it was "aware of."

A parliamentary commission had been formed in 1979 to carry out an investigation of Sindona based in part on the findings of Giorgio Ambrosoli. In July 1981, as the commission's investigation widened under the direction of the socialist Francesco De Martino (the same politician who had revealed the P-2 list to the press), Sindona was formally charged with ordering Ambrosoli's murder. In December, Roberto Calvi, called before the commission, testified that he had never been "a partner of Sindona."

In January 1982, in Palermo, Sindona was indicted, along with John Gambino and more than seventy others, on charges of conspiracy in a $600 million international heroin-trafficking plot.

Among the others indicted were Gambino's cousin Rosario Spatola and several relatives of Salvatore Inzerillo, the head of the Passo di Rigano Mafia, with whom Spatola's wife's uncle Rosario Di Maggio had been associated. Don Salvatore had been murdered the previous May by attackers who used Kalashnikov automatics to shoot through the armored Alfa-Romeo he drove. On January 22, Don Salvatore's sixty-seven-year-old brother, Pietro, was found dead in the trunk of a car in New York. Wads of dollars had been crammed in his mouth and between his legs. Less than two weeks later, on February 2, another brother, fifty-two-year-old Antonio Inzerillo of Delran Township, New Jersey, was reported missing by his wife. According to the government, the vanished Antonio (FBI Number 723997D) was the fellow South Jersey *caporegime* of John Gambino. His wife, Anna, was a Gambino by blood.

These indictments, along with the earlier, related indictments of Rosario Gambino and others, were the beginnings of the most massive proceedings ever undertaken against that thing called the Mafia. Following the 1983 arrest in Sao Paulo, Brazil, of Tommaso Buscetta, and his eventual decision to turn informer, these proceedings promised to surpass even the hopes of Giovanni Falcone, the driven magistrate of Palermo whose dream these proceedings were. Don Masino, as Buscetta was known, was the most exalted and knowing Mafioso to turn against his own kind. When he learned that the Brazilian authorities had agreed to extradite him to Italy, where he had escaped from prison in 1980 and where two of his sons had since been murdered in Sicily's heroin wars, Buscetta tried to kill himself with strychnine. He was flown to Italy on July 14, 1984, the day after his fifty-sixth birthday. Over the Atlantic, he decided to talk. Falcone met him the next day. Two months later, he emerged with a 3,000-page history of *la Nuova Mafia*. Using Don Masino's testimony, Falcone indicted more than 470 men. To accommodate their mass trial, which began on February 10, 1986, a special, fortress-like courthouse was built near the walls of the old Ucciardone prison. Buscetta, meanwhile, had been sent to testify in America, where the government was tending to its counterpart case against the Mafia, the so-called Pizza Connection trial, in New York.

Falcone's indictment against Sindona was begrudgingly dismissed. Of the hundreds of Mafiosi hauled in by the net Falcone fashioned from Buscetta's testimony, none implicated

Sindona. In the thousands of hours of wiretaps harvested on both sides of the Atlantic, his name was never mentioned. Buscetta himself denied any knowledge of him.

But Falcone did not relent. On the eve of the great trial in Palermo, it was reported that a new indictment of Sindona was being prepared. Buscetta, it was said, had recalled things he had heard about Sindona's meetings with certain now-deceased Mafiosi, such as Salvatore Inzerillo.

By then, the American government had signed a secret agreement with Buscetta. He and his family would become state-supported American citizens. The agreement, signed October 28, 1985, was dependent only on Buscetta's settling his affairs with Italian justice.

As he had been drawn in his ambition to Sindona, and in his delusions to Gelli and Ortolani, so Roberto Calvi, in his final desperation, had been drawn yet again to a man whose shadow was one of hidden power. Five months after Calvi retained him as a special consultant to the Ambrosiano group, Francesco Pazienza had been forced to leave SISMI, when it became known that General Giuseppe Santovito, his patron at the intelligence agency, was among those named, and thus ruined, by the P-2 list. Pazienza had promised to earn his extravagant $500,000 yearly retainer by helping to raise cash to cover the ruinous "loans" outstanding to the secret ghost-company network that had served as the funnel of gold for the baneful schemes of Calvi's P-2 mentors. After leaving SISMI, Pazienza, embracing Calvi with his shield arm, renewed his vows of saving him.

Pazienza's connections were impressive, ranging from U.S. Secretary of State Alexander Haig (under whom Pazienza's associate Michael Ledeen served) to Robert Armao, the Rockefeller family aide who also tended the fortunes of the deposed shah of Iran. One of Pazienza's less illustrious acquaintances was Flavio Carboni, a flamboyant, fifty-year-old Sardinian who ran a construction company called Prato Verde.

At the end of 1981, Pazienza and Calvi arranged for the Ambrosiano to loan Carboni's firm $3 million. A third of the money was passed back, *in nero,* to Calvi, who used it to try to bribe a judge involved in his appeal. Pazienza, for his part, received a $250,000 commission, with which he bought a yacht.

The Ambrosiano's deputy chairman, Roberto Rosone, had been with the bank as long as Calvi. In the stormy wake of Calvi's arrest and trial, Rosone had tried to have him overthrown. Rosone had failed, but he had not relented. He pressed Calvi, again and again, to explain the loans to the Vatican-tied ghost companies. But all Calvi did was chasten him for doubting the probity of the church.

On April 27, 1982, Rosone was walking near his home in the company of his bodyguard when several shots were fired into his legs. The bodyguard, drawing his .357 Magnum, killed the gunman where he stood. The dead attacker was identified as Danilo Abbruciati, a Roman hood who had been aligned with Domenico Balducci, a Sicilian Mafioso who had moved north to a position of power within the *malavita romana.* Balducci, murdered in October 1981, had been a companion of both Pazienza and Carboni.

Six weeks later, on June 10, Roberto Calvi vanished, eleven days before his appeal was due to be heard in court. Following his disappearance, the price of the Ambrosiano's stock plunged 13 percent on the Borsa, reducing the group's market value by $137 million.

"A particular question mark has long hung over the structure of Ambrosiano, and its extensive foreign shareholdings. Foreign-based concerns are also listed among the largest individual shareholders," *The Financial Times* of London stated on June 15, in a report concerning the "Calvi mystery." On that same day, Calvi, using a forged passport supplied through Flavio Carboni, arrived at Gatwick Airport from Austria and checked into Room 881 at the Chelsea Cloisters residential hotel.

Calvi called his wife, Clara, the next day. It was the last time she ever heard his voice.

"A crazy, marvelous thing is about to explode," he said. "It could solve everything."

On June 17, in a burnt-gold summer dusk, there was a silhouette in a fourth-floor office window of the Ambrosiano headquarters in Milan. It was Calvi's longtime secretary, fifty-five-year-old Graziella Teresa Corrocher. A moment later, she lay dead on the stones below. A note left behind said, "He should be twice-damned."

Less than twelve hours later, on the morning of June 18, Calvi was found hanging by the neck from a construction scaffold beneath Blackfriars Bridge, on the River Thames. In the pockets of his tide-drenched suit, along with Italian, Swiss, Austrian, British, and American currency totaling $15,000, there were four pieces of brick and concrete. A fifth piece of brick was stuck down the front of his trousers.

Calvi's luggage was found undisturbed in his room at the Chelsea Cloisters. But there was no trace of the black briefcase that Calvi always carried with him. That missing briefcase and the circumstances of Calvi's death gave rise to mystery without end. The bricks led many to think of the Masons. So did the name of the bridge he had been hanged from: P-2 members had been known to wear black robes and address one another as *"fratello"* ("brother"), a word very close to *"frate"* ("friar"). Blackfriars was also the name of a Masonic lodge in Newcastle-on-Tyne. And where was the vanished Gelli? No one knew, though he was rumored to be hiding in Buenos Aires, where he was close to the ruling military junta established by his fellow Mason and friend, Lieutenant General Videla. That military regime came to an end with the resignation of Leopoldo Galtieri, who recently had ordered the invasion of the British-held Falkland Islands. President Galtieri had stepped down on June 17, the date of Calvi's death. Even the last paint job Blackfriars Bridge had received seemed to contribute to the air of uncanny conspiracy. It was pale blue and white, Argentina's national colors.

"Calvi's death was certainly not suicide, as the British coroner suggested," Sindona said. "In the first place, Calvi was terrified of heights. He would never have climbed over a bridge onto high scaffolding, even if he could have done so with his pockets full of rocks. In the second place, why would he have gone to London to kill himself? He could have gotten drugs, whatever he wanted, right in Milan. Calvi was murdered, and those who killed him made it appear to be some sort of ritual Masonic execution.

"You will remember that, when Calvi was in jail, he said that he had given $30 million to Bettino Craxi, the head of the Partito Socialista. He believed—he had told me this—that Craxi was 'the rising star' who would command Italy's political future. As it turned out, he was right: Craxi came into power a year later as Italy's first socialist prime minister. Calvi's great error was to reveal his bribes to the socialists.

"I was interested to see that, after he retracted his statements, *Avanti!*, the official newspaper of the PSI, came out in defense of him. Calvi, by showing that his silence was precarious, had rendered himself a risk to the ascending powers.

"After his provisional release from jail, Calvi turned to mercenaries, who demanded unimaginable payments in exchange for fruitless and often harmful services. He shared their demented notions of replenishing the lost Ambrosiano money through extortion. At the same time, he clung to the hope of finding a legitimate purchaser for the Ambrosiano stock he controlled. That was the hope that sent him to London, the financial center of the world. But he carried with him also, in the black case he never laid aside, his weapon of last resort—the documentation of his black-money payments to Craxi and the others. What he did not see was that it was the warrant of his own death.

"Those documents had to be destroyed, and Calvi with

245

them. The fate of an immense political force—and of certain interests in South America, as well—was perceived to be resting in his none-too-steady hand.

"In Italy, you see, corruption is a high-stakes game. In America, there are judges and politicians one can buy for a million dollars. In Italy, that is only pocket money as far as corruption is concerned. Calvi ended up paying $30 million—and more, I'm sure—for his own death."

On Easter Sunday 1986, Calvi's missing briefcase turned up, sold to a Milanese politician by two mysterious and unnamed northern Italians. All documents of importance had obviously long since been removed from it.

The month after Calvi's death, the Banca d'Italia commissioners who were appointed to care for the fallen Ambrosiano met with Archbishop Paul Marcinkus and other officials of the IOR. They confronted them with the Vatican comfort letters acknowledging control of Manic Holding, Bellatrix, Erin, Laramie, World Wide Trading, and other ghost companies through which an estimated $1.4 billion had vanished from the Ambrosiano group in the form of unsecured loans. The IOR officials responded by producing Calvi's secret counterletter absolving the IOR. Archbishop Marcinkus concluded by telling the commissioners that the Banca d'Italia had no power within the state of the Vatican.

"The government," declared Treasury Minister Beniamino Andreatta, "is waiting for a clear assumption of responsibility by the IOR." While waiting, the government indicted Luigi Mennini and twenty-three others besides Sindona on further charges relating to the fall of Banca Privata. The indictments were filed on July 22, the day Carlo Bordoni was allowed to vanish from Italy, never to be heard from again.

Italy increased its pressure on the IOR in the months that followed. Archbishop Marcinkus, declared to be under formal investigation as a result of Banco Ambrosiano's collapse, took sanctuary within the walls of the Vatican. In the summer of

1983, desperate to drive down the rising scandal at its gates, the Vatican capitulated. It would pay some $250 million toward the settlement of the ghost companies' debts. Pope John Paul II, in anticipation of this eventuality, already had moved to raise Vatican revenue by hurriedly proclaiming 1983 to be an "extraordinary Holy Year" in celebration of—his face was straight—the 1,950th anniversary of Redemption by Jesus.

"It was a bad thing," Sindona said. "Andreatta, the treasury minister, had told the Ambrosiano's foreign creditors that neither the Banca d'Italia nor the Nuovo Banco Ambrosiano would be responsible for the debts produced by the ghost-company loans, as they had been transacted outside Italy, through Ambrosiano Holding of Luxembourg. The international banking community—with the odd exception of the Federal Reserve—criticized the Italian government for taking this stance instead of respecting the gentlemen's agreement of Berne, which set forth that central banks would not allow the collapse of foreign entities owned by national banking institutions.

"Andreatta knew that the Vatican comfort letters were insufficient to establish liability on the part of the IOR. But Andreatta also knew that the Vatican fears nothing so much as scandal. The media did his work for him. The Vatican's payment of $250 million to the Nuovo Banco Ambrosiano was considered, *urbi et orbi*, to be due punishment. But a more courageous and competent defense would have done the IOR —and the church—far less damage in the long run, in terms of both money and prestige.

"You see, the IOR has always had far less capital than most people think. The Vatican's fabled gold reserves are just that —a fable. The IOR's most valuable asset was its prestige. At any given time, its capital has never been more than $200 million, at most. So, in conceding to pay $250 million, the IOR was driven to seek money on the market.

"Calvi—no one knows this, but it is true—paid the Vatican, through Marcinkus, $20 million for those two letters of

247

comfort. He knew that Marcinkus would be lured by that $20 million, which he could then offer up to the pope as proof of his money-making abilities. But the fact that Calvi was even willing, let alone eager, to pay $20 million for those letters, which he knew to be meaningless, offers some indication of the worth of the Vatican's prestige. Now, to a certain degree, that prestige has been lost. And the archbishop who helped lose it lost also his chance to win the purple cloth that had been the object of his every ambition.

"In 1983, Marcinkus sent me a message through a prison chaplain. He perhaps did not wish to be caught corresponding directly with me. 'Tell him personally,' he wrote, 'I wish him peace.'"

On September 12, 1982, Licio Gelli, who had dyed his silver hair brown and grown a moustache, arrived in Madrid from Buenos Aires, then took a flight to Geneva. He checked into the Noga Hilton International, at 19 Quai du Mont-Blanc. On the next afternoon, he walked across the way to the Union de Banques Suisses, accompanied by a lawyer and P-2 member named Augusto Sinagra. Gelli told an officer of the bank that he wanted to transfer some $50 million that he had deposited in a numbered account at the bank some time ago. The officer asked the two men to sit, then excused himself. Some moments later, two policemen entered and asked Gelli for identification. He showed them an Argentine passport with a false name. They took him away. He had learned the hard way what Sindona had tried to tell him: There was no such thing as an anonymous numbered account.

Gelli was incarcerated in the five-year-old Champ Dollon prison outside Geneva. Almost a year passed before a hearing was scheduled to rule on his extradition to Italy. On August 10, 1983, nine days before that hearing was to take place, Gelli escaped with the help of a prison official. He was not seen again; but, in May 1984, he sent a memorandum to the parliamentary commission of inquiry into P-2. In it, he said that the infamous P-2 list contained the names not only of members, but also of "sympathizers and my friends."

He had once cultivated an aura of mystery and unstated power. In the years after his disappearance, that self-kindled aura grew into a fantastic darkness no man could crave. Considered one of the world's most wanted men, he was accused of everything, from terrorist bombings to the murder of Princess Grace of Monaco. Some, less prone to romance, presumed that Gelli alone knew the truth about the missing Ambrosiano millions, that he knew how much of the $1.4 billion had been lost in South America, how much in the takeover of Ambrosiano stock, and that he knew how much remained, and where.

"But if that were true," Sindona said, "why would he have so endangered himself by trying to withdraw $50 million from a bank? No, I think there is a treasure yet out there, among the ghosts."

I asked him if he had any idea where Gelli was these days.

"I don't know," he said. Then he grinned. "But you must bear in mind that this is one thing, if I did know, I would not tell."

"How smart a man is he?"

"Less smart than people think." He grinned again. It was a different grin.

XII.
The Exterminator's Secret

ON ONE OF MY LAST VISITS TO VOGHERA—it was the dead of August—I was told that Oreste Dominioni, the attorney who was defending Sindona in his trial for the murder of Giorgio Ambrosoli, had shown up unexpectedly to meet with him. One of the young guards invited me to wait in the guardhouse, out of the noontide sun.

Inside the guardhouse, another young guard sat at a desk. Several of his co-workers stood gathered around him, watching over his hunched shoulders. He pushed aside a couple of the Mini Uzi automatics that lay near his elbow. Slowly, he taped together two large sheets of blank paper; then he leaned back. When he leaned forward again, the guards at his shoulders livened. He began to draw something. His observers offered encouragement and suggestions, pointing here and there upon the surface of his work. Then, with a flourish, he was done. There was laughter and a smattering of applause. Someone commented that it was the biggest and ugliest one he had ever drawn. The vein was especially good. The work was then folded, sealed, and addressed. There was another suggestion, more laughter. The words "IMPORTANTE-MAFIA" were added. A passing guard—new to the job—was summoned and directed to deliver the oversized letter to the indicated woman within the prison walls. The guard I was with looked at his watch, then to me. *"Vuol bere?"* he asked—did I care for a drink? He suggested that we take a stroll *"al bar."* I looked around at the stretches of gravel and parched dirt that surrounded the prison, which was in the middle of nowhere; but I rose and walked with him—into, rather than away from, the prison. Soon, beyond another guardpost, I began to hear music. Then, surely enough, in the heart of the prison, we came to a bar. I had coffee; he had Crodino. Others were drinking Scotch, and wine. There were Uzis scattered about, and newspapers opened to the sports section. The barmaid wasn't bad, and the prices were cheaper than anywhere on the outside. I remembered what Sindona had said the previous spring: The tortellini was good in this place.

By this time, he had been imprisoned for more than five years. The best of all possible prisons, he told me, would be a federal prison in America staffed by Italian guards.

"Here, in the winter, you freeze," he said, "but here, at least, there is respect. In American prisons, everyone is treated like an animal.

"First, after the Franklin trial, they sent me to Springfield. I had problems because everyone believed I still had money. Many men threatened to kill me if I did not give them money. 'Go ahead,' I told them. 'I don't give a damn.' There was one gang that was especially bad. Always shoving, always threatening. Then, one day, I was approached by a black man with many tattoos. He was the second in command of the black Mafia in Kansas City. He wanted advice about his lawyer. I was able to show him where the lawyer was screwing him. It turned out that his lawyer was working as much for the federal prosecutor as for him. He was very grateful, and he told me I would not have any more problems at Springfield. Overnight, the men who had been tormenting me turned servile."

In August 1982, he was transferred from Springfield to the Federal Correctional Institution in Otisville, New York. Federal prisons are classified by the government according to a numerical-ranking system. Minimum-security prisons are Number 1's; penitentiaries are Number 5's; and the institution in Marion, Ohio, is Number 6. ("Marion," a federal warden told me, "is the end of the line. For a guy to get there, he has to be worse than bad.") The prison at Otisville, in Orange County, is a Number 4. Sindona was assigned there to the prison library. He read through every volume of the Macmillan *Encyclopedia of Philosophy,* pausing at the essay on Nietzsche in volume 5—"Socrates before his judges, Socrates in prison, Socrates meeting death is a paragon of power"— remembering his arguments with Cardinal Montini in that tapestried chamber half a lifetime ago. He continued to subscribe to *The Wall Street Journal.* He gave lessons in business and Italian to his fellow inmates.

"One black guy who took my basic business course was hired by American Express when he got out," Sindona said proudly. "He gave me a subscription to *The Economist* when he got his first paycheck." But his students were few. "Baseball, baseball, that's all they were interested in at that place."

In Otisville, Sindona had no trouble from prisoners, as he had in the beginning at Springfield. But there was a guard, he said, who attempted to shake him down.

"He was a captain who instructed one of the female workers to ingratiate herself with me. She would come to me and tell me how hard it was for her to get by. She would ask for a piece of candy, and tell me she could not afford her own. The oldest trick in the book. The trouble was, she was one of the ugliest women I had ever seen. All the while, the captain would drop hints to me about the fortune he imagined me to have hidden away somewhere. Finally, I got sick of his games. I confronted him in the administrative office, in front of seven or so other officers. 'You know,' I told him, 'I am not stupid. I am an international lawyer. You can't do certain things. There are laws.' 'Shut up!' he shouted. 'Here, I am the law.' Then he sent me to isolation.

"And today that man who proclaimed himself to be the law has an even bigger job."

The alleged Mafiosi at Otisville, as at all other federal prisons, were distinguished by identification numbers that bore the prefix "O.C.," for "Organized Crime." Though Sindona's number had no prefix, the O.C. inmates sought his company.

"They wanted me to study their case histories and counsel them. One day, after going through a pile of their legal documents, I told them, 'They should change the "O.C." to "D.C."' 'Perchè?' 'Dis organized Crime,' I said. A few of them got upset, but most of them laughed.

"They showed *The Godfather* while I was there. These men loved it. 'This stupid movie is why you got your time,' I told them. A few of them saw the light. 'Maybe you're right,' one of the big shots said."

Tony Scotto, the Brooklyn boss of the International Longshoremen's Association, was at Otisville finishing a five-year sentence for labor racketeering. One of Scotto's frequent visitors was Anthony G. Di Falco.

"I crossed his path one day," Sindona said, "and he blanched. 'You are a traitor to your father and to me,' I told him."

As his first Christmas at Otisville approached, Sindona granted an interview to *The New York Times*. The photograph of him the *Times* printed on its front page a few days later was a good one, but it was from before the fall. The Sindona who watched the snow come down in the woods and dairy farms surrounding Otisville had the look of a revenant. "When you are on top, everybody comes to you and wants to help you," he told the interviewer. "When you are down, everybody abandons you." He mentioned no one in particular, but was thinking of some letters he had written.

Back in September 1981, he had sent a long letter to President Reagan asking that his case be reconsidered. The letter had been delivered to the White House by David Kennedy, the former ambassador and secretary of the treasury. Three months later, Sindona received a reply from Fred F. Fielding, the president's counsel. "Thank you very much for your petition," Fielding said. "I have taken the liberty of forwarding your material to Mr. David Stephenson, Acting Pardon Attorney." In November of the next year, he sent a four-page letter to the Federal Plaza office of Richard Nixon. He reminded the former president of "the meetings we had in the mid-1960's" and of "my generous offer" during the 1972 campaign. "I now turn to you for assistance," Sindona wrote. There was no reply at all. Sindona then asked Randolph Guthrie, Nixon's former partner, to speak to him. Nixon told Guthrie that he was afraid to help Sindona, as it might further harm his image.

"That same November, Mario Cuomo was elected governor of New York. I saw him on television talking about justice. I wrote him a note, which I had Joseph Macaluso deliver to him. In it, I reminded Cuomo of the great esteem he had expressed for me. He told Macaluso that, in his position, he could not be concerned about me."

In midsummer of 1984, Sindona was visited at Otisville by James D. Harmon, Jr., the executive director of the President's Commission on Organized Crime. Accompanying Harmon was Assistant U.S. Attorney Andrew Maloney. The two men were friends and fellow West Point graduates. After consulting with Raymond Dearie, the U.S. attorney in Brooklyn, Maloney had told Harmon that there was no evidence connecting Sindona to organized crime. At the same time, he had also told Harmon that Sindona would be willing to explain the procedures of money laundering, which continued to elude the government. At the end of that meeting at Otisville, Harmon told Sindona that he wanted him to come to Washington.

"I was brought down during the last week of August," Sindona remembered. "They put me in a local jail, where one of the prisoners threatened to cut off my finger to get at my wedding ring. When Harmon showed up, he asked me to forgive him, saying that he he had only been in Washington a brief time and didn't yet know the city's prison system.

"In October of the previous year, I had read an article called 'Money Laundering' in *New York* magazine. It was one of the most foolish things I had ever seen. It had nothing to do with money laundering. It was all about little men running around Florida with shoeboxes of cash. I wrote a letter to the author, Nick Pileggi, and explained to him that he, like almost everyone else, confused the hiding of money with the laundering of money. In fact, he had even dealt with the simple hiding of money in an incomplete and naïve way.

"In Washington, I saw that the Drug Enforcement Agency, the FBI, and the President's Commission all had copies of that article lying around in their offices. I was stunned. It was then that Harmon admitted to me that he knew close to nothing about the international monetary system. It was insane.

"I explained to them, in detail, how large sums of money are actually laundered. I told them the things that very few men know. And they sat, and they listened, and they did not comprehend a thing.

"A few months later, after I was extradited to Italy, I managed to obtain a copy of the commission's *Interim Report to the President*. It was a creation of profoundest, irredeemable stupidity. I had shown them that, in the true laundering of money, taxes had to be paid on that money. Yet still—perhaps unwilling to accept that the IRS is a conduit for dirty money—the commission spoke of the tax-revenue losses caused by money laundering. I had explained to them that, in true laundering, the dirty cash must be transformed during the process into quasi-money through a series of sophisticated financial transactions. Yet the report gave as an example of money laundering—this is true—a drug dealer who exchanges small-denomination bills for large-denomination bills. I realized then that the government would never succeed in its lofty quest. I had wasted my breath before the commission, as surely as the commission was wasting the millions of dollars in taxes which it worried might be lost through crimes it did not understand."

On January 10, 1985, after reading the report, Sindona sent a letter from Voghera to James Harmon in Washington, professing pity for him as well as scorn. At the same time, he sent a letter to President Reagan's White House counsel, saying that "the commission, in continuing the path taken thus far, will not reach the aims established and will be nothing more than a useless and costly duplicate of other, already existing offices."

But, by now, he had other things to think about. His trials at the Palace of Justice had begun; and they were taking him in the back way, where there was no Latin in the rock.

After ten years, they had him back. He was tried first for the crime of *bancarotta fraudolenta*, fraudulent bankruptcy. The oldest Roman code of law, the Twelve Tables, had looked harshly upon this crime, decreeing that bankrupt debtors be taken "across the Tiber" and killed. "On the third market day, creditors shall cut pieces. Should they have cut more or less than their due, it shall be with impunity." Though the letter of Roman law had changed, its spirit retained something of the old vigor. Three weeks before the start of the trial, the cover of Italy's biggest-selling magazine, *Panorama*, hailed Sindona's return with the striking photograph of a lifeless hand painted the colors of Italy. The red ran from a gash in the white wrist. To the left of this *mano morto*, in large yellow letters beneath Sindona's name, were the words *"Un assassino e i suoi amici"* —"An assassin and his friends."

The trial began on Monday, December 3. He was brought to the Palace of Justice at ten o'clock that morning in a convoy of seven police vans. He smiled for the photographers as he was led into the courtroom and put into a twenty-foot-high cage with brown metal bars. At the outset, he made a motion that this trial and the trial for Ambrosoli's murder be combined, that it all be gotten over with in one fell swoop. The motion was denied, and the trial was adjourned until December 12. When that day came, Sindona declined to attend. He stayed in Voghera and let his trial proceed without him. Toward the end of January, the press reported that the unseen Sindona was fasting from mortal fear. There were allusions to the dreaded *"caffè tipo Ucciardone,"* the poison cup of jailhouse coffee that was traditionally symbolic of the Mafia's ability to kill through stone walls and locked cells. In truth, he was eating well and working every day. He returned to the trial in February, bringing with him "The Hilton Report" and other documents, among them secret internal papers from the Banco di Roma.

"I demonstrated, beyond any possible doubt," he claimed, "that the sums missing from my Italian banks—on which the prosecution centered—had ended up in the numbered accounts of Carlo Bordoni and his wife and friends in Switzerland, and that more than $60 million belonging to me had been robbed from the Banco di Roma on the orders of Giuseppe Petrilli, the former chairman of IRI.

"The president of the tribunal, Mario Chiarolla, who had been given orders to condemn me, was interested only in how I had obtained these documents. He would not take them in his hand. At that point, I announced that it was obvious that the outcome of my trial had been predetermined and I, just as obviously, foredoomed."

On the ides of March, he was sentenced to twelve years in prison.

The trial for the murder of Giorgio Ambrosoli began ten weeks later, on June 4, 1985. It was to be what is known as a *processo indiziario,* a trial based on circumstantial evidence. Contrary to the American legal system, Italian law considers hearsay to be admissible evidence in court. Enough of it, pieced together, constitutes *indizio,* or indirect proof of guilt or innocence. It was the prosecutor Guido Viola's intent to establish, through *indizio,* that Sindona was the *mandante* of Ambrosoli's murder. If Viola could demonstrate that Sindona had a criminal mentality and criminal connections, he would be able to postulate that Sindona could have had Ambrosoli killed. After that, it would be easy to convict him with the right circumstantial evidence, which the American government had promised to deliver.

Sharing the courtroom cage with Sindona this time was Robert Venetucci, a Long Island man whom Sindona had come to know after his fall. Venetucci, who had a previous conviction, on drug charges, was a few years younger than Sindona. Their relationship, Venetucci said, was limited to a loan to two small businesses, a real estate firm and Mini Mart Film on Staten Island. Venetucci had been extradited to Italy on charges of aggravated extortion: His voice had been identified on one of the taped telephone threats to Enrico Cuccia.

"After he was extradited," Venetucci's lawyer, Paul Goldberger, said, "we got hold of a voiceprint expert who was willing to testify for us. Then, all of a sudden, once Venetucci was over there, they slapped him with a murder rap, charging him with being the middleman between Sindona and Arico, the killer. To do this, the Italian authorities had to move for what's called a waiver of the rule of speciality. This means that they needed permission from our government to try him on charges other than those he'd been extradited for. It was obvious that this had been their scheme all along. On September 1, 1985, I filed a complaint with the U.S. State Department, charging that the waiver was requested on the basis of preexisting plans. October came and went, November came and went, December came and went. Here it is February 1986, the trial is almost over, and the State Department still hasn't gotten back to me."

Venetucci, all the while, before and after the change of charges, remained silent. He sat in the cage, and he watched. Since he did not understand Italian very well, every once in a while he would ask Sindona what was going on.

In his attempt to establish Sindona's guilt by association, Guido Viola summoned the Spatola brothers to testify. "I have nothing to say," the younger one, Vincenzo, declared. "I know only my brother." Rosario was not so taciturn that June day.

"I have served the state. I have won contracts for public works." He glowered at the bearded communist prosecutor. "I came from nothing. I sweated seven shirts."

Viola asked him how Sindona had come to stay at Torretta during his disappearance.

"Simple courtesy," Spatola answered. "He had been hospitable to me at the Hotel Pierre, and I reciprocated."

Hadn't Spatola been aware that there was a warrant out for Sindona's arrest, that he was a fugitive from justice?

"It wasn't written on his forehead."

Viola asked him about the alleged threats that had been made to Enrico Cuccia.

"Who is Cuccia?" He brought his fingers together and shook his hand, *chiedere*.

The press relished the Spatolas' appearance at the Palace of Justice. The *Corriere della Sera* spoke of the courtroom being pervaded by a *"forte odore di mafia."* *La Stampa* said that Rosario's presence was like something out of *Il Giorno della Civetta,* the classic Mafia novel by Leonardo Sciasca. The *indizio* Viola sought seemed to be gaining in the summer wind.

After the Spatolas left the courtroom, the trial was adjourned until September 18. It was the *pausa estiva,* the summer break, when justice rested.

That same June, in Rome, a group of Bulgarian officials were being tried. The star witness was Mehmet Ali Agca, the Turk who had already been convicted of shooting Pope John Paul II. On June 19, to quiet the courtroom, the judge had shouted, *"Pazienza!"*—"Patience!"

"Yes!" Agca's eyes widened. "Francesco Pazienza! That's the one who promised me freedom if I would say the Bulgarians were behind me."

By then, Pazienza had been in the Metropolitan Correctional Center for more than three months. On March 5, the day after his arrest, Prime Minister Bettino Craxi (who, in earlier days, had been a visitor to Pazienza's home in Rome, according to Pazienza's former girlfriend Marina De Laurentiis, the niece of Sindona's friend Dino) met in Washington with President Reagan. After that meeting, it was announced that Prime Minister Craxi would now be a public supporter of the president's Star Wars space-defense program, for which he had in the past expressed disapproval. As Italy pressed for Pazienza's extradition, neither the White House nor the Department of Justice would comment on his case in any way. A federal judge in New York, however, was told by Assistant U.S. Attorney David W. Denton, that there was "a significant national interest in having Mr. Pazienza held."

Though they had traveled many of the same roads, Pazienza and Sindona had never met. Now Pazienza sent a message to him, expressing a desire that they might someday meet. The meeting never came about.

The first breeze of September came through the barred window in Voghera. Sindona was laughing, talking about the differences between American and Italian jurisprudence.

"Like all legal systems, they're based on the same principle: If they want you, they get you. That is the real *lex mundi.*

"Lawyers in Italy are much less diligent than in America, but they are also less crooked. When is the last time anyone heard of a lawyer being disbarred by the American Bar Association? But it is not that way in Italy. Many American lawyers would not be tolerated by the Associazione di Avvocati. But, then again"—he smiled—"if the verdict predates the trial, what does the lawyer matter?

"The lawyers I have now, Costello in New York and Dominioni in Milan, are fine men and fine lawyers both. They are working practically for free, and they are working hard. They tell me that there is no way I can be convicted for Ambrosoli's murder. But I think I understand the *lex mundi* better than they."

It was getting late; the Lombardy light was falling. A guard knocked, then turned a key in the bolted door. Our time was up.

* * *

Bob Costello, U. S. Attorney Rudolph W. Giuliani, and Billy Martin, in a New York Yankees uniform, stood grinning in a framed picture atop a wooden cabinet in Costello's midtown Manhattan office.

"A few summers ago," he said.

He and Giuliani had worked together at the U.S. Attorney's Office in the 1970s. In June 1981, after six years there, Costello had left to join the firm of Lombard & Phelan. Today, the sign on the door said Phelan & Costello. He had just turned thirty-four when he began representing Sindona, in January 1982. He had been one of three criminal attorneys recommended to Sindona by Mudge, Rose, Guthrie & Alexander.

Rudy Giuliani's smiling face and the knowledge that Costello was with the U.S. Attorney's Office at the time of Sindona's prosecution brought to mind a question. Did the government actually believe that Sindona was a Mafioso, or was it just a comfortable pretense?

"Well," Costello said, "it depends on who you define the government to be. Do I think that the U.S. Attorney's Office for the Southern District of New York believes he's a part of the Mafia? No, I don't think so. At the same time, I can tell you that representing him has not made me one of the most popular guys at the dinner gatherings of the U.S. Attorneys Association."

Later, a few blocks away, we ate and drank and talked about the enigma that sat in a cell in a place neither of us had ever heard of a year ago.

"I've been surprised before in my life," Costello said, "but I would be astounded if he really had anything to do with this murder. It's not him.

"If you stop to consider, it would have been very stupid of him to be involved, even if he were of such a nature. Besides, he knew that Ambrosoli, at the time of his murder, had already completed his reports.

"I honestly don't know what happened. Maybe no one alive today does. I do know that there are people out on the street who view Michele Sindona as one of the most famous and most powerful Sicilians of all time; people who think that they would be greatly rewarded if they were to perform some favor for him, even without his request or knowledge. This is not logical thinking, but it is a type of thinking that surely exists out there, especially among certain people.

"Another intriguing aspect of this whole thing—this occurred to me after talking to Bill Gabler, the guy who claims Luigi Ronsisvalle told him he'd been hired to kill Sindona—is that all of Sindona's accusers are people from the Witness Protection Program. This is a murder that took place in Milan, but the solution of it seems to be coiled in some dark corner of the third floor of the MCC."

Sindona's attorney John J. Kirby, Jr., had been in Milan on the day of Ambrosoli's death. In October 1985, at Costello's request, he supplied an affidavit recalling that day.

"In an effort to prepare Mr. Sindona's defense," Kirby said in that affidavit, "we had requested the issuance of Letters Rogatory to Dr. Ambrosoli and others. Said Letters having been issued by the United States Court, I was in attendance at their execution in front of Judge Dr. Giovanni Galati in the Tribunal in Milan, Italy, commencing July 9, 1979. Others in attendance included: Mr. Steven Stein of the Proskauer law firm, Mr. Walter Mack of the U.S. Attorney's Office of the Southern District of New York, and a special master representing the United States judge.

"With the permission of Judge Galati, counsel for Mr. Sindona were allowed to put questions to Dr. Ambrosoli supplementing and clarifying the written Rogatories; such questions were put to Dr. Ambrosoli throughout the proceedings, including the 11th of July. The proceedings were adjourned that afternoon to be commenced again the following day.

"That evening I conferred by telephone with Mr. Sindona, reporting to him on the progress of the proceedings, and received suggestions from him with respect to additional questions to be put to Dr. Ambrosoli on the following day. There

263

were a number of questions still pending, including the production of documents which, while not precisely called for by
the Letters Rogatory, were within the substance of the request. It was also the custom of Judge Galati, after hearing
discussion on the need for additional questions for clarification,
to allow such questions to be put to the witness. Therefore, I
anticipated being able to put further questions to Dr. Ambrosoli before the completion of the Rogatory to him and so
advised by Mr. Sindona.

"The following morning, I was advised that Dr. Ambrosoli
had been murdered on the night of July 11. Together with the
other attorneys, I appeared before Judge Galati and agreed
that the record of the testimony of Dr. Ambrosoli rendered on
July 9, 10, and 11, pursuant to Letters Rogatory of the American
Judicial Authority, were accurate. It was my opinion then as it
is now that the inability of Dr. Ambrosoli to sign the record of
his interrogation would have no effect on the question of the
admissibility of that interrogation in the United States proceedings.

"The primary purpose of addressing Letters Rogatory to
Dr. Ambrosoli was to secure access to the entire files of Banca
Privata Italiana. It was anticipated that only with such access
could the defense of Mr. Sindona be prepared properly in the
United States proceedings. Only a portion of the BPI file was
made available in connection with the Rogatory to Dr. Ambrosoli."

William Joseph Arico, the man who shot Giorgio Ambrosoli, had met a man named Henry Hill in 1974, at the federal penitentiary in Lewisburg, Pennsylvania. Arico, then
thirty-seven years old, was serving time for manslaughter and
bank robbery. Hill, who was seven years younger than Arico,
had been sent to Lewisburg for selling dope. The two men got
along. Arico introduced Hill to another Lewisburg inmate,
Robert Venetucci, a friend of his from Long Island who, like
Hill, had been convicted on drug charges. In 1978, on the

outside, the three of them became neighbors on Long Island. Arico worked with Hill, delivering drugs and committing armed robberies in the New York area. Venetucci, after his release, was introduced to Sindona in a Manhattan office by an important Italian manufacturer of mopeds.

On December 8, 1979, five months after he killed Ambrosoli, Billy Arico robbed a jewelry store in Brooklyn, got caught, and was sent to the penitentiary on Riker's Island in New York. On May 22, 1980, Henry Hill, once again under federal indictment, decided to strike a bargain with the government and join the Witness Protection Program.

It was Henry Hill who told the government that Billy Arico had murdered Giorgio Ambrosoli. According to Hill's story, Arico had told him, in the autumn of 1978, that he needed some weapons. Hill later sold him five handguns and an Ingram M-11 submachine gun equipped with a silencer. Arico then told Hill—or so Hill claimed—that he had been hired to do a job for Michele Sindona, whom he had met through Robert Venetucci. The following summer, after the killing, Arico had visited Hill at his home in Rockville Centre, Long Island. "This is the guy I whacked out over there," he said, showing him an Italian clipping about the Ambrosoli murder.

It was Hill's testimony upon which the Italian authorities based their July 1981 indictment of Sindona. On June 28, 1980, five weeks after Henry Hill joined the Witness Protection Program, Billy Arico escaped from the Riker's Island penitentiary, swimming across the East River to Hunts Point in the Bronx. On June 16, 1982, he was arrested by the FBI at his stepson's home near Philadelphia. A month later, on July 16, he was interrogated at the Metropolitan Correctional Center by the FBI agent Michael Mott and the assistant U.S. attorney Charles Rose.

"The first thing we asked Arico was whether he killed Giorgio Ambrosoli," Charles Rose later recounted. "He asked his lawyer if it was all right to respond. The lawyer told him to go ahead, and he said, 'Yes.' We then asked him if he had been following the orders of Michele Sindona. He looked to his lawyer again, and then he said, 'Yes.'"

According to Rose, Arico stated that he had been introduced to Sindona by Robert Venetucci in the dining room of the Conca d'Oro Motel on Staten Island. Robert Venetucci, later questioned, said that, yes, he knew Arico and, yes, he had known Sindona, but he had never introduced them, and had known nothing about the murder of Giorgio Ambrosoli.

"So," Costello was saying, "there they were on the third floor of the MCC: Carlo Bordoni, Luigi Ronsisvalle, and then Henry Hill. And the one thing we know for a fact is that Carlo Bordoni was Sindona's enemy.

"I have wondered, and I have not been able to understand, why William Arico would, for no apparent reason, admit to a murder to a fellow like Henry Hill, who has been described as a well-known liar who would say anything to get out of trouble. And I have wondered why Carlo Bordoni, who has so conveniently disappeared, has been the object of so little speculation in this case."

Six months after Arico was questioned by Mott and Rose, Costello talked with Louis Freeman, the Federal Defenders Service Unit attorney who had been assigned by the court to represent Arico. In January 1985, Costello prepared an affidavit concerning that discussion and the events that followed:

"On February 10, 1983, I spoke to Mr. Freeman, who informed me that William Arico was not cooperating with the United States Attorney's Office; that Arico had not accused Michele Sindona of any complicity in the death of Giorgio Ambrosoli but that Arico had received pressure from the prosecutors to make accusations against Michele Sindona. Mr. Freeman told me that Mr. Arico was informed that unless he agreed to cooperate and to make accusations against Mr. Sindona, he would be extradited to Italy. Mr. Freeman told me that despite that pressure, Mr. Arico had not made any such accusations against Mr. Sindona, and that he would communicate my request to Mr. Arico that I be permitted to interview him.

"Sometime during the period between February 1983 and July 1983, Louis Freeman left the Federal Defenders Office and entered the private practice of law with the newly created firm of Freeman, Nooter and Ginsberg. Mr. Freeman was also representing Mr. Arico's stepson, Charles Arico, in connection with the extradition request from Italy. Apparently, William Arico desired to have Mr. Freeman remain as his attorney, and at that point in time he began requesting that Michele Sindona or the Sindona family pay for the legal fees for both Charles and William Arico. Mr. Sindona declined despite threats by William Arico to do something to Mr. Sindona or a member of Mr. Sindona's family. At that time, I advised Louis Freeman about these discussions and Mr. Freeman immediately instructed William Arico to stop making any such requests or threats.

"In late June 1983, Mr. Freeman informed me that Mr. Arico was willing to meet with me to discuss the Ambrosoli matter. On July 1, 1983, I met with William Arico in the presence of his attorney, Louis Freeman, at the Metropolitan Correctional Center. I interviewed Mr. Arico concerning his knowledge and familiarity with Michele Sindona and Nino Sindona for approximately one hour in the attorney conference room in the presence of Louis Freeman. During the course of that interview, William Arico stated unequivocally that he never did anything with respect to Giorgio Ambrosoli for Michele Sindona. I asked him if he was familiar with Henry Hill's statements to the effect that Arico had made these admissions to Henry Hill. Mr. Arico stated that Hill's statements were outright lies. Arico stated that he had never met Michele Sindona but that he had, on one occasion, met Nino Sindona at a social function but was introduced to Nino under a different name. Arico stated that he had no other contact with Nino

267

Sindona or anyone else in the Sindona family. During that interview, Arico again discussed the fact that the authorities were putting considerable pressure on him concerning his stepson, Charles Arico, who was also arrested and housed at the same jail. William Arico again suggested that Michele Sindona should pay his legal fees. I again questioned Arico as to whether or not Michele Sindona had anything to do with the Ambrosoli murder and Arico stated that Michele Sindona did not."

At the end of 1983, Sindona was transferred from Otisville to the Metropolitan Correctional Center, to await what was thought to be the imminent ratification of the new treaty under which he was to be extradited. The government placed Sindona in Nine-South, the unit where Arico was.

While imprisoned at the MCC during the Franklin trial a few years before, Sindona had met a young man named Michael O'Rourke, an IRA partisan who had been captured in New York after escaping from Green Street Courthouse in Dublin, where he had been convicted for possessing explosives. O'Rourke was still there, and it was he who introduced Sindona to Arico.

"I hear you are an exterminator," Sindona said to him, grinning coolly.

"Yeah," Arico said. "Cockroaches, rats. I do all right."

At about twenty minutes after eight on the Sunday night of February 19, 1984, Billy Arico and another prisoner, Miguel Sepulveda, a thirty-nine-year-old South American who was serving twenty-seven years on a narcotics conviction, finished cutting through the cell window they had been working on. They climbed out onto a roof. The South American was very fat, and it took awhile. On the roof, they were met by guards with rifles drawn. Arico and his companion moved suddenly to the roof's edge; there was another roof below. They either fell or jumped—the guards could not tell. In any case, it was the end of William Arico. The fat dope dealer landed on top of him, crushing him to death.

Michael O'Rourke, the IRA terrorist who introduced Arico to Sindona, was extradited to Ireland in June 1984. A year and a half later, Costello was able to locate him through the Brehon Society, the organization of New York lawyers that provides legal assistance to the IRA. In December 1985, at Arbour Hill Prison in Dublin, O'Rourke swore an affidavit:

"From on or about 29th September 1979 until on or about 19th June 1984, a period of about four years and eight months, I was detained in the United States of America and during the said period I was held at the Metropolitan Correctional Center (hereinafter referred to as 'the MCC') in New York City, where I was at all material times incarcerated in a high-security unit known as Nine-South.

"I say and believe that during the said period I came to know one Michele Sindona, first during the period of his trial in connection with the Franklin National Bank and later upon his return to the MCC for the hearings connected with his proposed extradition to Italy.

"Before Michele Sindona's return to the MCC for the aforementioned extradition proceedings, I this Deponent became friendly with one William 'Bill' Arico, who informed me of his escape from a New York Prison known as Riker's Island Prison by swimming from the island on which the said Prison is located. The said William Arico also informed me that he was once detained by the U.S. Immigration authorities on his return to Italy. In the course of various conversations with me, the said William Arico mentioned an individual named Henry Hill who he said was a Government Informer in the Federal Protection Organization. In the course of the said conversations, the said William Arico informed me of some of his attempts to escape from the MCC, including the attempt which subsequently resulted in his death.

"I say and believe that I was in the company of the said William Arico on the evening when Michele Sindona arrived back to face his extradition hearing, on which occasion I walked over and greeted the said Michele Sindona. I this Deponent informed the said William Arico that this was Michele Sindona, 'The Banker.' I this Deponent have no doubt that until that moment the said William Arico had never seen or met Michele Sindona.

"Later the said Michele Sindona came over to me and William Arico and asked me to turn the heating valve on in his cell. William Arico accompanied me to the cell being occupied by the said Michele Sindona, and again I this Deponent perceived no indication that these two persons actually knew each other.

"Sometime subsequently, the said William Arico informed me that he had found out that Michele Sindona 'had plenty of money.' He also informed me that he was putting pressure on the said Michele Sindona to have him come up with money to pay lawyers opposing his stepson's extradition to Italy, and that he the said William Arico was looking for $5,000 payment from Michele Sindona. I say and believe that on one occasion William Arico accompanied me to the Law Library in the MCC where I spent much time during my said detention. In the course of that visit to the library, the said William Arico had me draw out the miscellaneous reports concerning the earlier trial of Michele Sindona.

"I say and believe that I this Deponent have received no money or inducement of any kind in consideration for swearing this Affidavit. I have done so of my own free will."

That fall, Costello also obtained the affidavit of Bill Gabler, the former protected witness who said Luigi Ronsisvalle had told him he had been hired to kill Sindona and someone whose "first name was Enrico" and whose last name "began with a C." In late October, Costello was notified that he would able to testify at Sindona's trial. He was also told that the Court of Assize in Milan had agreed to hear Gabler's testimony.

"I called up Gabler and asked him if he would go to Italy," Costello recalled. "He said, 'Sure.' The only problem was, he didn't have a passport, and he couldn't find his birth certificate. This meant trouble, because Gabler had previously been in the Witness Protection Program, and the first thing the government does when someone joins the program is to destroy all records of that person's existence. Protected witnesses become people without pasts, people without identities.

"Since Gabler was now out of the program and was back using his real name, I assumed that his identity would have been in some way restored. So, what we did was, we sent an agency that specializes in obtaining birth certificates and passports and so on to Brooklyn, where Gabler was born. They came back to us the next day and said they'd encountered something strange. They said there was no record whatsoever of Gabler ever having been born or ever having existed. By this time, I had only two days to get Gabler a passport. I called the head of the marshals' service in Virginia in charge of the Witness Protection Program, and I explained the problem. I called Alfred McNeil, who is the deputy in charge of the Witness Protection Program here in New York and under whose direct care Gabler once had been. McNeil was already aware that I had sent someone out to Brooklyn for Gabler's birth certificate. Apparently a flag on the file had caused the government to be alerted that someone was looking for one of their men without identities. I explained my problem, and, basically, the people I talked to were very nice.

"Furthermore, since Gabler was still on parole, I had to get permission from his federal parole officer in Uniondale, who in turn had to get permission from the parole commission in Washington, D.C. To the credit of the government people, all this was attended to within two days. With his new birth certificate in hand, one of my associates marched him over to the passport office in Rockefeller Center, where it was arranged for him to be issued a passport immediately, on the day we left for Italy."

As soon as the existence and nature of Gabler's affidavit were known, the government went to Ronsisvalle and obtained a counteraffidavit. "Certain of the statements Mr. Gabler attributes to me are neither accurate accounts of any conversations I had with Mr. Gabler nor consistent with the truth," Ronsisvalle swore. "Furthermore, I never told Mr. Gabler, or anyone else, that I had been hired to kill these two people."

Luigi Ronsisvalle's next testimony under oath would be delivered in January 1986, at the federal courthouse in downtown Manhattan. As a star government witness in the Pizza Connection trial, he was cross-examined by Ivan S. Fisher, the attorney for the defendant Salvatore Catalano. Fisher, the lawyer whom Sindona had sued and accused of swindling him, brought up the alleged plot to kill John Kenney, the federal prosecutor in the Franklin case. In the past, Ronsisvalle had claimed that a mysterious associate of Sindona's had told him that Sindona was willing to pay $100,000 for Kenney's death, and that he, Ronsisvalle, had set out to find someone to perform the murder. Now, in 1986, Ronsisvalle's story was different. He himself, he now said, had agreed to kill Kenney for Sindona.

On the eve of his departure to testify in Italy, Costello, by chance, obtained the most startling of the affidavits he was able to deliver to the tribunal.

"I am an American citizen and I make my home in Nutley, New Jersey," stated the affidavit of George Gregory Korkola. "I am currently an inmate at the Green Haven Correctional Facility in Stormville, New York, serving a five-to-fifteen-year sentence for possession and transportation of weapons in the third degree. I am forty-four years old, married with two children. Prior to being arrested on the charges which led to my current incarceration, I made my living designing, manufacturing, and selling security systems. I was active in community affairs in Nutley, New Jersey, and was elected a town committeeman for that community.

"While I was incarcerated at the Metropolitan Correctional Center, I became friendly with another inmate by the name of William Arico. During a conversation that we had during either late April or early May 1983 concerning the Vatican and the pope, Mr. Arico mentioned the name Michele Sindona. Arico told me that he went to Italy and killed an Italian prosecutor by the name of Ambrosoli. Arico told me he shot him pointblank and that he did not feel sorry about it. 'He was a scumbag,' Arico said. Arico told me that he was paid by someone to kill Ambrosoli. Arico told me that the authorities believe that Michele Sindona had something to do with the murder of Ambrosoli, but Arico insisted that Michele Sindona did not have anything to do with the murder. William Arico told me that Michele Sindona did not ask for or pay for the killing of Ambrosoli. Arico further stated that while it was his personal opinion that Sindona may not have been unhappy about this, he absolutely had nothing to do with it.

"During the course of our conversations, Mr. Arico's possible extradition to Italy came up often. Arico was emphatic that he would never go to Italy. He was very concerned about his stepson, Charles Arico, being extradited to Italy. Arico told me that if he went to Italy he would surely be convicted of murder because they had plenty of evidence against him. Arico also told me that he was going to be getting out of jail. He did not tell me specifically that he intended to escape but he emphasized that he would never go to Italy and he would do whatever he had to do to make sure he did not go. Arico confided in me because he knew of my expertise in electronics and he wanted to know how he could maintain contact with his family after he was out of jail without the authorities being able to recognize his voice or tell his whereabouts. Arico was interested in any information I had about electronic scramblers. We also had discussions about revolvers since Arico became aware that I was in jail on a weapons charge. During the course of those conversations, Arico told me that he preferred a 9-millimeter pistol. Arico at one point referred to a magazine article on the Ambrosoli murder and told me that they had the story all wrong. Arico again said that he killed Ambrosoli but he did not do it for Michele Sindona. Arico said he was paid by someone else and that it had no connection with Sindona.

"I have never met or talked to Michele Sindona. I knew from the newspapers that he was extradited to Italy, but I had no knowledge of what had become of him. This recently changed when I saw an article in the New York *Daily News* which indicated that Mr. Sindona was on trial in Italy and charged with this murder. I decided that I could no longer keep silent and I therefore wrote to Mr. Costello. I am reluctant to become involved in this proceeding since I expect to be released on parole next year. I could not, however, sit idly by and not inform the Court of these admissions by Arico. I have nothing to gain in return for providing this information. I have received no favors of any kind nor do I expect to receive any favors from anyone. Indeed, my only hope is that this will not interfere with my parole opportunity next year.

"In order to demonstrate my truthfulness, I am willing to be examined and cross-examined by anyone the Italian Court designates. i am willing to undergo any polygraph or other chemical or psychological examination. In short, I am at the Italian Court's disposal for whatever proceedings it desires."

Costello's day to testify at the Palace of Justice came on November 6, 1985. The trial was developing as Guido Viola had hoped, and Sindona had surmised, it would. On October 3, making a rare public appearance, Enrico Cuccia had been questioned in court about the threatening calls he had received. In reporting his testimony, the *Corriere della Sera* had referred to *"la voce di uno dei 'santoni' della finanza italiana"* ("the voice of one of the 'saintly hermits' of Italian finance"). When Costello testified in court, however, there was little coverage of his revelations.

"That really drove home the truth of what Sindona had often told me," Costello said. "That whole day at the Palace of Justice was like nothing I had ever experienced in a courtroom. It was like a Fellini movie. To begin with, the court-appointed translator they gave me—I had no choice—was an out-of-work opera singer from America who garbled everything I said. Sindona was correcting her from his cage. People across the courtroom were yelling out corrections. Even I, who don't understand Italian, could tell she was transposing names.

"Then, after all my testimony, after reading into evidence all the affidavits I had collected, there was not a single question from the prosecution. Nothing. Guido Viola just sat there the whole time looking as if he were suffering a migraine attack. I had ripped apart their case and they just sat there in silence waiting to get rid of me. I was astounded."

The next day, the Assistant U.S. attorney Charles Rose and the FBI agent Michael Mott testified that Arico had told them that Sindona had ordered the murder of Giorgio Ambrosoli.

A month later, on the afternoon of December 6, George Korkola was writted out of the Green Haven prison and brought before Charles Rose. With Rose were two FBI agents, three Italian magistrates, and a translator.

"This is the man who wrote an affidavit in opposition to my affidavit," Rose said in Italian to the magistrates, not knowing that Korkola understood Italian.

Rose then told Korkola that the Italian authorities were very upset over the fact that, out of the blue, Bob Costello had arrived in Milan waving an affidavit from a prisoner in New York.

"His closing statement to me," Korkola said, "was that I should not go to Italy for a couple of years, because they were very disturbed about my affidavit."

The prosecution rested its case on December 10. After recalling Rose's testimony and evoking the image of Ambrosoli *"steso sul freddo tavolo dell'obitorio"* ("laid out on the cold mortuary table"), Viola asked that Sindona be sentenced to prison for the rest of his days on earth.

Viola asked the same for Robert Venetucci, then he cast his wrath further in the name of the state. Rodolfo Guzzi, Sindona's lawyer in Rome, should be sentenced to ten years; John Gambino, to nine. Eight each should be given to Rosario Spatola and Joseph Macaluso; seven to Rosario's brother, Vincenzo; six to Joseph Miceli Crimi and Sindona's son-in-law, Piersandro Magnoni. Sindona's daughter should be given five, for she had stood by her father in his opprobrium. And there were more.

Meanwhile, the first snowfall of the season had blanketed Milan. In a letter dated December 12, two days after the prosecution's summation, Sindona rendered a summation of his own. It was the last Latin lesson, his gloss on the words in the rock: "Big illusion."

Christmas passed, and the winds of another year rode down through the Po valley. Sindona sat in his cell, awaiting the inevitable, final dooming: the end of the journey that had begun forty years ago, when he crossed the straits of Scylla and Charybdis, heading north, toward fortune. This was the north, this his fortune.

"Carlo Bordoni and his friends in that land of the free arranged the murder of Giorgio Ambrosoli. Today Bordoni, freed with the aid and approval of two governments, is off somewhere with the money that I am supposed to have stolen. Tommaso Buscetta, death's merchant and a *picciotto* of the nameless few at the end of the world, was extradited under the same treaty as I. He has been made an American citizen and given a home and a lavish income at the taxpayers' expense. All my accusers have been rewarded. Luigi Ronsisvalle, who has admitted to thirteen murders, has now been paroled and provided for. And here I am," he smiled, "the Devil. Don't ever believe, as I did, that there is no such thing as forbidden knowledge."

* * *

The last days of winter grew longer, and they warmed to spring. On March 18, 1986, the final dooming came: found guilty of arranging the murder of Giorgio Ambrosoli, Sindona was sentenced to spend the rest of his life in prison.

Later that Lenten afternoon, he sat in his cell and he wrote me a letter. "The Corte d'Assise of Milan decided today to convict me for life," he began in English. He turned then to Italian.

"You know me well enough," his words said, "to know that I am not afraid to die. I believe in God and in eternal life, and I await the passage with serenity; and, therefore, any possible violent act against me does not worry me at all."

He ended by expressing his hope that he soon would be returned to the United States, where we might be able to meet again. It was the last I would ever hear from him.

On the morning of March 20—two years to the very day after I first met him—Sindona rose to take his breakfast. As always, the plate and coffee cup were sealed. It was eight-thirty. He carried the plastic cup with him through the swinging doors that led to his toilet. Moments later, he staggered forth.

"Mi hanno avvelenato," he said. "They have poisoned me."

Those were his final words. At eight-forty, a Red Cross ambulance rushed him to the little hospital in Voghera, where he was declared to be in an irreversible coma. Potassium cyanide—a more-than-lethal dose of it—was found to be in his blood. That afternoon, a chaplain administered the last rites. Forty-eight hours later, at twelve minutes after two on the afternoon of March 22, Michele Sindona was pronounced dead.

His life, lived in mystery, had been ended in mystery. Was he murdered or did he kill himself? This is something the world will never know for certain. His son Marco, who saw him the day before, said that he did not seem to be on the brink of any new darkness. And there was the letter, expressing a hope to return to America. I thought of these things, as I

277

thought of the fact that Sindona had long and calmly foreseen his final dooming in the Palace of Justice. But I thought, too, of the Sindona who esteemed as the noblest of men the Socrates of the *Phaedo*, the Socrates who raised the cup of hemlock to his own lips.

So, what had begun in shadows ended in shadows. It was spring again. Almost a year had passed since I had sat on that bench in Voghera. When I left there after seeing him last, the light of day was waning. I stopped at the garden where the pines were, and I tried to recall a spring night there without stars, and a certain breeze from the west. When I did, I walked away. I was right. That breeze was older than the stones.

Index

INDEX